SECOND EDITION

# Learning React
*Modern Patterns for Developing React Apps*

*Alex Banks and Eve Porcello*

Beijing · Boston · Farnham · Sebastopol · Tokyo

**Learning React**

by Alex Banks and Eve Porcello

Published by O'Reilly Media, Inc., 1005 Gravenstein Highway North, Sebastopol, CA 95472.

O'Reilly books may be purchased for educational, business, or sales promotional use. Online editions are also available for most titles (*http://oreilly.com*). For more information, contact our corporate/institutional sales department: 800-998-9938 or *corporate@oreilly.com*.

**Acquisitions Editor:** Jennifer Pollock
**Development Editor:** Angela Rufino
**Production Editor:** Kristen Brown
**Copyeditor:** Holly Bauer Forsyth
**Proofreader:** Abby Wheeler

**Indexer:** Judith McConville
**Interior Designer:** David Futato
**Cover Designer:** Karen Montgomery
**Illustrator:** Rebecca Demarest

May 2017:          First Edition
June 2020:         Second Edition

**Revision History for the Second Edition**
2020-06-12:   First Release

See *http://oreilly.com/catalog/errata.csp?isbn=9781492051725* for release details.

978-1-492-05172-5

[LSI]

# Table of Contents

# Preface

This book is for developers who want to learn the React library while learning the latest techniques currently emerging in the JavaScript language. This is an exciting time to be a JavaScript developer. The ecosystem is exploding with new tools, syntax, and best practices that promise to solve many of our development problems. Our aim with this book is to organize these techniques so you can get to work with React right away. We'll get into state management, React Router, testing, and server rendering, so we promise not to introduce only the basics and then throw you to the wolves.

This book does not assume any knowledge of React at all. We'll introduce all of React's basics from scratch. Similarly, we won't assume that you've worked with the latest JavaScript syntax. This will be introduced in Chapter 2 as a foundation for the rest of the chapters.

You'll be better prepared for the contents of the book if you're comfortable with HTML, CSS, and JavaScript. It's almost always best to be comfortable with these big three before diving into a JavaScript library.

Along the way, check out the GitHub repository (*http://github.com/moonhighway/learning-react*). All of the examples are there and will allow you to practice hands-on.

## Conventions Used in This Book

The following typographical conventions are used in this book:

*Italic*
:   Indicates new terms, URLs, email addresses, filenames, and file extensions.

`Constant width`
:   Used for program listings, as well as within paragraphs to refer to program elements such as variable or function names, databases, data types, environment variables, statements, and keywords.

**Constant width bold**
> Shows commands or other text that should be typed literally by the user.

 This element signifies a tip or suggestion.

 This element signifies a general note.

 This element indicates a warning or caution.

# Using Code Examples

Supplemental material (code examples, exercises, etc.) is available for download at *https://github.com/moonhighway/learning-react*.

If you have a technical question or a problem using the code examples, please send email to *bookquestions@oreilly.com*.

This book is here to help you get your job done. In general, if example code is offered with this book, you may use it in your programs and documentation. You do not need to contact us for permission unless you're reproducing a significant portion of the code. For example, writing a program that uses several chunks of code from this book does not require permission. Selling or distributing examples from O'Reilly books does require permission. Answering a question by citing this book and quoting example code does not require permission. Incorporating a significant amount of example code from this book into your product's documentation does require permission.

We appreciate, but generally do not require, attribution. An attribution usually includes the title, author, publisher, and ISBN. For example: "*Learning React* by Alex Banks and Eve Porcello (O'Reilly). Copyright 2020 Alex Banks and Eve Porcello, 978-1-492-05172-5."

If you feel your use of code examples falls outside fair use or the permission given above, feel free to contact us at *permissions@oreilly.com*.

## O'Reilly Online Learning

 For more than 40 years, *O'Reilly Media* has provided technology and business training, knowledge, and insight to help companies succeed.

Our unique network of experts and innovators share their knowledge and expertise through books, articles, and our online learning platform. O'Reilly's online learning platform gives you on-demand access to live training courses, in-depth learning paths, interactive coding environments, and a vast collection of text and video from O'Reilly and 200+ other publishers. For more information, visit *http://oreilly.com*.

## How to Contact Us

Please address comments and questions concerning this book to the publisher:

> O'Reilly Media, Inc.
> 1005 Gravenstein Highway North
> Sebastopol, CA 95472
> 800-998-9938 (in the United States or Canada)
> 707-829-0515 (international or local)
> 707-829-0104 (fax)

We have a web page for this book, where we list errata, examples, and any additional information. You can access this page at *https://oreil.ly/learningReact_2e*.

Email *bookquestions@oreilly.com* to comment or ask technical questions about this book.

For news and information about our books and courses, visit *http://oreilly.com*.

Find us on Facebook: *http://facebook.com/oreilly*

Follow us on Twitter: *http://twitter.com/oreillymedia*

Watch us on YouTube: *http://www.youtube.com/oreillymedia*

## Acknowledgments

Our journey with React wouldn't have started without some good old-fashioned luck. We used YUI when we created the training materials for the full-stack JavaScript program we taught internally at Yahoo. Then in August 2014, development on YUI ended. We had to change all our course files, but to what? What were we supposed to use on the front-end now? The answer: React. We didn't fall in love with React immediately; it took us a couple hours to get hooked. It looked like React could potentially change everything. We got in early and got really lucky.

We appreciate the help of Angela Rufino and Jennifer Pollock for all the support in developing this second edition. We also want to acknowledge Ally MacDonald for all her editing help in the first edition. We're grateful to our tech reviewers, Scott Iwako, Adam Rackis, Brian Sletten, Max Firtman, and Chetan Karande.

There's also no way this book could have existed without Sharon Adams and Marilyn Messineo. They conspired to purchase Alex's first computer, a Tandy TRS 80 Color Computer. It also wouldn't have made it to book form without the love, support, and encouragement of Jim and Lorri Porcello and Mike and Sharon Adams.

We'd also like to acknowledge Coffee Connexion in Tahoe City, California, for giving us the coffee we needed to finish this book, and its owner, Robin, who gave us the timeless advice: "A book on programming? Sounds boring!"

# Welcome to React

What makes a JavaScript library good? Is it the number of stars on GitHub? The number of downloads on npm? Is the number of tweets that ThoughtLeaders™ write about it on a daily basis important? How do we pick the best tool to use to build the best thing? How do we know it's worth our time? How do we know it's good?

When React was first released, there was a lot of conversation around whether it was good, and there were many skeptics. It was new, and the new can often be upsetting.

To respond to these critiques, Pete Hunt from the React team wrote an article called "Why React?" that recommended that you "give it [React] five minutes." He wanted to encourage people to work with React first before thinking that the team's approach was too wild.

Yes, React is a small library that doesn't come with everything you might need out of the box to build your application. Give it five minutes.

Yes, in React, you write code that looks like HTML right in your JavaScript code. And yes, those tags require preprocessing to run in a browser. And you'll probably need a build tool like webpack for that. Give it five minutes.

As React approaches a decade of use, a lot of teams decided that it's good because they gave it five minutes. We're talking Uber, Twitter, Airbnb, and Twitter—huge companies that tried React and realized that it could help teams build better products faster. At the end of the day, isn't that what we're all here for? Not for the tweets. Not for the stars. Not for the downloads. We're here to build cool stuff with tools that we like to use. We're here for the glory of shipping stuff that we're proud to say we built. If you like doing those types of things, you'll probably like working with React.

# A Strong Foundation

Whether you're brand new to React or looking to this text to learn some of the latest features, we want this book to serve as a strong foundation for all your future work with the library. The goal of this book is to avoid confusion in the learning process by putting things in a sequence: a learning roadmap.

Before digging into React, it's important to know JavaScript. Not all of JavaScript, not every pattern, but having a comfort with arrays, objects, and functions before jumping into this book will be useful.

In the next chapter, we'll look at newer JavaScript syntax to get you acquainted with the latest JavaScript features, especially those that are frequently used with React. Then we'll give an introduction to functional JavaScript so you can understand the paradigm that gave birth to React. A nice side effect of working with React is that it can make you a stronger JavaScript developer by promoting patterns that are readable, reusable, and testable. Sort of like a gentle, helpful brainwashing.

From there, we'll cover foundational React knowledge to understand how to build out a user interface with components. Then we'll learn to compose these components and add logic with props and state. We'll cover React Hooks, which allow us to reuse stateful logic between components.

Once the basics are in place, we'll build a new application that allows users to add, edit, and delete colors. We'll learn how Hooks and Suspense can help us with data fetching. Throughout the construction of that app, we'll introduce a variety of tools from the broader React ecosystem that are used to handle common concerns like routing, testing, and server-side rendering.

We hope to get you up to speed with the React ecosystem faster by approaching it this way—not just to scratch the surface, but to equip you with the tools and skills necessary to build real-world React applications.

# React's Past and Future

React was first created by Jordan Walke, a software engineer at Facebook. It was incorporated into Facebook's newsfeed in 2011 and later on Instagram when it was acquired by Facebook in 2012. At JSConf 2013, React was made open source, and it joined the crowded category of UI libraries like jQuery, Angular, Dojo, Meteor, and others. At that time, React was described as "the V in MVC." In other words, React components acted as the view layer or the user interface for your JavaScript applications.

From there, community adoption started to spread. In January 2015, Netflix announced that they were using React to power their UI development. Later that month, React Native, a library for building mobile applications using React, was released. Facebook also released ReactVR, another tool that brought React to a broader range of rendering targets. In 2015 and 2016, a huge number of popular tools like React Router, Redux, and Mobx came on the scene to handle tasks like routing and state management. After all, React was billed as a library: concerned with implementing a specific set of features, not providing a tool for every use case.

Another huge event on the timeline was the release of React Fiber in 2017. Fiber was a rewrite of React's rendering algorithm that was sort of magical in its execution. It was a full rewrite of React's internals that changed barely anything about the public API. It was a way of making React more modern and performant without affecting its users.

More recently in 2019, we saw the release of Hooks, a new way of adding and sharing stateful logic across components. We also saw the release of Suspense, a way to optimize asynchronous rendering with React.

In the future, we'll inevitably see more change, but one of the reasons for React's success is the strong team that has worked on the project over the years. The team is ambitious yet cautious, pushing forward-thinking optimizations while constantly considering the impact any changes to the library will send cascading through the community.

As changes are made to React and related tools, sometimes there are breaking changes. In fact, future versions of these tools may break some of the example code in this book. You can still follow along with the code samples. We'll provide exact version information in the *package.json* file so that you can install these packages at the correct version.

Beyond this book, you can stay on top of changes by following along with the official React blog (*https://facebook.github.io/react/blog*). When new versions of React are released, the core team will write a detailed blog post and changelog about what's new. The blog has also been translated into an ever-expanding list of languages, so if English isn't your native language, you can find localized versions of the docs on the languages page (*https://reactjs.org/languages*) of the docs site.

## Learning React: Second Edition Changes

This is the second edition of *Learning React*. We felt it was important to update the book because React has evolved quite a bit over the past few years. We intend to focus on all the current best practices that are advocated by the React team, but we'll also share information about deprecated React features. There's a lot of React code that was written years ago using old styles that still works well and must be maintained. In all cases, we'll make mention of these features in a sidebar in case you find yourself working with legacy React applications.

# Working with the Files

In this section, we'll discuss how to work with the files for this book and how to install some useful React tools.

## File Repository

The GitHub repository associated with this book (*https://github.com/moonhighway/learning-react*) provides all the code files organized by chapter.

## React Developer Tools

We'd highly recommend installing React Developer Tools to support your work on React projects. These tools are available as a browser extension for Chrome and Firefox and as a standalone app for use with Safari, IE, and React Native. Once you install the dev tools, you'll be able to inspect the React component tree, view props and state details, and even view which sites are currently using React in production. These are really useful when debugging and when learning about how React is used in other projects.

To install, head over to the GitHub repository (*https://oreil.ly/5tizT*). There, you'll find links to the Chrome (*https://oreil.ly/Or3pH*) and Firefox extensions (*https://oreil.ly/uw3uv*).

Once installed, you'll be able to see which sites are using React. Anytime the React icon is illuminated in the browser toolbar as shown in Figure 1-1, you'll know that the site has React on the page.

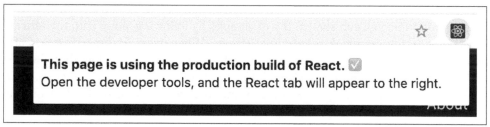

*Figure 1-1. Viewing the React Developer Tools in Chrome*

Then, when you open the developer tools, there will be a new tab visible called React, as shown in Figure 1-2. Clicking on that will show all the components that make up the page you're currently viewing.

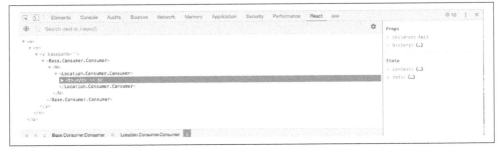

*Figure 1-2. Inspecting the DOM with the React Developer Tools*

# Installing Node.js

Node.js is a JavaScript runtime environment used to build full-stack applications. Node is open source and can be installed on Windows, macOS, Linux, and other platforms. We'll be using Node in Chapter 12 when we build an Express server.

You need to have Node installed, but you do not need to be a Node expert in order to use React. If you're not sure if Node.js is installed on your machine, you can open a Terminal or Command Prompt window and type:

```
node -v
```

When you run this command, you should see a node version number returned to you, ideally 8.6.2 or higher. If you type the command and see an error message that says "Command not found," Node.js is not installed. This is easily fixed by installing Node.js from the Node.js website (*http://nodejs.org*). Just go through the installer's automated steps, and when you type in the node -v command again, you'll see the version number.

## npm

When you installed Node.js, you also installed npm, the Node package manager. In the JavaScript community, engineers share open source code projects to avoid having to rewrite frameworks, libraries, or helper functions on their own. React itself is an example of a useful npm library. We'll use npm to install a variety of packages throughout this book.

Most JavaScript projects you encounter today will contain an assorted collection of files plus a *package.json* file. This file describes the project and all its dependencies. If you run npm install in the folder that contains the *package.json* file, npm will install all the packages listed in the project.

If you're starting your own project from scratch and want to include dependencies, simply run the command:

```
npm init -y
```

This will initialize the project and create a *package.json* file. From there, you can install your own dependencies with npm. To install a package with npm, you'll run:

```
npm install package-name
```

To remove a package with npm, you'll run:

```
npm remove package-name
```

## Yarn

An alternative to npm is Yarn. It was released in 2016 by Facebook in collaboration with Exponent, Google, and Tilde. The project helps Facebook and other companies manage their dependencies reliably. If you're familiar with the npm workflow, getting up to speed with Yarn is fairly simple. First, install Yarn globally with npm:

```
npm install -g yarn
```

Then, you're ready to install packages. When installing dependencies from *package.json*, in place of npm install, you can run yarn.

To install a specific package with yarn, run:

```
yarn add package-name
```

To remove a dependency, the command is familiar, too:

```
yarn remove package-name
```

Yarn is used in production by Facebook and is included in projects like React, React Native, and Create React App. If you ever find a project that contains a *yarn.lock* file, the project uses yarn. Similar to the npm install command, you can install all the dependencies of the project by typing yarn.

Now that you have your environment set up for React development, you're ready to start walking the path of learning React. In Chapter 2, we'll get up to speed with the latest JavaScript syntax that's most commonly found in React code.

# JavaScript for React

Since its release in 1995, JavaScript has gone through many changes. At first, we used JavaScript to add interactive elements to web pages: button clicks, hover states, form validation, etc.. Later, JavaScript got more robust with DHTML and AJAX. Today, with Node.js, JavaScript has become a real software language that's used to build full-stack applications. JavaScript is everywhere.

JavaScript's evolution has been guided by a group of individuals from companies that use JavaScript, browser vendors, and community leaders. The committee in charge of shepherding the changes to JavaScript over the years is the European Computer Manufacturers Association (ECMA). Changes to the language are community-driven, originating from proposals written by community members. Anyone can submit a proposal (*https://tc39.github.io/process-document*) to the ECMA committee. The responsibility of the ECMA committee is to manage and prioritize these proposals to decide what's included in each spec.

The first release of ECMAScript was in 1997, ECMAScript1. This was followed in 1998 by ECMAScript2. ECMAScript3 came out in 1999, adding regular expressions, string handling, and more. The process of agreeing on an ECMAScript4 became a chaotic, political mess that proved to be impossible. It was never released. In 2009, ECMAScript5(ES5) was released, bringing features like new array methods, object properties, and library support for JSON.

Since then, there has been a lot more momentum in this space. After ES6 or ES2015 was released in, yes, 2015, there have been yearly releases of new JS features. Anything that's part of the stage proposals is typically called ESNext, which is a simplified way of saying this is the next stuff that will be part of the JavaScript spec.

Proposals are taken through clearly defined stages, from stage 0, which represents the newest proposals, up through stage 4, which represents the finished proposals. When a proposal gains traction, it's up to the browser vendors like Chrome and Firefox to implement the features. Consider the const keyword. When creating variables, we used to use var in all cases. The ECMA committee decided there should be a const keyword to declare constants (more on that later in the chapter). When const was first introduced, you couldn't just write const in JavaScript code and expect it to run in a browser. Now you can because browser vendors have changed the browser to support it.

Many of the features we'll discuss in this chapter are already supported by the newest browsers, but we'll also be covering how to compile your JavaScript code. This is the process of transforming new syntax that the browser doesn't recognize into older syntax that the browser understands. The kangax compatibility table (*https://oreil.ly/oe7la*) is a great place to stay informed about the latest JavaScript features and their varying degrees of support by browsers.

In this chapter, we'll show you all the JavaScript syntax we'll be using throughout the book. We hope to provide a good baseline of JavaScript syntax knowledge that will carry you through all of your work with React. If you haven't made the switch to the latest syntax yet, now would be a good time to get started. If you're already comfortable with the latest language features, skip to the next chapter.

# Declaring Variables

Prior to ES2015, the only way to declare a variable was with the var keyword. We now have a few different options that provide improved functionality.

## The const Keyword

A constant is a variable that cannot be overwritten. Once declared, you cannot change its value. A lot of the variables that we create in JavaScript should not be overwritten, so we'll be using const a lot. Like other languages had done before it, JavaScript introduced constants with ES6.

Before constants, all we had were variables, and variables could be overwritten:

```
var pizza = true;
pizza = false;
console.log(pizza); // false
```

We cannot reset the value of a constant variable, and it will generate a console error (as shown in Figure 2-1) if we try to overwrite the value:

```
const pizza = true;
pizza = false;
```

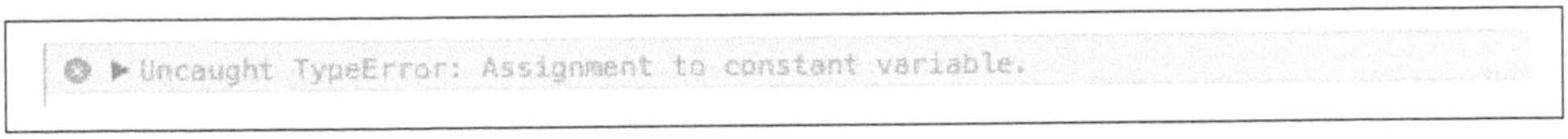

*Figure 2-1. An attempt at overwriting a constant*

## The let Keyword

JavaScript now has *lexical variable scope*. In JavaScript, we create code blocks with curly braces ({}). In functions, these curly braces block off the scope of any variable declared with var. On the other hand, consider if/else statements. If you're coming from other languages, you might assume that these blocks would also block variable scope. This was not the case until let came along.

If a variable is created inside of an if/else block, that variable is not scoped to the block:

```
var topic = "JavaScript";

if (topic) {
  var topic = "React";
  console.log("block", topic); // block React
}

console.log("global", topic); // global React
```

The topic variable inside the if block resets the value of topic outside of the block.

With the let keyword, we can scope a variable to any code block. Using let protects the value of the global variable:

```
var topic = "JavaScript";

if (topic) {
  let topic = "React";
  console.log("block", topic); // React
}

console.log("global", topic); // JavaScript
```

The value of topic is not reset outside of the block.

Another area where curly braces don't block off a variable's scope is in for loops:

```
var div,
    container = document.getElementById("container");

for (var i = 0; i < 5; i++) {
  div = document.createElement("div");
  div.onclick = function() {
    alert("This is box #" + i);
  };
```

```
      container.appendChild(div);
    }
```

In this loop, we create five divs to appear within a container. Each div is assigned an onclick handler that creates an alert box to display the index. Declaring i in the for loop creates a global variable named i, then iterates over it until its value reaches 5. When you click on any of these boxes, the alert says that i is equal to 5 for all divs, because the current value for the global i is 5 (see Figure 2-2).

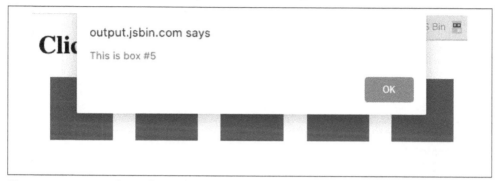

*Figure 2-2. i is equal to 5 for each box*

Declaring the loop counter i with let instead of var does block off the scope of i. Now clicking on any box will display the value for i that was scoped to the loop iteration (see Figure 2-3):

```
    const container = document.getElementById("container");
    let div;
    for (let i = 0; i < 5; i++) {
      div = document.createElement("div");
      div.onclick = function() {
        alert("This is box #: " + i);
      };
      container.appendChild(div);
    }
```

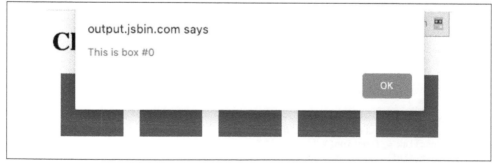

*Figure 2-3. The scope of i is protected with let*

The scope of i is protected with let.

## Template Strings

Template strings provide us with an alternative to string concatenation. They also allow us to insert variables into a string. You'll hear these referred to as template strings, template literals, or string templates interchangeably.

Traditional string concatenation uses plus signs to compose a string using variable values and strings:

```
console.log(lastName + ", " + firstName + " " + middleName);
```

With a template, we can create one string and insert the variable values by surrounding them with ${ }:

```
console.log(`${lastName}, ${firstName} ${middleName}`);
```

Any JavaScript that returns a value can be added to a template string between the ${ } in a template string.

Template strings honor whitespace, making it easier to draft up email templates, code examples, or anything else that contains whitespace. Now you can have a string that spans multiple lines without breaking your code:

```
const email = `
Hello ${firstName},

Thanks for ordering ${qty} tickets to ${event}.

Order Details
${firstName} ${middleName} ${lastName}
     ${qty} x $${price} = $${qty*price} to ${event}

You can pick your tickets up 30 minutes before
the show.

Thanks,

${ticketAgent}
`
```

Previously, using an HTML string directly in our JavaScript code was not so easy to do because we'd need to run it together on one line. Now that the whitespace is recognized as text, you can insert formatted HTML that is easy to read and understand:

```
document.body.innerHTML = `
<section>
  <header>
      <h1>The React Blog</h1>
  </header>
  <article>
```

```
      <h2>${article.title}</h2>
      ${article.body}
   </article>
   <footer>
      <p>copyright ${new Date().getYear()} | The React Blog</p>
   </footer>
</section>
`;
```

Notice that we can include variables for the page title and article text as well.

# Creating Functions

Any time you want to perform some sort of repeatable task with JavaScript, you can use a function. Let's take a look at some of the different syntax options that can be used to create a function and the anatomy of those functions.

## Function Declarations

A function declaration or function definition starts with the `function` keyword, which is followed by the name of the function, `logCompliment`. The JavaScript statements that are part of the function are defined between the curly braces:

```
function logCompliment() {
   console.log("You're doing great!");
}
```

Once you've declared the function, you'll invoke or call it to see it execute:

```
function logCompliment() {
   console.log("You're doing great!");
}

logCompliment();
```

Once invoked, you'll see the compliment logged to the console.

## Function Expressions

Another option is to use a function expression. This just involves creating the function as a variable:

```
const logCompliment = function() {
   console.log("You're doing great!");
};

logCompliment();
```

The result is the same, and `You're doing great!` is logged to the console.

One thing to be aware of when deciding between a function declaration and a function expression is that function declarations are hoisted and function expressions are not. In other words, you can invoke a function before you write a function declaration. You cannot invoke a function created by a function expression. This will cause an error. For example:

```
// Invoking the function before it's declared
hey();
// Function Declaration
function hey() {
  alert("hey!");
}
```

This works. You'll see the alert appear in the browser. It works because the function is hoisted, or moved up, to the top of the file's scope. Trying the same exercise with a function expression will cause an error:

```
// Invoking the function before it's declared
hey();
// Function Expression
const hey = function() {
  alert("hey!");
};

TypeError: hey is not a function
```

This is obviously a small example, but this TypeError can occasionally arise when importing files and functions in a project. If you see it, you can always refactor as a declaration.

## Passing arguments

The `logCompliment` function currently takes in no arguments or parameters. If we want to provide dynamic variables to the function, we can pass named parameters to a function simply by adding them to the parentheses. Let's start by adding a `first Name` variable:

```
const logCompliment = function(firstName) {
  console.log(`You're doing great, ${firstName}`);
};

logCompliment("Molly");
```

Now when we call the `logCompliment` function, the `firstName` value sent will be added to the console message.

We could add to this a bit by creating another argument called `message`. Now, we won't hard-code the message. We'll pass in a dynamic value as a parameter:

```
const logCompliment = function(firstName, message) {
  console.log(`${firstName}: ${message}`);
```

```
};

logCompliment("Molly", "You're so cool");
```

### Function returns

The logCompliment function currently logs the compliment to the console, but more often, we'll use a function to return a value. Let's add a return statement to this function. A return statement specifies the value returned by the function. We'll rename the function createCompliment:

```
const createCompliment = function(firstName, message) {
  return `${firstName}: ${message}`;
};

createCompliment("Molly", "You're so cool");
```

If you wanted to check to see if the function is executing as expected, just wrap the function call in a console.log:

```
console.log(createCompliment("You're so cool", "Molly"));
```

## Default Parameters

Languages including C++ and Python allow developers to declare default values for function arguments. Default parameters are included in the ES6 spec, so in the event that a value is not provided for the argument, the default value will be used.

For example, we can set up default strings for the parameters name and activity:

```
function logActivity(name = "Shane McConkey", activity = "skiing") {
  console.log(`${name} loves ${activity}`);
}
```

If no arguments are provided to the logActivity function, it will run correctly using the default values. Default arguments can be any type, not just strings:

```
const defaultPerson = {
  name: {
    first: "Shane",
    last: "McConkey"
  },
  favActivity: "skiing"
};

function logActivity(person = defaultPerson) {
  console.log(`${person.name.first} loves ${person.favActivity}`);
}
```

## Arrow Functions

Arrow functions are a useful new feature of ES6. With arrow functions, you can create functions without using the `function` keyword. You also often do not have to use the `return` keyword. Let's consider a function that takes in a `firstName` and returns a string, turning the person into a lord. Anyone can be a lord:

```
const lordify = function(firstName) {
  return `${firstName} of Canterbury`;
};

console.log(lordify("Dale")); // Dale of Canterbury
console.log(lordify("Gail")); // Gail of Canterbury
```

With an arrow function, we can simplify the syntax tremendously:

```
const lordify = firstName => `${firstName} of Canterbury`;
```

With the arrow, we now have an entire function declaration on one line. The `function` keyword is removed. We also remove `return` because the arrow points to what should be returned. Another benefit is that if the function only takes one argument, we can remove the parentheses around the arguments.

More than one argument should be surrounded by parentheses:

```
// Typical function
const lordify = function(firstName, land) {
  return `${firstName} of ${land}`;
};

// Arrow Function
const lordify = (firstName, land) => `${firstName} of ${land}`;

console.log(lordify("Don", "Piscataway")); // Don of Piscataway
console.log(lordify("Todd", "Schenectady")); // Todd of Schenectady
```

We can keep this as a one-line function because there is only one statement that needs to be returned. If there are multiple lines, you'll use curly braces:

```
const lordify = (firstName, land) => {
  if (!firstName) {
    throw new Error("A firstName is required to lordify");
  }

  if (!land) {
    throw new Error("A lord must have a land");
  }

  return `${firstName} of ${land}`;
};

console.log(lordify("Kelly", "Sonoma")); // Kelly of Sonoma
console.log(lordify("Dave")); // ! JAVASCRIPT ERROR
```

These if/else statements are surrounded with brackets but still benefit from the shorter syntax of the arrow function.

### Returning objects

What happens if you want to return an object? Consider a function called person that builds an object based on parameters passed in for firstName and lastName:

```
const person = (firstName, lastName) =>
    {
        first: firstName,
        last: lastName
    }

console.log(person("Brad", "Janson"));
```

As soon as you run this, you'll see the error: Uncaught SyntaxError: Unexpected token :. To fix this, just wrap the object you're returning with parentheses:

```
const person = (firstName, lastName) => ({
  first: firstName,
  last: lastName
});

console.log(person("Flad", "Hanson"));
```

These missing parentheses are the source of countless bugs in JavaScript and React apps, so it's important to remember this one!

### Arrow functions and scope

Regular functions do not block this. For example, this becomes something else in the setTimeout callback, not the tahoe object:

```
const tahoe = {
  mountains: ["Freel", "Rose", "Tallac", "Rubicon", "Silver"],
  print: function(delay = 1000) {
    setTimeout(function() {
      console.log(this.mountains.join(", "));
    }, delay);
  }
};

tahoe.print(); // Uncaught TypeError: Cannot read property 'join' of undefined
```

This error is thrown because it's trying to use the .join method on what this is. If we log this, we'll see that it refers to the Window object:

```
console.log(this); // Window {}
```

To solve this problem, we can use the arrow function syntax to protect the scope of this:

```
const tahoe = {
  mountains: ["Freel", "Rose", "Tallac", "Rubicon", "Silver"],
  print: function(delay = 1000) {
    setTimeout(() => {
      console.log(this.mountains.join(", "));
    }, delay);
  }
};

tahoe.print(); // Freel, Rose, Tallac, Rubicon, Silver
```

This works as expected, and we can `.join` the resorts with a comma. Be careful that you're always keeping scope in mind. Arrow functions do not block off the scope of this:

```
const tahoe = {
  mountains: ["Freel", "Rose", "Tallac", "Rubicon", "Silver"],
  print: (delay = 1000) => {
    setTimeout(() => {
      console.log(this.mountains.join(", "));
    }, delay);
  }
};

tahoe.print(); // Uncaught TypeError: Cannot read property 'join' of undefined
```

Changing the `print` function to an arrow function means that `this` is actually the window.

# Compiling JavaScript

When a new JavaScript feature is proposed and gains support, the community often wants to use it before it's supported by all browsers. The only way to be sure that your code will work is to convert it to more widely compatible code before running it in the browser. This process is called *compiling*. One of the most popular tools for JavaScript compilation is Babel (*http://www.babeljs.io*).

In the past, the only way to use the latest JavaScript features was to wait weeks, months, or even years until browsers supported them. Now, Babel has made it possible to use the latest features of JavaScript right away. The compiling step makes JavaScript similar to other languages. It's not quite traditional compiling: our code isn't compiled to binary. Instead, it's transformed into syntax that can be interpreted by a wider range of browsers. Also, JavaScript now has source code, meaning that there will be some files that belong to your project that don't run in the browser.

As an example, let's look at an arrow function with some default arguments:

```
const add = (x = 5, y = 10) => console.log(x + y);
```

If we run Babel on this code, it will generate the following:

```
"use strict";

var add = function add() {
  var x =
    arguments.length <= 0 || arguments[0] === undefined ? 5 : arguments[0];
  var y =
    arguments.length <= 1 || arguments[1] === undefined ? 10 : arguments[1];
  return console.log(x + y);
};
```

Babel added a "use strict" declaration to run in strict mode. The variables x and y are defaulted using the arguments array, a technique you may be familiar with. The resulting JavaScript is more widely supported.

A great way to learn more about how Babel works is to check out the Babel REPL (*https://babeljs.io/repl*) on the documentation website. Type some new syntax on the left side, then see some older syntax created.

The process of JavaScript compilation is typically automated by a build tool like webpack or Parcel. We'll discuss that in more detail later in the book.

# Objects and Arrays

Since ES2016, JavaScript syntax has supported creative ways of scoping variables within objects and arrays. These creative techniques are widely used among the React community. Let's take a look at a few of them, including destructuring, object literal enhancement, and the spread operator.

## Destructuring Objects

Destructuring assignment allows you to locally scope fields within an object and to declare which values will be used. Consider the sandwich object. It has four keys, but we only want to use the values of two. We can scope bread and meat to be used locally:

```
const sandwich = {
  bread: "dutch crunch",
  meat: "tuna",
  cheese: "swiss",
  toppings: ["lettuce", "tomato", "mustard"]
};

const { bread, meat } = sandwich;

console.log(bread, meat); // dutch crunch tuna
```

The code pulls bread and meat out of the object and creates local variables for them. Also, since we declared these destructed variables using let, the bread and meat variables can be changed without changing the original sandwich:

```
const sandwich = {
  bread: "dutch crunch",
  meat: "tuna",
  cheese: "swiss",
  toppings: ["lettuce", "tomato", "mustard"]
};

let { bread, meat } = sandwich;

bread = "garlic";
meat = "turkey";

console.log(bread); // garlic
console.log(meat); // turkey

console.log(sandwich.bread, sandwich.meat); // dutch crunch tuna
```

We can also destructure incoming function arguments. Consider this function that would log a person's name as a lord:

```
const lordify = regularPerson => {
  console.log(`${regularPerson.firstname} of Canterbury`);
};

const regularPerson = {
  firstname: "Bill",
  lastname: "Wilson"
};

lordify(regularPerson); // Bill of Canterbury
```

Instead of using dot notation syntax to dig into objects, we can destructure the values we need out of regularPerson:

```
const lordify = ({ firstname }) => {
  console.log(`${firstname} of Canterbury`);
};

const regularPerson = {
  firstname: "Bill",
  lastname: "Wilson"
};

lordify(regularPerson); // Bill of Canterbury
```

Let's take this one level farther to reflect a data change. Now, the regularPerson object has a new nested object on the spouse key:

```
const regularPerson = {
  firstname: "Bill",
  lastname: "Wilson",
  spouse: {
    firstname: "Phil",
```

```
      lastname: "Wilson"
    }
  };
```

If we wanted to lordify the spouse's first name, we'd adjust the function's destructured arguments slightly:

```
const lordify = ({ spouse: { firstname } }) => {
  console.log(`${firstname} of Canterbury`);
};

lordify(regularPerson); // Phil of Canterbury
```

Using the colon and nested curly braces, we can destructure the `firstname` from the `spouse` object.

## Destructuring Arrays

Values can also be destructured from arrays. Imagine that we wanted to assign the first value of an array to a variable name:

```
const [firstAnimal] = ["Horse", "Mouse", "Cat"];

console.log(firstAnimal); // Horse
```

We can also pass over unnecessary values with *list matching* using commas. List matching occurs when commas take the place of elements that should be skipped. With the same array, we can access the last value by replacing the first two values with commas:

```
const [, , thirdAnimal] = ["Horse", "Mouse", "Cat"];

console.log(thirdAnimal); // Cat
```

Later in this section, we'll take this example a step farther by combining array destructuring and the spread operator.

## Object Literal Enhancement

*Object literal enhancement* is the opposite of destructuring. It's the process of restructuring or putting the object back together. With object literal enhancement, we can grab variables from the global scope and add them to an object:

```
const name = "Tallac";
const elevation = 9738;

const funHike = { name, elevation };

console.log(funHike); // {name: "Tallac", elevation: 9738}
```

`name` and `elevation` are now keys of the `funHike` object.

We can also create object methods with object literal enhancement or restructuring:

```
const name = "Tallac";
const elevation = 9738;
const print = function() {
  console.log(`Mt. ${this.name} is ${this.elevation} feet tall`);
};

const funHike = { name, elevation, print };

funHike.print(); // Mt. Tallac is 9738 feet tall
```

Notice we use this to access the object keys.

When defining object methods, it's no longer necessary to use the function keyword:

```
// Old
var skier = {
  name: name,
  sound: sound,
  powderYell: function() {
    var yell = this.sound.toUpperCase();
    console.log(`${yell} ${yell} ${yell}!!!`);
  },
  speed: function(mph) {
    this.speed = mph;
    console.log("speed:", mph);
  }
};

// New
const skier = {
  name,
  sound,
  powderYell() {
    let yell = this.sound.toUpperCase();
    console.log(`${yell} ${yell} ${yell}!!!`);
  },
  speed(mph) {
    this.speed = mph;
    console.log("speed:", mph);
  }
};
```

Object literal enhancement allows us to pull global variables into objects and reduces typing by making the function keyword unnecessary.

## The Spread Operator

The spread operator is three dots (...) that perform several different tasks. First, the spread operator allows us to combine the contents of arrays. For example, if we had two arrays, we could make a third array that combines the two arrays into one:

```
const peaks = ["Tallac", "Ralston", "Rose"];
const canyons = ["Ward", "Blackwood"];
const tahoe = [...peaks, ...canyons];

console.log(tahoe.join(", ")); // Tallac, Ralston, Rose, Ward, Blackwood
```

All of the items from peaks and canyons are pushed into a new array called tahoe.

Let's take a look at how the spread operator can help us deal with a problem. Using the peaks array from the previous sample, let's imagine that we wanted to grab the last item from the array rather than the first. We could use the Array.reverse method to reverse the array in combination with array destructuring:

```
const peaks = ["Tallac", "Ralston", "Rose"];
const [last] = peaks.reverse();

console.log(last); // Rose
console.log(peaks.join(", ")); // Rose, Ralston, Tallac
```

See what happened? The reverse function has actually altered or mutated the array. In a world with the spread operator, we don't have to mutate the original array. Instead, we can create a copy of the array and then reverse it:

```
const peaks = ["Tallac", "Ralston", "Rose"];
const [last] = [...peaks].reverse();

console.log(last); // Rose
console.log(peaks.join(", ")); // Tallac, Ralston, Rose
```

Since we used the spread operator to copy the array, the peaks array is still intact and can be used later in its original form.

The spread operator can also be used to get the remaining items in the array:

```
const lakes = ["Donner", "Marlette", "Fallen Leaf", "Cascade"];

const [first, ...others] = lakes;

console.log(others.join(", ")); // Marlette, Fallen Leaf, Cascade
```

We can also use the three-dot syntax to collect function arguments as an array. When used in a function, these are called rest parameters. Here, we build a function that takes in *n* number of arguments using the spread operator, then uses those arguments to print some console messages:

```
function directions(...args) {
  let [start, ...remaining] = args;
  let [finish, ...stops] = remaining.reverse();

  console.log(`drive through ${args.length} towns`);
  console.log(`start in ${start}`);
  console.log(`the destination is ${finish}`);
  console.log(`stopping ${stops.length} times in between`);
```

```
}

directions("Truckee", "Tahoe City", "Sunnyside", "Homewood", "Tahoma");
```

The `directions` function takes in the arguments using the spread operator. The first argument is assigned to the `start` variable. The last argument is assigned to a `finish` variable using `Array.reverse`. We then use the length of the `arguments` array to display how many towns we're going through. The number of stops is the length of the `arguments` array minus the `finish` stop. This provides incredible flexibility because we could use the `directions` function to handle any number of stops.

The spread operator can also be used for objects (see the GitHub page for Rest/ Spread Properties (*https://oreil.ly/kCpEL*)). Using the spread operator with objects is similar to using it with arrays. In this example, we'll use it the same way we combined two arrays into a third array, but instead of arrays, we'll use objects:

```
const morning = {
  breakfast: "oatmeal",
  lunch: "peanut butter and jelly"
};

const dinner = "mac and cheese";

const backpackingMeals = {
  ...morning,
  dinner
};

console.log(backpackingMeals);

// {
//    breakfast: "oatmeal",
//    lunch: "peanut butter and jelly",
//    dinner: "mac and cheese"
// }
```

# Asynchronous JavaScript

The code samples that have been part of this chapter so far have been synchronous. When we write synchronous JavaScript code, we're providing a list of instructions that execute immediately in order. For example, if we wanted to use JavaScript to handle some simple DOM manipulation, we'd write the code to do so like this:

```
const header = document.getElementById("heading");
header.innerHTML = "Hey!";
```

These are instructions. "Yo, go select that element with an id of `heading`. Then when you're done with that, how about you set that inner HTML to *Hey*." It works synchronously. While each operation is happening, nothing else is happening.

With the modern web, we need to perform asynchronous tasks. These tasks often have to wait for some work to finish before they can be completed. We might need to access a database. We might need to stream video or audio content. We might need to fetch data from an API. With JavaScript, asynchronous tasks do not block the main thread. JavaScript is free to do something else while we wait for the API to return data. JavaScript has evolved a lot over the past few years to make handling these asynchronous actions easier. Let's explore some of the features that make this possible.

## Simple Promises with Fetch

Making a request to a REST API used to be pretty cumbersome. We'd have to write 20+ lines of nested code just to load some data into our app. Then the `fetch()` function showed up and simplified our lives. Thanks to the ECMAScript committee for making fetch happen.

Let's get some data from the randomuser.me API. This API has information like email address, name, phone number, location, and so on for fake members and is great to use as dummy data. `fetch` takes in the URL for this resource as its only parameter:

```
console.log(fetch("https://api.randomuser.me/?nat=US&results=1"));
```

When we log this, we see that there is a pending promise. *Promises* give us a way to make sense out of asynchronous behavior in JavaScript. The promise is an object that represents whether the async operation is pending, has been completed, or has failed. Think of this like the browser saying, "Hey, I'm going to try my best to go get this data. Either way, I'll come back and let you know how it went."

So back to the `fetch` result. The pending promise represents a state before the data has been fetched. We need to chain on a function called `.then()`. This function will take in a callback function that will run if the previous operation was successful. In other words, fetch some data, then do something else.

The something else we want to do is turn the response into JSON:

```
fetch("https://api.randomuser.me/?nat=US&results=1").then(res =>
  console.log(res.json())
);
```

The `then` method will invoke the callback function once the promise has resolved. Whatever you return from this function becomes the argument of the next `then` function. So we can chain together `then` functions to handle a promise that has been successfully resolved:

```
fetch("https://api.randomuser.me/?nat=US&results=1")
  .then(res => res.json())
  .then(json => json.results)
```

```
.then(console.log)
.catch(console.error);
```

First, we use `fetch` to make a GET request to randomuser.me. If the request is successful, we'll then convert the response body to JSON. Next, we'll take the JSON data and return the results, then we'll send the results to the `console.log` function, which will log them to the console. Finally, there is a `catch` function that invokes a callback if the `fetch` did not resolve successfully. Any error that occurred while fetching data from randomuser.me will be based on that callback. Here, we simply log the error to the console using `console.error`.

## Async/Await

Another popular approach for handling promises is to create an async function. Some developers prefer the syntax of async functions because it looks more familiar, like code that's found in a synchronous function. Instead of waiting for the results of a promise to resolve and handling it with a chain of `then` functions, async functions can be told to wait for the promise to resolve before further executing any code found in the function.

Let's make another API request but wrap the functionality with an async function:

```
const getFakePerson = async () => {
  let res = await fetch("https://api.randomuser.me/?nat=US&results=1");
  let { results } = res.json();
  console.log(results);
};

getFakePerson();
```

Notice that the `getFakePerson` function is declared using the `async` keyword. This makes it an asynchronous function that can wait for promises to resolve before executing the code any further. The `await` keyword is used before promise calls. This tells the function to wait for the promise to resolve. This code accomplishes the exact same task as the code in the previous section that uses `then` functions. Well, almost the exact same task…

```
const getFakePerson = async () => {
  try {
    let res = await fetch("https://api.randomuser.me/?nat=US&results=1");
    let { results } = res.json();
    console.log(results);
  } catch (error) {
    console.error(error);
  }
};

getFakePerson();
```

There we go—now this code accomplishes the exact same task as the code in the previous section that uses `then` functions. If the `fetch` call is successful, the results are logged to the console. If it's unsuccessful, then we'll log the error to the console using `console.error`. When using `async` and `await`, you need to surround your promise call in a `try…catch` block to handle any errors that may occur due to an unresolved promise.

## Building Promises

When making an asynchronous request, one of two things can happen: everything goes as we hope, or there's an error. There can be many different types of successful or unsuccessful requests. For example, we could try several ways to obtain the data to reach success. We could also receive multiple types of errors. Promises give us a way to simplify back to a simple pass or fail.

The `getPeople` function returns a new promise. The promise makes a request to the API. If the promise is successful, the data will load. If the promise is unsuccessful, an error will occur:

```
const getPeople = count =>
  new Promise((resolves, rejects) => {
    const api = `https://api.randomuser.me/?nat=US&results=${count}`;
    const request = new XMLHttpRequest();
    request.open("GET", api);
    request.onload = () =>
      request.status === 200
        ? resolves(JSON.parse(request.response).results)
        : reject(Error(request.statusText));
    request.onerror = err => rejects(err);
    request.send();
  });
```

With that, the promise has been created, but it hasn't been used yet. We can use the promise by calling the `getPeople` function and passing in the number of members that should be loaded. The `then` function can be chained on to do something once the promise has been fulfilled. When a promise is rejected, any details are passed back to the `catch` function, or the `catch` block if using `async`/`await` syntax:

```
getPeople(5)
  .then(members => console.log(members))
  .catch(error => console.error(`getPeople failed: ${error.message}`))
);
```

Promises make dealing with asynchronous requests easier, which is good, because we have to deal with a lot of asynchronicity in JavaScript. A solid understanding of asynchronous behavior is essential for the modern JavaScript engineer.

# Classes

Prior to ES2015, there was no official class syntax in the JavaScript spec. When classes were introduced, there was a lot of excitement about how similar the syntax of classes was to traditional object-oriented languages like Java and C++. The past few years saw the React library leaning on classes heavily to construct user interface components. Today, React is beginning to move away from classes, instead using functions to construct components. You'll still see classes all over the place, particularly in legacy React code and in the world of JavaScript, so let's take a quick look at them.

JavaScript uses something called prototypical inheritance. This technique can be wielded to create structures that feel object-oriented. For example, we can create a Vacation constructor that needs to be invoked with a new operator:

```
function Vacation(destination, length) {
  this.destination = destination;
  this.length = length;
}

Vacation.prototype.print = function() {
  console.log(this.destination + " | " + this.length + " days");
};

const maui = new Vacation("Maui", 7);

maui.print(); // Maui | 7 days
```

This code creates something that feels like a custom type in an object-oriented language. A Vacation has properties (destination, length), and it has a method (print). The maui instance inherits the print method through the prototype. If you are or were a developer accustomed to more standard classes, this might fill you with a deep rage. ES2015 introduced class declaration to quiet that rage, but the dirty secret is that JavaScript still works the same way. Functions are objects, and inheritance is handled through the prototype. Classes provide a syntactic sugar on top of that gnarly prototype syntax:

```
class Vacation {
  constructor(destination, length) {
    this.destination = destination;
    this.length = length;
  }

  print() {
    console.log(`${this.destination} will take ${this.length} days.`);
  }
}
```

When you're creating a class, the class name is typically capitalized. Once you've created the class, you can create a new instance of the class using the new keyword. Then you can call the custom method on the class:

```
const trip = new Vacation("Santiago, Chile", 7);

trip.print(); // Chile will take 7 days.
```

Now that a class object has been created, you can use it as many times as you'd like to create new vacation instances. Classes can also be extended. When a class is extended, the subclass inherits the properties and methods of the superclass. These properties and methods can be manipulated from here, but as a default, all will be inherited.

You can use Vacation as an abstract class to create different types of vacations. For instance, an Expedition can extend the Vacation class to include gear:

```
class Expedition extends Vacation {
  constructor(destination, length, gear) {
    super(destination, length);
    this.gear = gear;
  }

  print() {
    super.print();
    console.log(`Bring your ${this.gear.join(" and your ")}`);
  }
}
```

That's simple inheritance: the subclass inherits the properties of the superclass. By calling the print method of Vacation, we can append some new content onto what is printed in the print method of Expedition. Creating a new instance works the exact same way—create a variable and use the new keyword:

```
const trip = new Expedition("Mt. Whitney", 3, [
  "sunglasses",
  "prayer flags",
  "camera"
]);

trip.print();

// Mt. Whitney will take 3 days.
// Bring your sunglasses and your prayer flags and your camera
```

# ES6 Modules

A JavaScript *module* is a piece of reusable code that can easily be incorporated into other JavaScript files without causing variable collisions. JavaScript modules are stored in separate files, one file per module. There are two options when creating and exporting a module: you can export multiple JavaScript objects from a single module or one JavaScript object per module.

In *text-helpers.js*, two functions are exported:

```
export const print=(message) => log(message, new Date())

export const log=(message, timestamp) =>
  console.log(`${timestamp.toString()}: ${message}`)
```

export can be used to export any JavaScript type that will be consumed in another module. In this example, the print function and log function are being exported. Any other variables declared in *text-helpers.js* will be local to that module.

Modules can also export a single main variable. In these cases, you can use export default. For example, the *mt-freel.js* file can export a specific expedition:

```
export default new Expedition("Mt. Freel", 2, ["water", "snack"]);
```

export default can be used in place of export when you wish to export only one type. Again, both export and export default can be used on any JavaScript type: primitives, objects, arrays, and functions.

Modules can be consumed in other JavaScript files using the import statement. Modules with multiple exports can take advantage of object destructuring. Modules that use export default are imported into a single variable:

```
import { print, log } from "./text-helpers";
import freel from "./mt-freel";

print("printing a message");
log("logging a message");

freel.print();
```

You can scope module variables locally under different variable names:

```
import { print as p, log as l } from "./text-helpers";

p("printing a message");
l("logging a message");
```

You can also import everything into a single variable using *:

```
import * as fns from './text-helpers`
```

This import and export syntax is not yet fully supported by all browsers or by Node. However, like any emerging JavaScript syntax, it's supported by Babel. This means you can use these statements in your source code and Babel will know where to find the modules you want to include in your compiled JavaScript.

# CommonJS

CommonJS is the module pattern that's supported by all versions of Node (see the Node.js documentation on modules (*https://oreil.ly/CN-gA*)). You can still use these modules with Babel and webpack. With CommonJS, JavaScript objects are exported using `module.exports`.

For example, in CommonJS, we can export the `print` and `log` functions as an object:

```
const print(message) => log(message, new Date())

const log(message, timestamp) =>
console.log(`${timestamp.toString()}: ${message}`}

module.exports = {print, log}
```

CommonJS does not support an `import` statement. Instead, modules are imported with the `require` function:

```
const { log, print } = require("./txt-helpers");
```

JavaScript is indeed moving quickly and adapting to the increasing demands that engineers are placing on the language, and browsers are quickly implementing new features. For up-to-date compatibility information, see the ESNext compatibility table (*https://oreil.ly/rxTcg*). Many of the features that are included in the latest JavaScript syntax are present because they support functional programming techniques. In functional JavaScript, we can think of our code as being a collection of functions that can be composed into applications. In the next chapter, we'll explore functional techniques in more detail and will discuss why you might want to use them.

# CHAPTER 3

# Functional Programming with JavaScript

When you start to explore React, you'll likely notice that the topic of functional programming comes up a lot. Functional techniques are being used more and more in JavaScript projects, particularly React projects.

It's likely that you've already written functional JavaScript code without thinking about it. If you've mapped or reduced an array, then you're already on your way to becoming a functional JavaScript programmer. Functional programming techniques are core not only to React but to many of the libraries in the React ecosystem as well.

If you're wondering where this functional trend came from, the answer is the 1930s, with the invention of *lambda calculus*, or λ-calculus.[1] Functions have been a part of calculus since it emerged in the 17th century. Functions can be sent to functions as arguments or returned from functions as results. More complex functions, called *higher-order functions*, can manipulate functions and use them as either arguments or results or both. In the 1930s, Alonzo Church was at Princeton experimenting with these higher-order functions when he invented lambda calculus.

In the late 1950s, John McCarthy took the concepts derived from λ-calculus and applied them to a new programming language called Lisp. Lisp implemented the concept of higher-order functions and functions as *first-class members* or *first-class citizens*. A function is considered a first-class member when it can be declared as a variable and sent to functions as an argument. These functions can even be returned from functions.

In this chapter, we're going to go over some of the key concepts of functional programming, and we'll cover how to implement functional techniques with JavaScript.

---

1 Dana S. Scott, "λ-Calculus: Then & Now" (*https://oreil.ly/k0EpX*).

# What It Means to Be Functional

JavaScript supports functional programming because JavaScript functions are first-class citizens. This means that functions can do the same things that variables can do. The latest JavaScript syntax adds language improvements that can beef up your functional programming techniques, including arrow functions, promises, and the spread operator.

In JavaScript, functions can represent data in your application. You may have noticed that you can declare functions with the var, let, or const keywords the same way you can declare strings, numbers, or any other variables:

```
var log = function(message) {
  console.log(message);
};

log("In JavaScript, functions are variables");

// In JavaScript, functions are variables
```

We can write the same function using an arrow function. Functional programmers write a lot of small functions, and the arrow function syntax makes that much easier:

```
const log = message => {
  console.log(message);
};
```

Since functions are variables, we can add them to objects:

```
const obj = {
  message: "They can be added to objects like variables",
  log(message) {
    console.log(message);
  }
};

obj.log(obj.message);

// They can be added to objects like variables
```

Both of these statements do the same thing: they store a function in a variable called log. Additionally, the const keyword was used to declare the second function, which will prevent it from being overwritten.

We can also add functions to arrays in JavaScript:

```
const messages = [
  "They can be inserted into arrays",
  message => console.log(message),
  "like variables",
  message => console.log(message)
];
```

```
messages[1](messages[0]); // They can be inserted into arrays
messages[3](messages[2]); // like variables
```

Functions can be sent to other functions as arguments, just like other variables:

```
const insideFn = logger => {
  logger("They can be sent to other functions as arguments");
};

insideFn(message => console.log(message));

// They can be sent to other functions as arguments
```

They can also be returned from other functions, just like variables:

```
const createScream = function(logger) {
  return function(message) {
    logger(message.toUpperCase() + "!!!");
  };
};

const scream = createScream(message => console.log(message));

scream("functions can be returned from other functions");
scream("createScream returns a function");
scream("scream invokes that returned function");

// FUNCTIONS CAN BE RETURNED FROM OTHER FUNCTIONS!!!
// CREATESCREAM RETURNS A FUNCTION!!!
// SCREAM INVOKES THAT RETURNED FUNCTION!!!
```

The last two examples were of higher-order functions: functions that either take or return other functions. We could describe the same `createScream` higher-order function with arrows:

```
const createScream = logger => message => {
  logger(message.toUpperCase() + "!!!");
};
```

If you see more than one arrow used during a function declaration, this means that you're using a higher-order function.

We can say that JavaScript supports functional programming because its functions are first-class citizens. This means that functions are data. They can be saved, retrieved, or flow through your applications just like variables.

# Imperative Versus Declarative

Functional programming is a part of a larger programming paradigm: *declarative programming*. Declarative programming is a style of programming where applications are structured in a way that prioritizes describing *what* should happen over defining *how* it should happen.

In order to understand declarative programming, we'll contrast it with *imperative programming*, or a style of programming that's only concerned with how to achieve results with code. Let's consider a common task: making a string URL-friendly. Typically, this can be accomplished by replacing all of the spaces in a string with hyphens, since spaces are not URL-friendly. First, let's examine an imperative approach to this task:

```
const string = "Restaurants in Hanalei";
const urlFriendly = "";

for (var i = 0; i < string.length; i++) {
  if (string[i] === " ") {
    urlFriendly += "-";
  } else {
    urlFriendly += string[i];
  }
}

console.log(urlFriendly); // "Restaurants-in-Hanalei"
```

In this example, we loop through every character in the string, replacing spaces as they occur. The structure of this program is only concerned with how such a task can be achieved. We use a `for` loop and an `if` statement and set values with an equality operator. Just looking at the code alone does not tell us much. Imperative programs require lots of comments in order to understand what's going on.

Now let's look at a declarative approach to the same problem:

```
const string = "Restaurants in Hanalei";
const urlFriendly = string.replace(/ /g, "-");

console.log(urlFriendly);
```

Here we are using `string.replace` along with a regular expression to replace all instances of spaces with hyphens. Using `string.replace` is a way of describing what's supposed to happen: spaces in the string should be replaced. The details of how spaces are dealt with are abstracted away inside the `replace` function. In a declarative program, the syntax itself describes what should happen, and the details of how things happen are abstracted away.

Declarative programs are easy to reason about because the code itself describes what is happening. For example, read the syntax in the following sample. It details what happens after members are loaded from an API:

```
const loadAndMapMembers = compose(
  combineWith(sessionStorage, "members"),
  save(sessionStorage, "members"),
```

```
      scopeMembers(window),
      logMemberInfoToConsole,
      logFieldsToConsole("name.first"),
      countMembersBy("location.state"),
      prepStatesForMapping,
      save(sessionStorage, "map"),
      renderUSMap
    );

    getFakeMembers(100).then(loadAndMapMembers);
```

The declarative approach is more readable and, thus, easier to reason about. The details of how each of these functions is implemented are abstracted away. Those tiny functions are named well and combined in a way that describes how member data goes from being loaded to being saved and printed on a map, and this approach does not require many comments. Essentially, declarative programming produces applications that are easier to reason about, and when it's easier to reason about an application, that application is easier to scale. Additional details about the declarative programming paradigm can be found at the Declarative Programming wiki (*https:// oreil.ly/7MbkB*).

Now, let's consider the task of building a document object model, or DOM (*https:// www.w3.org/DOM*). An imperative approach would be concerned with how the DOM is constructed:

```
const target = document.getElementById("target");
const wrapper = document.createElement("div");
const headline = document.createElement("h1");

wrapper.id = "welcome";
headline.innerText = "Hello World";

wrapper.appendChild(headline);
target.appendChild(wrapper);
```

This code is concerned with creating elements, setting elements, and adding them to the document. It would be very hard to make changes, add features, or scale 10,000 lines of code where the DOM is constructed imperatively.

Now let's take a look at how we can construct a DOM declaratively using a React component:

```
const { render } = ReactDOM;

const Welcome = () => (
  <div id="welcome">
    <h1>Hello World</h1>
  </div>
);

render(<Welcome />, document.getElementById("target"));
```

React is declarative. Here, the `Welcome` component describes the DOM that should be rendered. The `render` function uses the instructions declared in the component to build the DOM, abstracting away the details of how the DOM is to be rendered. We can clearly see that we want to render our `Welcome` component into the element with the ID of `target`.

# Functional Concepts

Now that you've been introduced to functional programming and what it means to be "functional" or "declarative," we'll move on to introducing the core concepts of functional programming: immutability, purity, data transformation, higher-order functions, and recursion.

## Immutability

To mutate is to change, so to be *immutable* is to be unchangeable. In a functional program, data is immutable. It never changes.

If you need to share your birth certificate with the public but want to redact or remove private information, you essentially have two choices: you can take a big Sharpie to your original birth certificate and cross out your private data, or you can find a copy machine. Finding a copy machine, making a copy of your birth certificate, and writing all over that copy with that big Sharpie would be preferable. This way you can have a redacted birth certificate to share and your original that's still intact.

This is how immutable data works in an application. Instead of changing the original data structures, we build changed copies of those data structures and use them instead.

To understand how immutability works, let's take a look at what it means to mutate data. Consider an object that represents the color `lawn`:

```
let color_lawn = {
  title: "lawn",
  color: "#00FF00",
  rating: 0
};
```

We could build a function that would rate colors and use that function to change the rating of the `color` object:

```
function rateColor(color, rating) {
  color.rating = rating;
  return color;
}

console.log(rateColor(color_lawn, 5).rating); // 5
console.log(color_lawn.rating); // 5
```

In JavaScript, function arguments are references to the actual data. Setting the color's rating like this changes or mutates the original color object. (Imagine if you tasked a business with redacting and sharing your birth certificate and they returned your original birth certificate with black marker covering the important details. You'd hope that a business would have the common sense to make a copy of your birth certificate and return the original unharmed.) We can rewrite the rateColor function so that it does not harm the original goods (the color object):

```
const rateColor = function(color, rating) {
  return Object.assign({}, color, { rating: rating });
};

console.log(rateColor(color_lawn, 5).rating); // 5
console.log(color_lawn.rating); // 0
```

Here, we used Object.assign to change the color rating. Object.assign is the copy machine. It takes a blank object, copies the color to that object, and overwrites the rating on the copy. Now we can have a newly rated color object without having to change the original.

We can write the same function using an arrow function along with the object spread operator. This rateColor function uses the spread operator to copy the color into a new object and then overwrite its rating:

```
const rateColor = (color, rating) => ({
  ...color,
  rating
});
```

This version of the rateColor function is exactly the same as the previous one. It treats color as an immutable object, does so with less syntax, and looks a little bit cleaner. Notice that we wrap the returned object in parentheses. With arrow functions, this is a required step since the arrow can't just point to an object's curly braces.

Let's consider an array of color names:

```
let list = [{ title: "Rad Red" }, { title: "Lawn" }, { title: "Party Pink" }];
```

We could create a function that will add colors to that array using Array.push:

```
const addColor = function(title, colors) {
  colors.push({ title: title });
  return colors;
};

console.log(addColor("Glam Green", list).length); // 4
console.log(list.length); // 4
```

However, Array.push is not an immutable function. This addColor function changes the original array by adding another field to it. In order to keep the colors array immutable, we must use Array.concat instead:

```
const addColor = (title, array) => array.concat({ title });

console.log(addColor("Glam Green", list).length); // 4
console.log(list.length); // 3
```

`Array.concat` concatenates arrays. In this case, it takes a new object with a new color title and adds it to a copy of the original array.

You can also use the spread operator to concatenate arrays in the same way it can be used to copy objects. Here's the emerging JavaScript equivalent of the previous add Color function:

```
const addColor = (title, list) => [...list, { title }];
```

This function copies the original list to a new array and then adds a new object containing the color's title to that copy. It is immutable.

## Pure Functions

A *pure function* is a function that returns a value that's computed based on its arguments. Pure functions take at least one argument and always return a value or another function. They do not cause side effects, set global variables, or change anything about application state. They treat their arguments as immutable data.

In order to understand pure functions, let's first take a look at an impure function:

```
const frederick = {
  name: "Frederick Douglass",
  canRead: false,
  canWrite: false
};

function selfEducate() {
  frederick.canRead = true;
  frederick.canWrite = true;
  return frederick;
}

selfEducate();
console.log(frederick);

// {name: "Frederick Douglass", canRead: true, canWrite: true}
```

The `selfEducate` function is not a pure function. It does not take any arguments, and it does not return a value or a function. It also changes a variable outside of its scope: `Frederick`. Once the `selfEducate` function is invoked, something about the "world" has changed. It causes side effects:

```
const frederick = {
  name: "Frederick Douglass",
  canRead: false,
  canWrite: false
};

const selfEducate = person => {
  person.canRead = true;
  person.canWrite = true;
  return person;
};

console.log(selfEducate(frederick));
console.log(frederick);

// {name: "Frederick Douglass", canRead: true, canWrite: true}
// {name: "Frederick Douglass", canRead: true, canWrite: true}
```

### Pure Functions Are Testable

Pure functions are naturally *testable*. They do not change anything about their environment or "world," and therefore do not require a complicated test setup or teardown. Everything a pure function needs to operate it accesses via arguments. When testing a pure function, you control the arguments, and thus you can estimate the outcome. This selfEducate function is also impure: it causes side effects. Invoking this function mutates the objects that are sent to it. If we could treat the arguments sent to this function as immutable data, then we would have a pure function.

Let's have this function take an argument:

```
const frederick = {
  name: "Frederick Douglass",
  canRead: false,
  canWrite: false
};

const selfEducate = person => ({
  ...person,
  canRead: true,
  canWrite: true
});

console.log(selfEducate(frederick));
console.log(frederick);

// {name: "Frederick Douglass", canRead: true, canWrite: true}
// {name: "Frederick Douglass", canRead: false, canWrite: false}
```

Finally, this version of selfEducate is a pure function. It computes a value based on the argument that was sent to it: the person. It returns a new person object without mutating the argument sent to it and therefore has no side effects.

Now let's examine an impure function that mutates the DOM:

```
function Header(text) {
  let h1 = document.createElement("h1");
  h1.innerText = text;
  document.body.appendChild(h1);
}

Header("Header() caused side effects");
```

The Header function creates a heading—one element with specific text—and adds it to the DOM. This function is impure. It does not return a function or a value, and it causes side effects: a changed DOM.

In React, the UI is expressed with pure functions. In the following sample, Header is a pure function that can be used to create h1 elements just like in the previous example. However, this function on its own does not cause side effects because it does not mutate the DOM. This function will create an h1 element, and it's up to some other part of the application to use that element to change the DOM:

```
const Header = props => <h1>{props.title}</h1>;
```

Pure functions are another core concept of functional programming. They will make your life much easier because they will not affect your application's state. When writing functions, try to follow these three rules:

1. The function should take in at least one argument.
2. The function should return a value or another function.
3. The function should not change or mutate any of its arguments.

## Data Transformations

How does anything change in an application if the data is immutable? Functional programming is all about transforming data from one form to another. We'll produce transformed copies using functions. These functions make our code less imperative and thus reduce complexity.

You do not need a special framework to understand how to produce one dataset that is based upon another. JavaScript already has the necessary tools for this task built into the language. There are two core functions that you must master in order to be proficient with functional JavaScript: Array.map and Array.reduce.

In this section, we'll take a look at how these and some other core functions transform data from one type to another.

Consider this array of high schools:

```
const schools = ["Yorktown", "Washington & Liberty", "Wakefield"];
```

We can get a comma-delimited list of these and some other strings by using the `Array.join` function:

```
console.log(schools.join(", "));

// "Yorktown, Washington & Liberty, Wakefield"
```

`Array.join` is a built-in JavaScript array method that we can use to extract a delimited string from our array. The original array is still intact; `join` simply provides a different take on it. The details of how this string is produced are abstracted away from the programmer.

If we wanted to create a function that creates a new array of the schools that begin with the letter "W," we could use the `Array.filter` method:

```
const wSchools = schools.filter(school => school[0] === "W");

console.log(wSchools);
// ["Washington & Liberty", "Wakefield"]
```

`Array.filter` is a built-in JavaScript function that produces a new array from a source array. This function takes a *predicate* as its only argument. A predicate is a function that always returns a Boolean value: `true` or `false`. `Array.filter` invokes this predicate once for every item in the array. That item is passed to the predicate as an argument, and the return value is used to decide if that item will be added to the new array. In this case, `Array.filter` is checking every school to see if its name begins with a "W."

When it's time to remove an item from an array, we should use `Array.filter` over `Array.pop` or `Array.splice` because `Array.filter` is immutable. In this next sample, the cutSchool function returns new arrays that filter out specific school names:

```
const cutSchool = (cut, list) => list.filter(school => school !== cut);

console.log(cutSchool("Washington & Liberty", schools).join(", "));

// "Yorktown, Wakefield"

console.log(schools.join("\n"));

// Yorktown
// Washington & Liberty
// Wakefield
```

In this case, the cutSchool function is used to return a new array that does not contain "Washington & Liberty." Then, the join function is used with this new array to create a string out of the remaining two school names. cutSchool is a pure function. It takes a list of schools and the name of the school that should be removed and returns a new array without that specific school.

Another array function that is essential to functional programming is Array.map. Instead of a predicate, the Array.map method takes a function as its argument. This function will be invoked once for every item in the array, and whatever it returns will be added to the new array:

```
const highSchools = schools.map(school => `${school} High School`);

console.log(highSchools.join("\n"));

// Yorktown High School
// Washington & Liberty High School
// Wakefield High School

console.log(schools.join("\n"));

// Yorktown
// Washington & Liberty
// Wakefield
```

In this case, the map function was used to append "High School" to each school name. The schools array is still intact.

In the last example, we produced an array of strings from an array of strings. The map function can produce an array of objects, values, arrays, other functions—any Java-Script type. Here's an example of the map function returning an object for every school:

```
const highSchools = schools.map(school => ({ name: school }));

console.log(highSchools);

// [
// { name: "Yorktown" },
// { name: "Washington & Liberty" },
// { name: "Wakefield" }
// ]
```

An array containing objects was produced from an array that contains strings.

If you need to create a pure function that changes one object in an array of objects, map can be used for this, too. In the following example, we'll change the school with the name of "Stratford" to "HB Woodlawn" without mutating the schools array:

```
let schools = [
  { name: "Yorktown" },
```

```
    { name: "Stratford" },
    { name: "Washington & Liberty" },
    { name: "Wakefield" }
];

let updatedSchools = editName("Stratford", "HB Woodlawn", schools);

console.log(updatedSchools[1]); // { name: "HB Woodlawn" }
console.log(schools[1]); // { name: "Stratford" }
```

The `schools` array is an array of objects. The `updatedSchools` variable calls the `edit Name` function and we send it the school we want to update, the new school, and the `schools` array. This changes the new array but makes no edits to the original:

```
const editName = (oldName, name, arr) =>
  arr.map(item => {
    if (item.name === oldName) {
      return {
        ...item,
        name
      };
    } else {
      return item;
    }
  });
```

Within `editName`, the `map` function is used to create a new array of objects based upon the original array. The `editName` function can be written entirely in one line. Here's an example of the same function using a shorthand `if/else` statement:

```
const editName = (oldName, name, arr) =>
  arr.map(item => (item.name === oldName ? { ...item, name } : item));
```

If you need to transform an array into an object, you can use `Array.map` in conjunction with `Object.keys`. `Object.keys` is a method that can be used to return an array of keys from an object.

Let's say we needed to transform the `schools` object into an array of schools:

```
const schools = {
  Yorktown: 10,
  "Washington & Liberty": 2,
  Wakefield: 5
};

const schoolArray = Object.keys(schools).map(key => ({
  name: key,
  wins: schools[key]
}));

console.log(schoolArray);
```

```
// [
//   {
// name: "Yorktown",
// wins: 10
//   },
//   {
// name: "Washington & Liberty",
// wins: 2
//   },
//   {
// name: "Wakefield",
// wins: 5
//   }
// ]
```

In this example, Object.keys returns an array of school names, and we can use map on that array to produce a new array of the same length. The name of the new object will be set using the key, and wins is set equal to the value.

So far, we've learned that we can transform arrays with Array.map and Array.filter. We've also learned that we can change arrays into objects by combining Object.keys with Array.map. The final tool that we need in our functional arsenal is the ability to transform arrays into primitives and other objects.

The reduce and reduceRight functions can be used to transform an array into any value, including a number, string, boolean, object, or even a function.

Let's say we need to find the maximum number in an array of numbers. We need to transform an array into a number; therefore, we can use reduce:

```
const ages = [21, 18, 42, 40, 64, 63, 34];

const maxAge = ages.reduce((max, age) => {
  console.log(`${age} > ${max} = ${age > max}`);
  if (age > max) {
    return age;
  } else {
    return max;
  }
}, 0);

console.log("maxAge", maxAge);

// 21 > 0 = true
// 18 > 21 = false
// 42 > 21 = true
// 40 > 42 = false
// 64 > 42 = true
// 63 > 64 = false
// 34 > 64 = false
// maxAge 64
```

The ages array has been reduced into a single value: the maximum age, 64. reduce takes two arguments: a callback function and an original value. In this case, the original value is 0, which sets the initial maximum value to 0. The callback is invoked once for every item in the array. The first time this callback is invoked, age is equal to 21, the first value in the array, and max is equal to 0, the initial value. The callback returns the greater of the two numbers, 21, and that becomes the max value during the next iteration. Each iteration compares each age against the max value and returns the greater of the two. Finally, the last number in the array is compared and returned from the previous callback.

If we remove the console.log statement from the preceding function and use a shorthand if/else statement, we can calculate the max value in any array of numbers with the following syntax:

```
const max = ages.reduce((max, value) => (value > max ? value : max), 0);
```

**Array.reduceRight**

Array.reduceRight works the same way as Array.reduce; the difference is that it starts reducing from the end of the array rather than the beginning.

Sometimes we need to transform an array into an object. The following example uses reduce to transform an array that contains colors into a hash:

```
const colors = [
  {
    id: "xekare",
    title: "rad red",
    rating: 3
  },
  {
    id: "jbwsof",
    title: "big blue",
    rating: 2
  },
  {
    id: "prigbj",
    title: "grizzly grey",
    rating: 5
  },
  {
    id: "ryhbhsl",
    title: "banana",
    rating: 1
  }
];

const hashColors = colors.reduce((hash, { id, title, rating }) => {
```

```
    hash[id] = { title, rating };
    return hash;
}, {});

console.log(hashColors);

// {
// "xekare": {
// title:"rad red",
// rating:3
// },
// "jbwsof": {
// title:"big blue",
// rating:2
// },
// "prigbj": {
// title:"grizzly grey",
// rating:5
// },
// "ryhbhsl": {
// title:"banana",
// rating:1
// }
// }
```

In this example, the second argument sent to the reduce function is an empty object. This is our initial value for the hash. During each iteration, the callback function adds a new key to the hash using bracket notation and sets the value for that key to the id field of the array. Array.reduce can be used in this way to reduce an array to a single value—in this case, an object.

We can even transform arrays into completely different arrays using reduce. Consider reducing an array with multiple instances of the same value to an array of unique values. The reduce method can be used to accomplish this task:

```
const colors = ["red", "red", "green", "blue", "green"];

const uniqueColors = colors.reduce(
  (unique, color) =>
    unique.indexOf(color) !== -1 ? unique : [...unique, color],
  []
);

console.log(uniqueColors);

// ["red", "green", "blue"]
```

In this example, the colors array is reduced to an array of distinct values. The second argument sent to the reduce function is an empty array. This will be the initial value for distinct. When the distinct array does not already contain a specific color, it will be added. Otherwise, it will be skipped, and the current `distinct` array will be returned.

`map` and `reduce` are the main weapons of any functional programmer, and JavaScript is no exception. If you want to be a proficient JavaScript engineer, then you must master these functions. The ability to create one dataset from another is a required skill and is useful for any type of programming paradigm.

## Higher-Order Functions

The use of *higher-order functions* is also essential to functional programming. We've already mentioned higher-order functions, and we've even used a few in this chapter. Higher-order functions are functions that can manipulate other functions. They can take functions in as arguments or return functions or both.

The first category of higher-order functions are functions that expect other functions as arguments. `Array.map`, `Array.filter`, and `Array.reduce` all take functions as arguments. They are higher-order functions.

Let's take a look at how we can implement a higher-order function. In the following example, we create an `invokeIf` callback function that will test a condition and invoke a callback function when it's true and another callback function when the condition is false:

```
const invokeIf = (condition, fnTrue, fnFalse) =>
  condition ? fnTrue() : fnFalse();

const showWelcome = () => console.log("Welcome!!!");

const showUnauthorized = () => console.log("Unauthorized!!!");

invokeIf(true, showWelcome, showUnauthorized); // "Welcome!!!"
invokeIf(false, showWelcome, showUnauthorized); // "Unauthorized!!!"
```

`invokeIf` expects two functions: one for true and one for false. This is demonstrated by sending both `showWelcome` and `showUnauthorized` to `invokeIf`. When the condition is true, `showWelcome` is invoked. When it's false, `showUnauthorized` is invoked.

Higher-order functions that return other functions can help us handle the complexities associated with asynchronicity in JavaScript. They can help us create functions that can be used or reused at our convenience.

*Currying* is a functional technique that involves the use of higher-order functions.

The following is an example of currying. The `userLogs` function hangs on to some information (the username) and returns a function that can be used and reused when the rest of the information (the message) is made available. In this example, log messages will all be prepended with the associated username. Notice that we're using the `getFakeMembers` function that returns a promise from Chapter 2:

```
const userLogs = userName => message =>
  console.log(`${userName} -> ${message}`);

const log = userLogs("grandpa23");

log("attempted to load 20 fake members");
getFakeMembers(20).then(
  members => log(`successfully loaded ${members.length} members`),
  error => log("encountered an error loading members")
);

// grandpa23 -> attempted to load 20 fake members
// grandpa23 -> successfully loaded 20 members

// grandpa23 -> attempted to load 20 fake members
// grandpa23 -> encountered an error loading members
```

`userLogs` is the higher-order function. The `log` function is produced from `userLogs`, and every time the `log` function is used, "grandpa23" is prepended to the message.

## Recursion

Recursion is a technique that involves creating functions that recall themselves. Often, when faced with a challenge that involves a loop, a recursive function can be used instead. Consider the task of counting down from 10. We could create a `for` loop to solve this problem, or we could alternatively use a recursive function. In this example, `countdown` is the recursive function:

```
const countdown = (value, fn) => {
  fn(value);
  return value > 0 ? countdown(value - 1, fn) : value;
};

countdown(10, value => console.log(value));

// 10
// 9
// 8
// 7
// 6
// 5
// 4
// 3
// 2
// 1
// 0
```

countdown expects a number and a function as arguments. In this example, it's invoked with a value of 10 and a callback function. When countdown is invoked, the callback is invoked, which logs the current value. Next, countdown checks the value to see if it's greater than 0. If it is, countdown recalls itself with a decremented value. Eventually, the value will be 0, and countdown will return that value all the way back up the call stack.

Recursion is a pattern that works particularly well with asynchronous processes. Functions can recall themselves when they're ready, like when the data is available or when a timer has finished.

The countdown function can be modified to count down with a delay. This modified version of the countdown function can be used to create a countdown clock:

```
const countdown = (value, fn, delay = 1000) => {
  fn(value);
  return value > 0
    ? setTimeout(() => countdown(value - 1, fn, delay), delay)
    : value;
};

const log = value => console.log(value);
countdown(10, log);
```

In this example, we create a 10-second countdown by initially invoking countdown once with the number 10 in a function that logs the countdown. Instead of recalling itself right away, the countdown function waits one second before recalling itself, thus creating a clock.

Recursion is a good technique for searching data structures. You can use recursion to iterate through subfolders until a folder that contains only files is identified. You can also use recursion to iterate though the HTML DOM until you find an element that does not contain any children. In the next example, we'll use recursion to iterate deeply into an object to retrieve a nested value:

```
const dan = {
  type: "person",
  data: {
    gender: "male",
    info: {
      id: 22,
      fullname: {
        first: "Dan",
        last: "Deacon"
      }
    }
  }
};
```

```
deepPick("type", dan); // "person"
deepPick("data.info.fullname.first", dan); // "Dan"
```

deepPick can be used to access Dan's type, stored immediately in the first object, or to dig down into nested objects to locate Dan's first name. Sending a string that uses dot notation, we can specify where to locate values that are nested deep within an object:

```
const deepPick = (fields, object = {}) => {
  const [first, ...remaining] = fields.split(".");
  return remaining.length
    ? deepPick(remaining.join("."), object[first])
    : object[first];
};
```

The deepPick function is either going to return a value or recall itself until it eventually returns a value. First, this function splits the dot-notated fields string into an array and uses array destructuring to separate the first value from the remaining values. If there are remaining values, deepPick recalls itself with slightly different data, allowing it to dig one level deeper.

This function continues to call itself until the fields string no longer contains dots, meaning that there are no more remaining fields. In this sample, you can see how the values for first, remaining, and object[first] change as deepPick iterates through:

```
deepPick("data.info.fullname.first", dan); // "Dan"

// First Iteration
// first = "data"
// remaining.join(".") = "info.fullname.first"
// object[first] = { gender: "male", {info} }

// Second Iteration
// first = "info"
// remaining.join(".") = "fullname.first"
// object[first] = {id: 22, {fullname}}

// Third Iteration
// first = "fullname"
// remaining.join("." = "first"
// object[first] = {first: "Dan", last: "Deacon" }

// Finally...
// first = "first"
// remaining.length = 0
// object[first] = "Deacon"
```

Recursion is a powerful functional technique that's fun to implement.

## Composition

Functional programs break up their logic into small, pure functions that are focused on specific tasks. Eventually, you'll need to put these smaller functions together. Specifically, you may need to combine them, call them in series or parallel, or compose them into larger functions until you eventually have an application.

When it comes to composition, there are a number of different implementations, patterns, and techniques. One that you may be familiar with is chaining. In JavaScript, functions can be chained together using dot notation to act on the return value of the previous function.

Strings have a replace method. The replace method returns a template string, which will also have a replace method. Therefore, we can chain together replace methods with dot notation to transform a string:

```
const template = "hh:mm:ss tt";
const clockTime = template
  .replace("hh", "03")
  .replace("mm", "33")
  .replace("ss", "33")
  .replace("tt", "PM");

console.log(clockTime);

// "03:33:33 PM"
```

In this example, the template is a string. By chaining replace methods to the end of the template string, we can replace hours, minutes, seconds, and time of day in the string with new values. The template itself remains intact and can be reused to create more clock time displays.

The both function is one function that pipes a value through two separate functions. The output of civilian hours becomes the input for appendAMPM, and we can change a date using both of these functions combined into one:

```
const both = date => appendAMPM(civilianHours(date));
```

However, this syntax is hard to comprehend and therefore tough to maintain or scale. What happens when we need to send a value through 20 different functions?

A more elegant approach is to create a higher-order function we can use to compose functions into larger functions:

```
const both = compose(
  civilianHours,
  appendAMPM
);

both(new Date());
```

This approach looks much better. It's easy to scale because we can add more functions at any point. This approach also makes it easy to change the order of the composed functions.

The `compose` function is a higher-order function. It takes functions as arguments and returns a single value:

```
const compose = (...fns) => arg =>
  fns.reduce((composed, f) => f(composed), arg);
```

`compose` takes in functions as arguments and returns a single function. In this implementation, the spread operator is used to turn those function arguments into an array called `fns`. A function is then returned that expects one argument, `arg`. When this function is invoked, the `fns` array is piped starting with the argument we want to send through the function. The argument becomes the initial value for `compose`, then each iteration of the reduced callback returns. Notice that the callback takes two arguments: composed and a function `f`. Each function is invoked with `compose`, which is the result of the previous function's output. Eventually, the last function will be invoked and the last result returned.

This is a simple example of a `compose` function designed to illustrate composition techniques. This function becomes more complex when it's time to handle more than one argument or deal with arguments that are not functions.

## Putting It All Together

Now that we've been introduced to the core concepts of functional programming, let's put those concepts to work for us and build a small JavaScript application.

Our challenge is to build a ticking clock. The clock needs to display hours, minutes, seconds, and time of day in civilian time. Each field must always have double digits, meaning leading zeros need to be applied to single-digit values like 1 or 2. The clock must also tick and change the display every second.

First, let's review an imperative solution for the clock:

```
// Log Clock Time every Second
setInterval(logClockTime, 1000);

function logClockTime() {
  // Get Time string as civilian time
  let time = getClockTime();

  // Clear the Console and log the time
  console.clear();
  console.log(time);
}

function getClockTime() {
```

```javascript
// Get the Current Time
let date = new Date();
let time = "";

// Serialize clock time
let time = {
  hours: date.getHours(),
  minutes: date.getMinutes(),
  seconds: date.getSeconds(),
  ampm: "AM"
};

// Convert to civilian time
if (time.hours == 12) {
  time.ampm = "PM";
} else if (time.hours > 12) {
  time.ampm = "PM";
  time.hours -= 12;
}

// Prepend a 0 on the hours to make double digits
if (time.hours < 10) {
  time.hours = "0" + time.hours;
}

// prepend a 0 on the minutes to make double digits
if (time.minutes < 10) {
  time.minutes = "0" + time.minutes;
}

// prepend a 0 on the seconds to make double digits
if (time.seconds < 10) {
  time.seconds = "0" + time.seconds;
}

// Format the clock time as a string "hh:mm:ss tt"
return time.hours + ":" + time.minutes + ":" + time.seconds + " " + time.ampm;
}
```

This solution works, and the comments help us understand what's happening. However, these functions are large and complicated. Each function does a lot. They're hard to comprehend, they require comments, and they're tough to maintain. Let's see how a functional approach can produce a more scalable application.

Our goal will be to break the application logic up into smaller parts: functions. Each function will be focused on a single task, and we'll compose them into larger functions that we can use to create the clock.

First, let's create some functions that give us values and manage the console. We'll need a function that gives us one second, a function that gives us the current time, and a couple of functions that will log messages on a console and clear the console. In functional programs, we should use functions over values wherever possible. We'll invoke the function to obtain the value when needed:

```
const oneSecond = () => 1000;
const getCurrentTime = () => new Date();
const clear = () => console.clear();
const log = message => console.log(message);
```

Next, we'll need some functions for transforming data. These three functions will be used to mutate the `Date` object into an object that can be used for our clock:

serializeClockTime

Takes a date object and returns an object for clock time that contains hours, minutes, and seconds.

civilianHours

Takes the clock time object and returns an object where hours are converted to civilian time. For example: 1300 becomes 1:00.

appendAMPM

Takes the clock time object and appends time of day (AM or PM) to that object.

```
const serializeClockTime = date => ({
  hours: date.getHours(),
  minutes: date.getMinutes(),
  seconds: date.getSeconds()
});

const civilianHours = clockTime => ({
  ...clockTime,
  hours: clockTime.hours > 12 ? clockTime.hours - 12 : clockTime.hours
});

const appendAMPM = clockTime => ({
  ...clockTime,
  ampm: clockTime.hours >= 12 ? "PM" : "AM"
});
```

These three functions are used to transform data without changing the original. They treat their arguments as immutable objects.

Next, we'll need a few higher-order functions:

display

Takes a target function and returns a function that will send a time to the target. In this example, the target will be `console.log`.

formatClock

Takes a template string and uses it to return clock time formatted based on the criteria from the string. In this example, the template is "hh:mm:ss tt". From there, `formatClock` will replace the placeholders with hours, minutes, seconds, and time of day.

`prependZero`

Takes an object's key as an argument and prepends a zero to the value stored under that object's key. It takes in a key to a specific field and prepends values with a zero if the value is less than 10.

```
const display = target => time => target(time);

const formatClock = format => time =>
  format
    .replace("hh", time.hours)
    .replace("mm", time.minutes)
    .replace("ss", time.seconds)
    .replace("tt", time.ampm);

const prependZero = key => clockTime => ({
  ...clockTime,
  key: clockTime[key] < 10 ? "0" + clockTime[key] : clockTime[key]
});
```

These higher-order functions will be invoked to create the functions that will be reused to format the clock time for every tick. Both `formatClock` and `prependZero` will be invoked once, initially setting up the required template or key. The inner functions they return will be invoked once every second to format the time for display.

Now that we have all of the functions required to build a ticking clock, we'll need to compose them. We'll use the `compose` function that we defined in the last section to handle composition:

`convertToCivilianTime`

A single function that takes clock time as an argument and transforms it into civilian time by using both civilian hours.

`doubleDigits`

A single function that takes civilian clock time and makes sure the hours, minutes, and seconds display double digits by prepending zeros where needed.

`startTicking`

Starts the clock by setting an interval that invokes a callback every second. The callback is composed using all our functions. Every second the console is cleared, `currentTime` is obtained, converted, civilianized, formatted, and displayed.

```
const convertToCivilianTime = clockTime =>
  compose(
    appendAMPM,
    civilianHours
  )(clockTime);
```

```
const doubleDigits = civilianTime =>
  compose(
    prependZero("hours"),
    prependZero("minutes"),
    prependZero("seconds")
  )(civilianTime);

const startTicking = () =>
  setInterval(
    compose(
      clear,
      getCurrentTime,
      serializeClockTime,
      convertToCivilianTime,
      doubleDigits,
      formatClock("hh:mm:ss tt"),
      display(log)
    ),
    oneSecond()
  );

startTicking();
```

This declarative version of the clock achieves the same results as the imperative version. However, there quite a few benefits to this approach. First, all of these functions are easily testable and reusable. They can be used in future clocks or other digital displays. Also, this program is easily scalable. There are no side effects. There are no global variables outside of functions themselves. There could still be bugs, but they'll be easier to find.

In this chapter, we've introduced functional programming principles. Throughout the book when we discuss best practices in React, we'll continue to demonstrate how many React concepts are based in functional techniques. In the next chapter, we'll dive into React officially with an improved understanding of the principles that guided its development.

# CHAPTER 4

# How React Works

So far on your journey, you've brushed up on the latest syntax. You've reviewed the functional programming patterns that guided React's creation. These steps have prepared you to take the next step, to do what you came here to do: to learn how React works. Let's get into writing some real React code.

When you work with React, it's more than likely that you'll be creating your apps with JSX. JSX is a tag-based JavaScript syntax that looks a lot like HTML. It's a syntax we'll dive deep into in the next chapter and continue to use for the rest of the book. To truly understand React, though, we need to understand its most atomic units: React elements. From there, we'll get into React elements. From there, we'll get into React components by looking at how we can create custom components that compose other components and elements.

## Page Setup

In order to work with React in the browser, we need to include two libraries: React and ReactDOM. React is the library for creating views. ReactDOM is the library used to actually render the UI in the browser. Both libraries are available as scripts from the unpkg CDN (links are included in the following code). Let's set up an HTML document:

```
<!DOCTYPE html>
<html>
  <head>
    <meta charset="utf-8" />
    <title>React Samples</title>
  </head>
  <body>
    <!-- Target container -->
    <div id="root"></div>
```

```
<!-- React library & ReactDOM (Development Version)-->
  <script
src="https://unpkg.com/react@16/umd/react.development.js">
</script>
  <script
src="https://unpkg.com/react-dom@16/umd/react-dom.development.js">
</script>

  <script>
    // Pure React and JavaScript code
  </script>
</body>
</html>
```

These are the minimum requirements for working with React in the browser. You can place your JavaScript in a separate file, but it must be loaded somewhere in the page after React has been loaded. We're going to be using the development version of React to see all of the error messages and warnings in the browser console. You can choose to use the minified production version using *react.production.min.js* and *react-dom.production.min.js*, which will strip away those warnings.

# React Elements

HTML is simply a set of instructions that a browser follows when constructing the DOM. The elements that make up an HTML document become DOM elements when the browser loads HTML and renders the user interface.

Let's say you have to construct an HTML hierarchy for a recipe. A possible solution for such a task might look something like this:

```
<section id="baked-salmon">
  <h1>Baked Salmon</h1>
  <ul class="ingredients">
    <li>2 lb salmon</li>
    <li>5 sprigs fresh rosemary</li>
    <li>2 tablespoons olive oil</li>
    <li>2 small lemons</li>
    <li>1 teaspoon kosher salt</li>
    <li>4 cloves of chopped garlic</li>
  </ul>
  <section class="instructions">
    <h2>Cooking Instructions</h2>
    <p>Preheat the oven to 375 degrees.</p>
    <p>Lightly coat aluminum foil with oil.</p>
    <p>Place salmon on foil</p>
    <p>Cover with rosemary, sliced lemons, chopped garlic.</p>
    <p>Bake for 15-20 minutes until cooked through.</p>
    <p>Remove from oven.</p>
```

```
    </section>
  </section>
```

In HTML, elements relate to one another in a hierarchy that resembles a family tree. We could say that the root element (in this case, a section) has three children: a heading, an unordered list of ingredients, and a section for the instructions.

In the past, websites consisted of independent HTML pages. When the user navigated these pages, the browser would request and load different HTML documents. The invention of AJAX (Asynchronous JavaScript and XML) brought us the single-page application, or SPA (*https://oreil.ly/z6Saj*). Since browsers could request and load tiny bits of data using AJAX, entire web applications could now run out of a single page and rely on JavaScript to update the user interface.

In an SPA, the browser initially loads one HTML document. As users navigate through the site, they actually stay on the same page. JavaScript destroys and creates a new user interface as the user interacts with the application. It may feel as though you're jumping from page to page, but you're actually still on the same HTML page, and JavaScript is doing the heavy lifting.

The DOM API (*https://mzl.la/2m1oQDJ*) is a collection of objects that JavaScript can use to interact with the browser to modify the DOM. If you've used `document.crea teElement` or `document.appendChild`, you've worked with the DOM API.

React is a library that's designed to update the browser DOM for us. We no longer have to be concerned with the complexities associated with building high-performing SPAs because React can do that for us. With React, we do not interact with the DOM API directly. Instead, we provide instructions for what we want React to build, and React will take care of rendering and reconciling the elements we've instructed it to create.

The browser DOM is made up of DOM elements. Similarly, the React DOM is made up of React elements. DOM elements and React elements may look the same, but they're actually quite different. A React element is a description of what the actual DOM element should look like. In other words, React elements are the instructions for how the browser DOM should be created.

We can create a React element to represent an h1 using `React.createElement`:

```
React.createElement("h1", { id: "recipe-0" }, "Baked Salmon");
```

The first argument defines the type of element we want to create. In this case, we want to create an h1 element. The second argument represents the element's properties. This h1 currently has an id of recipe-0. The third argument represents the element's children: any nodes that are inserted between the opening and closing tag (in this case, just some text).

During rendering, React will convert this element to an actual DOM element:

```
<h1 id="recipe-0">Baked Salmon</h1>
```

The properties are similarly applied to the new DOM element: the properties are added to the tag as attributes, and the child text is added as text within the element. A React element is just a JavaScript literal that tells React how to construct the DOM element.

If you were to log this element, it would look like this:

```
{
  $$typeof: Symbol(React.element),
  "type": "h1",
  "key": null,
  "ref": null,
  "props": {id: "recipe-0", children: "Baked Salmon"},
  "_owner": null,
  "_store": {}
}
```

This is the structure of a React element. There are fields that are used by React: _owner, _store, and $$typeof. The key and ref fields are important to React elements, but we'll introduce those later. For now, let's take a closer look at the type and props fields.

The type property of the React element tells React what type of HTML or SVG element to create. The props property represents the data and child elements required to construct a DOM element. The children property is for displaying other nested elements as text.

**Creating Elements**

We're taking a peek at the object that React.createElement returns. You won't actually create these elements by hand; instead, you'll use the React.createElement function.

# ReactDOM

Once we've created a React element, we'll want to see it in the browser. ReactDOM contains the tools necessary to render React elements in the browser. ReactDOM is where we'll find the `render` method.

We can render a React element, including its children, to the DOM with `React DOM.render`. The element we want to render is passed as the first argument, and the second argument is the target node, where we should render the element:

```
const dish = React.createElement("h1", null, "Baked Salmon");

ReactDOM.render(dish, document.getElementById("root"));
```

Rendering the title element to the DOM would add an h1 element to the div with the id of root, which we would already have defined in our HTML. We build this div inside the body tag:

```
<body>
  <div id="root">
    <h1>Baked Salmon</h1>
  </div>
</body>
```

Anything related to rendering elements to the DOM is found in the `ReactDOM` package. In versions of React earlier than React 16, you could only render one element to the DOM. Today, it's possible to render arrays as well. When the ability to do this was announced at ReactConf 2017, everyone clapped and screamed. It was a big deal. This is what that looks like:

```
const dish = React.createElement("h1", null, "Baked Salmon");
const dessert = React.createElement("h2", null, "Coconut Cream Pie");

ReactDOM.render([dish, dessert], document.getElementById("root"));
```

This will render both of these elements as siblings inside of the root container. We hope you just clapped and screamed!

In the next section, we'll get an understanding of how to use `props.children`.

## Children

React renders child elements using `props.children`. In the previous section, we rendered a text element as a child of the h1 element, and thus `props.children` was set to Baked Salmon. We could render other React elements as children, too, creating a tree of elements. This is why we use the term *element tree*: the tree has one root element from which many branches grow.

Let's consider the unordered list that contains ingredients:

```
<ul>
  <li>2 lb salmon</li>
  <li>5 sprigs fresh rosemary</li>
  <li>2 tablespoons olive oil</li>
  <li>2 small lemons</li>
  <li>1 teaspoon kosher salt</li>
  <li>4 cloves of chopped garlic</li>
</ul>
```

In this sample, the unordered list is the root element, and it has six children. We can represent this `ul` and its children with `React.createElement`:

```
React.createElement(
  "ul",
  null,
  React.createElement("li", null, "2 lb salmon"),
  React.createElement("li", null, "5 sprigs fresh rosemary"),
  React.createElement("li", null, "2 tablespoons olive oil"),
  React.createElement("li", null, "2 small lemons"),
  React.createElement("li", null, "1 teaspoon kosher salt"),
  React.createElement("li", null, "4 cloves of chopped garlic")
);
```

Every additional argument sent to the `createElement` function is another child element. React creates an array of these child elements and sets the value of `props.chil dren` to that array.

If we were to inspect the resulting React element, we would see each list item represented by a React element and added to an array called `props.children`. If you console log this element:

```
const list = React.createElement(
  "ul",
  null,
  React.createElement("li", null, "2 lb salmon"),
  React.createElement("li", null, "5 sprigs fresh rosemary"),
  React.createElement("li", null, "2 tablespoons olive oil"),
  React.createElement("li", null, "2 small lemons"),
  React.createElement("li", null, "1 teaspoon kosher salt"),
  React.createElement("li", null, "4 cloves of chopped garlic")
);

console.log(list);
```

The result will look like this:

```
{
  "type": "ul",
  "props": {
  "children": [
  { "type": "li", "props": { "children": "2 lb salmon" } … },
```

```
      { "type": "li", "props": { "children": "5 sprigs fresh rosemary"} … },
      { "type": "li", "props": { "children": "2 tablespoons olive oil" } … },
      { "type": "li", "props": { "children": "2 small lemons"} … },
      { "type": "li", "props": { "children": "1 teaspoon kosher salt"} … },
      { "type": "li", "props": { "children": "4 cloves of chopped garlic"} … }
    ]
    ...
  }
}
```

We can now see that each list item is a child. Earlier in this chapter, we introduced HTML for an entire recipe rooted in a `section` element. To create this using React, we'll use a series of `createElement` calls:

```
React.createElement(
  "section",
  { id: "baked-salmon" },
  React.createElement("h1", null, "Baked Salmon"),
  React.createElement(
    "ul",
    { className: "ingredients" },
    React.createElement("li", null, "2 lb salmon"),
    React.createElement("li", null, "5 sprigs fresh rosemary"),
    React.createElement("li", null, "2 tablespoons olive oil"),
    React.createElement("li", null, "2 small lemons"),
    React.createElement("li", null, "1 teaspoon kosher salt"),
    React.createElement("li", null, "4 cloves of chopped garlic")
  ),
  React.createElement(
    "section",
    { className: "instructions" },
    React.createElement("h2", null, "Cooking Instructions"),
    React.createElement("p", null, "Preheat the oven to 375 degrees."),
    React.createElement("p", null, "Lightly coat aluminum foil with oil."),
    React.createElement("p", null, "Place salmon on foil."),
    React.createElement(
      "p",
      null,
      "Cover with rosemary, sliced lemons, chopped garlic."
    ),
    React.createElement(
      "p",
      null,
      "Bake for 15-20 minutes until cooked through."
    ),
    React.createElement("p", null, "Remove from oven.")
  )
);
```

**className in React**

Any element that has an HTML `class` attribute is using `className` for that property instead of `class`. Since `class` is a reserved word in JavaScript, we have to use `className` to define the `class` attribute of an HTML element. This sample is what pure React looks like. Pure React is ultimately what runs in the browser. A React app is a tree of React elements all stemming from a single root element. React elements are the instructions React will use to build a UI in the browser.

## Constructing elements with data

The major advantage of using React is its ability to separate data from UI elements. Since React is just JavaScript, we can add JavaScript logic to help us build the React component tree. For example, ingredients can be stored in an array, and we can map that array to the React elements.

Let's go back and think about the unordered list for a moment:

```
React.createElement(
  "ul",
  null,
  React.createElement("li", null, "2 lb salmon"),
  React.createElement("li", null, "5 sprigs fresh rosemary"),
  React.createElement("li", null, "2 tablespoons olive oil"),
  React.createElement("li", null, "2 small lemons"),
  React.createElement("li", null, "1 teaspoon kosher salt"),
  React.createElement("li", null, "4 cloves of chopped garlic")
);
```

The data used in this list of ingredients can easily be represented using a JavaScript array:

```
const items = [
  "2 lb salmon",
  "5 sprigs fresh rosemary",
  "2 tablespoons olive oil",
  "2 small lemons",
  "1 teaspoon kosher salt",
  "4 cloves of chopped garlic"
];
```

We want to use this data to generate the correct number of list items without having to hard-code each one. We can map over the array and create list items for as many ingredients as there are:

```
React.createElement(
  "ul",
  { className: "ingredients" },
  items.map(ingredient => React.createElement("li", null, ingredient))
);
```

This syntax creates a React element for each ingredient in the array. Each string is displayed in the list item's children as text. The value for each ingredient is displayed as the list item.

When running this code, you'll see a console warning like the one shown in Figure 4-1.

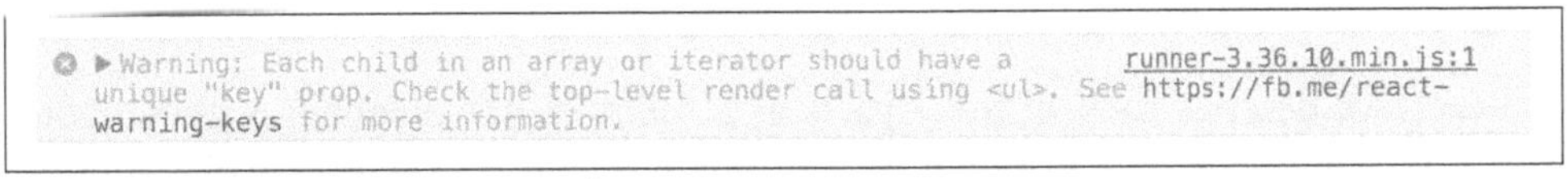

⊗ ▶ Warning: Each child in an array or iterator should have a    <u>runner-3.36.10.min.js:1</u>
   unique "key" prop. Check the top-level render call using <ul>. See https://fb.me/react-
   warning-keys for more information.

*Figure 4-1. Console warning*

When we build a list of child elements by iterating through an array, React likes each of those elements to have a key property. The key property is used by React to help it update the DOM efficiently. You can make this warning go away by adding a unique key property to each of the list item elements. You can use the array index for each ingredient as that unique value:

```
React.createElement(
  "ul",
  { className: "ingredients" },
  items.map((ingredient, i) =>
    React.createElement("li", { key: i }, ingredient)
  )
);
```

We'll cover keys in more detail when we discuss JSX, but adding this to each list item will clear the console warning.

# React Components

No matter its size, its contents, or what technologies are used to create it, a user interface is made up of parts. Buttons. Lists. Headings. All of these parts, when put together, make up a user interface. Consider a recipe application with three different recipes. The data is different in each box, but the parts needed to create a recipe are the same (see Figure 4-2).

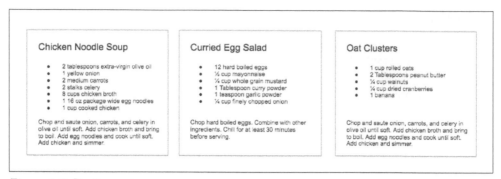

*Figure 4-2. Recipes app*

In React, we describe each of these parts as a *component*. Components allow us to reuse the same structure, and then we can populate those structures with different sets of data.

When considering a user interface you want to build with React, look for opportunities to break down your elements into reusable pieces. For example, the recipes in Figure 4-3 have a title, ingredients list, and instructions. All are part of a larger recipe or app component. We could create a component for each of the highlighted parts: ingredients, instructions, and so on.

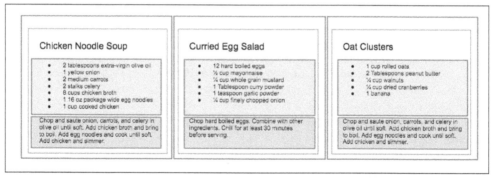

*Figure 4-3. Each component is outlined: `App`, `IngredientsList`, `Instructions`*

Think about how scalable this is. If we want to display one recipe, our component structure will support this. If we want to display 10,000 recipes, we'll just create 10,000 new instances of that component.

We'll create a component by writing a function. That function will return a reusable part of a user interface. Let's create a function that returns an unordered list of ingredients. This time, we'll make dessert with a function called `IngredientsList`:

```
function IngredientsList() {
  return React.createElement(
    "ul",
```

```
    { className: "ingredients" },
    React.createElement("li", null, "1 cup unsalted butter"),
    React.createElement("li", null, "1 cup crunchy peanut butter"),
    React.createElement("li", null, "1 cup brown sugar"),
    React.createElement("li", null, "1 cup white sugar"),
    React.createElement("li", null, "2 eggs"),
    React.createElement("li", null, "2.5 cups all purpose flour"),
    React.createElement("li", null, "1 teaspoon baking powder"),
    React.createElement("li", null, "0.5 teaspoon salt")
  );
}

ReactDOM.render(
  React.createElement(IngredientsList, null, null),
  document.getElementById("root")
);
```

The component's name is IngredientsList, and the function outputs elements that look like this:

```
<IngredientsList>
  <ul className="ingredients">
    <li>1 cup unsalted butter</li>
    <li>1 cup crunchy peanut butter</li>
    <li>1 cup brown sugar</li>
    <li>1 cup white sugar</li>
    <li>2 eggs</li>
    <li>2.5 cups all purpose flour</li>
    <li>1 teaspoon baking powder</li>
    <li>0.5 teaspoon salt</li>
  </ul>
</IngredientsList>
```

This is pretty cool, but we've hardcoded this data into the component. What if we could build one component and then pass data into that component as properties? And then what if that component could render the data dynamically? Maybe someday that will happen!

Just kidding—that day is now. Here's an array of secretIngredients needed to put together a recipe:

```
const secretIngredients = [
  "1 cup unsalted butter",
  "1 cup crunchy peanut butter",
  "1 cup brown sugar",
  "1 cup white sugar",
  "2 eggs",
  "2.5 cups all purpose flour",
  "1 teaspoon baking powder",
  "0.5 teaspoon salt"
];
```

Then we'll adjust the `IngredientsList` component to map over these `items`, constructing an `li` for however many items are in the `items` array:

```
function IngredientsList() {
  return React.createElement(
    "ul",
    { className: "ingredients" },
    items.map((ingredient, i) =>
      React.createElement("li", { key: i }, ingredient)
    )
  );
}
```

Then we'll pass those `secretIngredients` as a property called `items`, which is the second argument used in `createElement`:

```
ReactDOM.render(
  React.createElement(IngredientsList, { items: secretIngredients }, null),
  document.getElementById("root")
);
```

Now, let's look at the DOM. The data property `items` is an array with eight ingredients. Because we made the `li` tags using a loop, we were able to add a unique key using the index of the loop:

```
<IngredientsList items="[...]">
  <ul className="ingredients">
    <li key="0">1 cup unsalted butter</li>
    <li key="1">1 cup crunchy peanut butter</li>
    <li key="2">1 cup brown sugar</li>
    <li key="3">1 cup white sugar</li>
    <li key="4">2 eggs</li>
    <li key="5">2.5 cups all purpose flour</li>
    <li key="6">1 teaspoon baking powder</li>
    <li key="7">0.5 teaspoon salt</li>
  </ul>
</IngredientsList>
```

Creating our component this way will make the component more flexible. Whether the `items` array is one item or a hundred items long, the component will render each as a list item.

Another adjustment we can make here is to reference the `items` array from React props. Instead of mapping over the global `items`, we'll make `items` available on the `props` object. Start by passing `props` to the function, then mapping over `props.items`:

```
function IngredientsList(props) {
  return React.createElement(
    "ul",
    { className: "ingredients" },
    props.items.map((ingredient, i) =>
```

```
      React.createElement("li", { key: i }, ingredient)
    )
  );
}
```

We could also clean up the code a bit by destructuring items from props:

```
function IngredientsList({ items }) {
  return React.createElement(
    "ul",
    { className: "ingredients" },
    items.map((ingredient, i) =>
      React.createElement("li", { key: i }, ingredient)
    )
  );
}
```

Everything that's associated with the UI for IngredientsList is encapsulated into one component. Everything we need is right there.

# React Components: A Historical Tour

Before there were function components, there were other ways to create components. While we won't spend a great deal of time on these approaches, it's important to understand the history of React components, particularly when dealing with these APIs in legacy codebases. Let's take a little historical tour of React APIs of times gone by.

## Tour stop 1: createClass

When React was first made open source in 2013, there was one way to create a component: createClass. The use of React.createClass to create a component looks like this:

```
const IngredientsList = React.createClass({
  displayName: "IngredientsList",
  render() {
    return React.createElement(
      "ul",
      { className: "ingredients" },
      this.props.items.map((ingredient, i) =>
        React.createElement("li", { key: i }, ingredient)
      )
    );
  }
});
```

Components that used createClass would have a render() method that described the React element(s) that should be returned and rendered. The idea of the component was the same: we'd describe a reusable bit of UI to render.

In React 15.5 (April 2017), React started throwing warnings if `createClass` was used. In React 16 (September 2017), `React.createClass` was officially deprecated and was moved to its own package, `create-react-class`.

### Tour stop 2: class components

When class syntax was added to JavaScript with ES 2015, React introduced a new method for creating React components. The `React.Component` API allowed you to use class syntax to create a new component instance:

```
class IngredientsList extends React.Component {
  render() {
    return React.createElement(
      "ul",
      { className: "ingredients" },
      this.props.items.map((ingredient, i) =>
        React.createElement("li", { key: i }, ingredient)
      )
    );
  }
}
```

It's still possible to create a React component using class syntax, but be forewarned that `React.Component` is on the path to deprecation as well. Although it's still supported, you can expect this to go the way of `React.createClass`, another old friend who shaped you but who you won't see as often because they moved away and you moved on. From now on, we'll use functions to create components in this book and only briefly point out older patterns for reference.

# CHAPTER 5

# React with JSX

In the last chapter, we dove deep into how React works, breaking down our React applications into small reusable pieces called components. These components render trees of elements and other components. Using the `createElement` function is a good way to see how React works, but as React developers, that's not what we do. We don't go around composing complex, barely readable trees of JavaScript syntax and call it fun. In order to work efficiently with React, we need one more thing: JSX.

JSX combines the *JS* from JavaScript and the *X* from XML. It is a JavaScript extension that allows us to define React elements using a tag-based syntax directly within our JavaScript code. Sometimes JSX is confused with HTML because they look similar. JSX is just another way of creating React elements, so you don't have to pull your hair out looking for the missing comma in a complex `createElement` call.

In this chapter, we're going to discuss how to use JSX to construct a React application.

## React Elements as JSX

Facebook's React team released JSX when they released React to provide a concise syntax for creating complex DOM trees with attributes. They also hoped to make React more readable like HTML and XML. In JSX, an element's type is specified with a tag. The tag's attributes represent the properties. The element's children can be added between the opening and closing tags.

You can also add other JSX elements as children. If you have an unordered list, you can add child list item elements to it with JSX tags. It looks very similar to HTML:

```
<ul>
  <li>1 lb Salmon</li>
  <li>1 cup Pine Nuts</li>
  <li>2 cups Butter Lettuce</li>
  <li>1 Yellow Squash</li>
  <li>1/2 cup Olive Oil</li>
  <li>3 Cloves of Garlic</li>
</ul>
```

JSX works with components as well. Simply define the component using the class name. We pass an array of ingredients to the `IngredientsList` as a property with JSX, as shown in Figure 5-1.

*Figure 5-1. Creating the IngredientsList with JSX*

When we pass the array of ingredients to this component, we need to surround it with curly braces. This is called a JavaScript *expression*, and we must use these when passing JavaScript values to components as properties. Component properties will take two types: either a string or a JavaScript expression. JavaScript expressions can include arrays, objects, and even functions. In order to include them, you must surround them in curly braces.

## JSX Tips

JSX might look familiar, and most of the rules result in syntax that's similar to HTML. However, there are a few considerations you should understand when working with JSX.

### Nested components

JSX allows you to add components as children of other components. For example, inside the `IngredientsList`, we can render another component called `Ingredient` multiple times:

```
<IngredientsList>
  <Ingredient />
  <Ingredient />
  <Ingredient />
</IngredientsList>
```

### className

Since `class` is a reserved word in JavaScript, `className` is used to define the `class` attribute instead:

```
<h1 className="fancy">Baked Salmon</h1>
```

### JavaScript expressions

JavaScript expressions are wrapped in curly braces and indicate where variables will be evaluated and their resulting values returned. For example, if we want to display the value of the `title` property in an element, we can insert that value using a JavaScript expression. The variable will be evaluated and its value returned:

```
<h1>{title}</h1>
```

Values of types other than string should also appear as JavaScript expressions:

```
<input type="checkbox" defaultChecked={false} />
```

### Evaluation

The JavaScript that's added in between the curly braces will get evaluated. This means that operations such as concatenation or addition will occur. This also means that functions found in JavaScript expressions will be invoked:

```
<h1>{"Hello" + title}</h1>
```

```
<h1>{title.toLowerCase().replace}</h1>
```

## Mapping Arrays with JSX

JSX is JavaScript, so you can incorporate JSX directly inside of JavaScript functions. For example, you can map an array to JSX elements:

```
<ul>
  {props.ingredients.map((ingredient, i) => (
    <li key="{i}">{ingredient}</li>
  ))}
</ul>
```

JSX looks clean and readable, but it can't be interpreted with a browser. All JSX must be converted into `createElement` calls. Luckily, there's an excellent tool for this task: Babel.

# Babel

Many software languages require you to compile your source code. JavaScript is an interpreted language: the browser interprets the code as text, so there's no need to compile JavaScript. However, not all browsers support the latest JavaScript syntax, and no browser supports JSX syntax. Since we want to use the latest features of Java-Script along with JSX, we're going to need a way to convert our fancy source code into something that the browser can interpret. This process is called compiling, and it's what Babel (*https://babeljs.io*) is designed to do.

The first version of the project was called 6to5, and it was released in September 2014. 6to5 was a tool that could be used to convert ES6 syntax to ES5 syntax, which was more widely supported by web browsers. As the project grew, it aimed to be a platform to support all of the latest changes in ECMAScript. It also grew to support converting JSX into JavaScript. The project was renamed Babel in February 2015.

Babel is used in production at Facebook, Netflix, PayPal, Airbnb, and more. Previously, Facebook had created a JSX transformer that was their standard, but it was soon retired in favor of Babel.

There are many ways of working with Babel. The easiest way to get started is to include a link to the Babel CDN directly in your HTML, which will compile any code in script blocks that have a type of "text/babel." Babel will compile the source code on the client before running it. Although this may not be the best solution for production, it's a great way to get started with JSX:

```html
<!DOCTYPE html>
<html>
  <head>
    <meta charset="utf-8" />
    <title>React Examples</title>
  </head>
  <body>
    <div id="root"></div>

    <!-- React Library & React DOM -->
    <script
src="https://unpkg.com/react@16.8.6/umd/react.development.js">
</script>
    <script
src="https://unpkg.com/react-dom@16.8.6/umd/react-dom.development.js">
</script>
    <script
src="https://unpkg.com/@babel/standalone/babel.min.js">
</script>

    <script type="text/babel">
      // JSX code here. Or link to separate JavaScript file that contains JSX.
    </script>
  </body>
</html>
```

**Console Warning in the Browser with In-Browser Babel**

When using the in-browser transformer, you'll see a warning that says to precompile scripts for production. Don't worry about that warning for the purposes of this and any other small demos. We'll upgrade to production-ready Babel later in the chapter.

# Recipes as JSX

JSX provides us with a nice, clean way to express React elements in our code that makes sense to us and is immediately readable by developers. The drawback of JSX is that it's not readable by the browser. Before our code can be interpreted by the browser, it needs to be converted from JSX into JavaScript.

This data array contains two recipes, and this represents our application's current state:

```
const data = [
  {
    name: "Baked Salmon",
    ingredients: [
      { name: "Salmon", amount: 1, measurement: "l lb" },
      { name: "Pine Nuts", amount: 1, measurement: "cup" },
      { name: "Butter Lettuce", amount: 2, measurement: "cups" },
      { name: "Yellow Squash", amount: 1, measurement: "med" },
      { name: "Olive Oil", amount: 0.5, measurement: "cup" },
      { name: "Garlic", amount: 3, measurement: "cloves" }
    ],
    steps: [
      "Preheat the oven to 350 degrees.",
      "Spread the olive oil around a glass baking dish.",
      "Add the yellow squash and place in the oven for 30 mins.",
      "Add the salmon, garlic, and pine nuts to the dish.",
      "Bake for 15 minutes.",
      "Remove from oven. Add the lettuce and serve."
    ]
  },
  {
    name: "Fish Tacos",
    ingredients: [
      { name: "Whitefish", amount: 1, measurement: "l lb" },
      { name: "Cheese", amount: 1, measurement: "cup" },
      { name: "Iceberg Lettuce", amount: 2, measurement: "cups" },
      { name: "Tomatoes", amount: 2, measurement: "large" },
      { name: "Tortillas", amount: 3, measurement: "med" }
    ],
    steps: [
      "Cook the fish on the grill until cooked through.",
      "Place the fish on the 3 tortillas.",
      "Top them with lettuce, tomatoes, and cheese."
    ]
```

```
      }
    ];
```

The data is expressed in an array of two JavaScript objects. Each object contains the name of the recipe, a list of the ingredients required, and a list of steps necessary to cook the recipe.

We can create a UI for these recipes with two components: a Menu component for listing the recipes and a Recipe component that describes the UI for each recipe. It's the Menu component that we'll render to the DOM. We'll pass our data to the Menu component as a property called recipes:

```
// The data, an array of Recipe objects
const data = [ ... ];

// A function component for an individual Recipe
function Recipe (props) {
  ...
}

// A function component for the Menu of Recipes
function Menu (props) {
  ...
}

// A call to ReactDOM.render to render our Menu into the current DOM
ReactDOM.render(
  <Menu recipes={data} title="Delicious Recipes" />,
  document.getElementById("root")
);
```

The React elements within the Menu component are expressed as JSX. Everything is contained within an article element. A header element, an h1 element, and a div.recipes element are used to describe the DOM for our menu. The value for the title property will be displayed as text within the h1:

```
function Menu(props) {
  return (
    <article>
      <header>
        <h1>{props.title}</h1>
      </header>
      <div className="recipes" />
    </article>
  );
}
```

Inside of the div.recipes element, we add a component for each recipe:

```
<div className="recipes">
  {props.recipes.map((recipe, i) => (
    <Recipe
      key={i}
      name={recipe.name}
      ingredients={recipe.ingredients}
      steps={recipe.steps}
    />
  ))}
</div>
```

In order to list the recipes within the div.recipes element, we use curly braces to add a JavaScript expression that will return an array of children. We can use the map function on the props.recipes array to return a component for each object within the array. As mentioned previously, each recipe contains a name, some ingredients, and cooking instructions (steps). We'll need to pass this data to each Recipe as props. Also remember that we should use the key property to uniquely identify each element.

You could also refactor this to use spread syntax. The JSX spread operator works like the object spread operator. It will add each field of the recipe object as a property of the Recipe component. The syntax here will supply all properties to the component:

```
{
  props.recipes.map((recipe, i) => <Recipe key={i} {...recipe} />);
}
```

Remember that this shortcut will provide all the properties to the Recipe component. This could be a good thing but might also add too many properties to the component.

Another place we can make a syntax improvement to our Menu component is where we take in the props argument. We can use object destructuring to scope the variables to this function. This allows us to access the title and recipes variables directly, no longer having to prefix them with props:

```
function Menu({ title, recipes }) {
  return (
    <article>
      <header>
        <h1>{title}</h1>
      </header>
      <div className="recipes">
        {recipes.map((recipe, i) => (
          <Recipe key={i} {...recipe} />
        ))}
      </div>
    </article>
```

```
    );
  }
```

Now let's code the component for each individual recipe:

```
function Recipe({ name, ingredients, steps }) {
  return (
    <section id={name.toLowerCase().replace(/ /g, "-")}>
      <h1>{name}</h1>
      <ul className="ingredients">
        {ingredients.map((ingredient, i) => (
          <li key={i}>{ingredient.name}</li>
        ))}
      </ul>
      <section className="instructions">
        <h2>Cooking Instructions</h2>
        {steps.map((step, i) => (
          <p key={i}>{step}</p>
        ))}
      </section>
    </section>
  );
}
```

Each recipe has a string for the name, an array of objects for ingredients, and an array of strings for the steps. Using object destructuring, we can tell this component to locally scope those fields by name so we can access them directly without having to use props.name, props.ingredients, or props.steps.

The first JavaScript expression we see is being used to set the id attribute for the root section element. It's converting the recipe's name to a lowercase string and globally replacing spaces with dashes. The result is that "Baked Salmon" will be converted to "baked-salmon" (and likewise, if we had a recipe with the name "Boston Baked Beans," it would be converted to "boston-baked-beans") before it's used as the id attribute in our UI. The value for name is also being displayed in an h1 as a text node.

Inside of the unordered list, a JavaScript expression is mapping each ingredient to an li element that displays the name of the ingredient. Within our instructions section, we see the same pattern being used to return a paragraph element where each step is displayed. These map functions are returning arrays of child elements.

The complete code for the application should look like this:

```
const data = [
  {
    name: "Baked Salmon",
    ingredients: [
      { name: "Salmon", amount: 1, measurement: "l lb" },
      { name: "Pine Nuts", amount: 1, measurement: "cup" },
      { name: "Butter Lettuce", amount: 2, measurement: "cups" },
      { name: "Yellow Squash", amount: 1, measurement: "med" },
```

```
        { name: "Olive Oil", amount: 0.5, measurement: "cup" },
        { name: "Garlic", amount: 3, measurement: "cloves" }
      ],
      steps: [
        "Preheat the oven to 350 degrees.",
        "Spread the olive oil around a glass baking dish.",
        "Add the yellow squash and place in the oven for 30 mins.",
        "Add the salmon, garlic, and pine nuts to the dish.",
        "Bake for 15 minutes.",
        "Remove from oven. Add the lettuce and serve."
      ]
  },
  {
    name: "Fish Tacos",
    ingredients: [
      { name: "Whitefish", amount: 1, measurement: "l lb" },
      { name: "Cheese", amount: 1, measurement: "cup" },
      { name: "Iceberg Lettuce", amount: 2, measurement: "cups" },
      { name: "Tomatoes", amount: 2, measurement: "large" },
      { name: "Tortillas", amount: 3, measurement: "med" }
    ],
    steps: [
      "Cook the fish on the grill until hot.",
      "Place the fish on the 3 tortillas.",
      "Top them with lettuce, tomatoes, and cheese."
    ]
  }
];

function Recipe({ name, ingredients, steps }) {
  return (
    <section id={name.toLowerCase().replace(/ /g, "-")}>
      <h1>{name}</h1>
      <ul className="ingredients">
        {ingredients.map((ingredient, i) => (
          <li key={i}>{ingredient.name}</li>
        ))}
      </ul>
      <section className="instructions">
        <h2>Cooking Instructions</h2>
        {steps.map((step, i) => (
          <p key={i}>{step}</p>
        ))}
      </section>
    </section>
  );
}

function Menu({ title, recipes }) {
  return (
    <article>
      <header>
```

```
      <h1>{title}</h1>
    </header>
    <div className="recipes">
      {recipes.map((recipe, i) => (
        <Recipe key={i} {...recipe} />
      ))}
    </div>
  </article>
  );
}

ReactDOM.render(
  <Menu recipes={data} title="Delicious Recipes" />,
  document.getElementById("root")
);
```

When we run this code in the browser, React will construct a UI using our instructions with the recipe data as shown in Figure 5-2.

If you're using Google Chrome and have the React Developer Tools Extension installed, you can take a look at the present state of the component tree. To do this, open the developer tools and select the Components tab, as shown in Figure 5-3.

Here we can see the Menu and its child elements. The data array contains two objects for recipes, and we have two Recipe elements. Each Recipe element has properties for the recipe name, ingredients, and steps. The ingredients and steps are passed down to their own components as data.

The components are constructed based on the application's data being passed to the Menu component as a property. If we change the recipes array and rerender our Menu component, React will change this DOM as efficiently as possible.

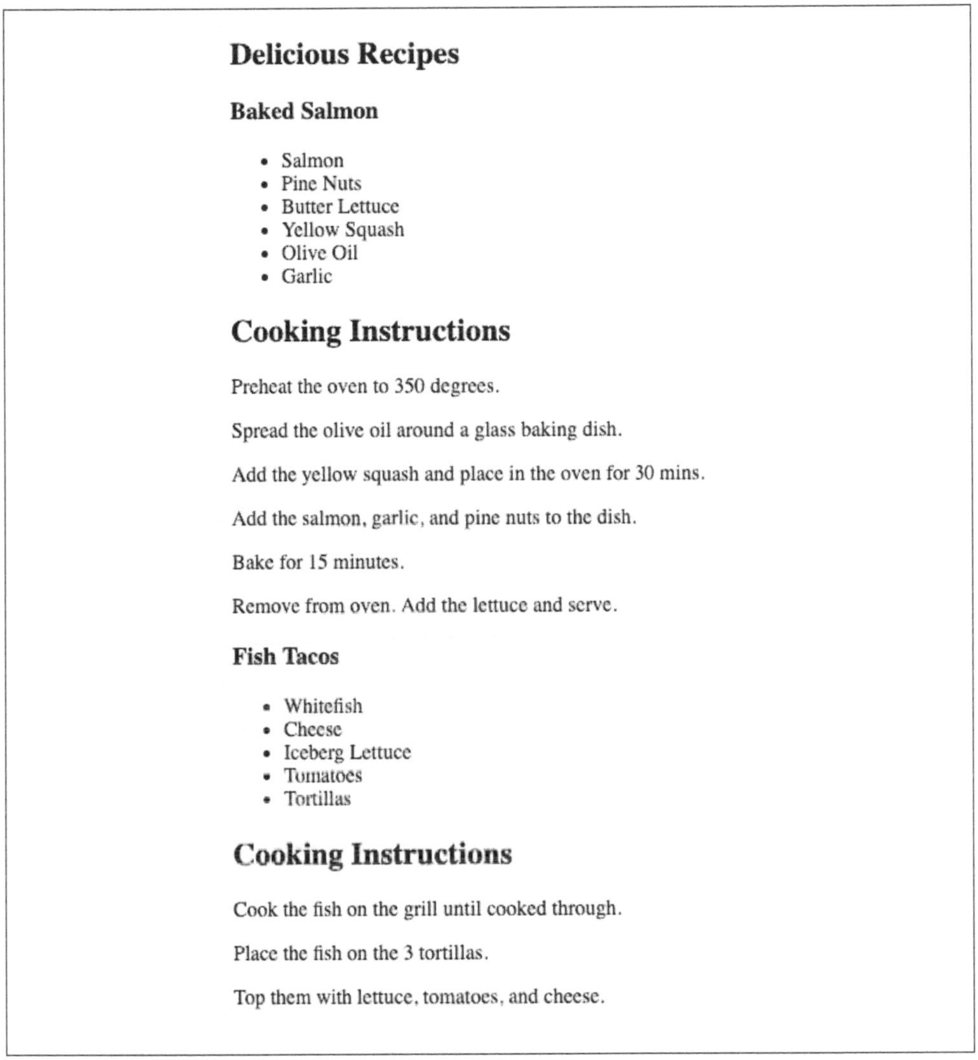

**Delicious Recipes**

**Baked Salmon**

- Salmon
- Pine Nuts
- Butter Lettuce
- Yellow Squash
- Olive Oil
- Garlic

## Cooking Instructions

Preheat the oven to 350 degrees.

Spread the olive oil around a glass baking dish.

Add the yellow squash and place in the oven for 30 mins.

Add the salmon, garlic, and pine nuts to the dish.

Bake for 15 minutes.

Remove from oven. Add the lettuce and serve.

**Fish Tacos**

- Whitefish
- Cheese
- Iceberg Lettuce
- Tomatoes
- Tortillas

## Cooking Instructions

Cook the fish on the grill until cooked through.

Place the fish on the 3 tortillas.

Top them with lettuce, tomatoes, and cheese.

*Figure 5-2. Delicious Recipes output*

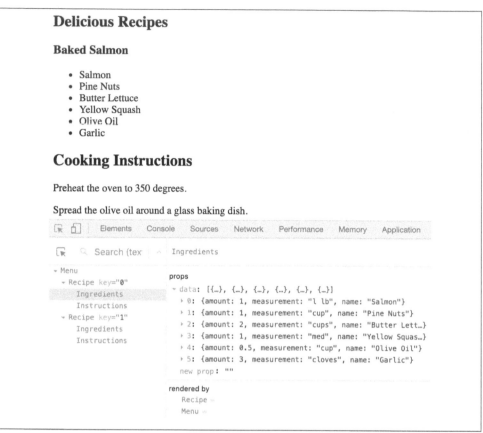

*Figure 5-3. Resulting virtual DOM in React Developer Tools*

# React Fragments

In the previous section, we rendered the Menu component, a parent component that rendered the Recipe component. We want to take a moment to look at a small example of rendering two sibling components using a React fragment. Let's start by creating a new component called Cat that we'll render to the DOM at the root:

```
function Cat({ name }) {
  return <h1>The cat's name is {name}</h1>;
}

ReactDOM.render(<Cat name="Jungle" />, document.getElementById("root"));
```

This will render the h1 as expected, but what might happen if we added a p tag to the Cat component at the same level as the h1?

```
function Cat({ name }) {
  return (
    <h1>The cat's name is {name}</h1>
    <p>He's good.</p>
  );
}
```

Immediately, we'll see an error in the console that reads `Adjacent JSX elements must be wrapped in an enclosing tag` and recommends using a fragment. This is where fragments come into play! React will not render two or more adjacent or sibling elements as a component, so we used to have to wrap these in an enclosing tag like a div. This led to a lot of unnecessary tags being created, though, and a bunch of wrappers without much purpose. If we use a React fragment, we can mimic the behavior of a wrapper without actually creating a new tag.

Start by wrapping the adjacent tags, the h1 and p, with a `React.Fragment` tag:

```
function Cat({ name }) {
  return (
    <React.Fragment>
      <h1>The cat's name is {name}</h1>
      <p>He's good.</p>
    </React.Fragment>
  );
}
```

Adding this clears the warning. You also can use a fragment shorthand to make this look even cleaner:

```
function Cat({ name }) {
  return (
    <>
      <h1>The cat's name is {name}</h1>
      <p>He's good.</p>
    </>
  );
}
```

If you look at the DOM, the fragment is not visible in the resulting tree:

```
<div id="root">
  <h1>The cat's name is Jungle</h1>
  <p>He's good</p>
</div>
```

Fragments are a relatively new feature of React and do away with the need for extra wrapper tags that can pollute the DOM.

# Intro to webpack

Once we start working with React in real projects, there are a lot of questions to consider: How do we want to deal with JSX and ESNext transformation? How can we manage our dependencies? How can we optimize our images and CSS?

Many different tools have emerged to answer these questions, including Browserify, gulp, Grunt, Prepack, and more. Due to its features and widespread adoption by large companies, *webpack* has also emerged as one of the leading tools for bundling.

The React ecosystem has matured to include tools like create-react-app, Gatsby, and Code Sandbox. When you use these tools, a lot of the details about how the code gets compiled are abstracted away. For the remainder of this chapter, we are going to set up our own webpack build. This day in age, understanding that your JavaScript/React code is being compiled by something like webpack is vital, but knowing *how* to compile your JavaScript/React with something like webpack is not as important. We understand if you want to skip ahead.

Webpack is billed as a module bundler. A module bundler takes all of our different files (JavaScript, LESS, CSS, JSX, ESNext, and so on) and turns them into a single file. The two main benefits of bundling are *modularity* and *network performance*.

Modularity will allow you to break down your source code into parts, or modules, that are easier to work with, especially in a team environment.

Network performance is gained by only needing to load one dependency in the browser: the bundle. Each `script` tag makes an HTTP request, and there's a latency penalty for each HTTP request. Bundling all the dependencies into a single file allows you to load everything with one HTTP request, thereby avoiding additional latency.

Aside from code compilation, webpack also can handle:

*Code splitting*
> Splits up your code into different chunks that can be loaded when you need them. Sometimes these are called *rollups* or *layers*; the aim is to break up code as needed for different pages or devices.

*Minification*
> Removes whitespace, line breaks, lengthy variable names, and unnecessary code to reduce the file size.

*Feature Flagging*
> Sends code to one or more—but not all—environments when testing out features.

*Hot Module Replacement (HMR)*
> Watches for changes in source code. Changes only the updated modules immediately.

The Recipes app we built earlier in this chapter has some limitations that webpack will help us alleviate. Using a tool like webpack to statically build client JavaScript makes it possible for teams to work together on large-scale web applications. We can also gain the following benefits by incorporating the webpack module bundler:

*Modularity*
> Using the module pattern to export modules that will later be imported or required by another part of the application makes source code more approachable. It allows development teams to work together, by allowing them to create and work with separate files that will be statically combined into a single file before sending to production.

*Composition*
> With modules, we can build small, simple, reusable React components that we can compose efficiently into applications. Smaller components are easier to comprehend, test, and reuse. They're also easier to replace down the line when enhancing applications.

*Speed*
> Packaging all the application's modules and dependencies into a single client bundle will reduce the load time of an application because there's latency associated with each HTTP request. Packaging everything together in a single file means that the client will only need to make a single request. Minifying the code in the bundle will improve load time as well.

*Consistency*
> Since webpack will compile JSX and JavaScript, we can start using tomorrow's JavaScript syntax today. Babel supports a wide range of ESNext syntax, which means we don't have to worry about whether the browser supports our code. It allows developers to consistently use cutting-edge JavaScript syntax.

## Creating the Project

To demonstrate how we might set up a React project from scratch, let's go ahead and create a new folder on our computer called *recipes-app*:

```
mkdir recipes-app
cd recipes-app
```

For this project, we're going to go through the following steps:

1. Create the project.

2. Break down the recipe app into components that live in different files.

3. Set up a webpack build that incorporates Babel.

**create-react-app**

There's a tool called Create React App that can be used to autogenerate a React project with all of this preconfigured. We're going to take a closer look at what's happening behind the scenes before abstracting these steps away with a tool.

## 1. Create the project

Next, we'll create the project and *package.json* file with npm, sending the -y flag to use all of the defaults. We'll also install webpack, webpack-cli, react, and react-dom:

```
npm init -y
npm install react react-dom serve
```

If we're using npm 5, we don't need to send the --save flag when installing. Next, we'll create the following directory structure to house the components:

```
recipes-app (folder)
    > node_modules (already added with npm install command)
    > package.json (already added with npm init command)
    > package-lock.json (already added with npm init command)
    > index.html
    > /src (folder)
      > index.js
      > /data (folder)
        > recipes.json
      > /components (folder)
        > Recipe.js
        > Instructions.js
        > Ingredients.js
```

**File Organization**

There's no one way to organize the files in a React project. This is just one possible strategy.

## 2. Break components into modules

Currently, the Recipe component is doing quite a bit. We're displaying the name of the recipe, constructing an unordered list of ingredients, and displaying the instructions, with each step getting its own paragraph element. This component should be placed in the *Recipe.js* file. In any file where we're using JSX, we'll need to import React at the top:

```
// ./src/components/Recipe.js

import React from "react";

export default function Recipe({ name, ingredients, steps }) {
  return (
    <section id="baked-salmon">
      <h1>{name}</h1>
      <ul className="ingredients">
        {ingredients.map((ingredient, i) => (
          <li key={i}>{ingredient.name}</li>
        ))}
      </ul>
      <section className="instructions">
        <h2>Cooking Instructions</h2>
        {steps.map((step, i) => (
          <p key={i}>{step}</p>
        ))}
      </section>
    </section>
  );
}
```

A more functional approach to the `Recipe` component would be to break it down into smaller, more focused function components and compose them together. We can start by pulling the instructions out into their own component and creating a module in a separate file we can use for any set of instructions.

In that new file called *Instructions.js*, create the following component:

```
// ./src/components/Instructions.js

import React from "react";

export default function Instructions({ title, steps }) {
  return (
    <section className="instructions">
      <h2>{title}</h2>
      {steps.map((s, i) => (
        <p key={i}>{s}</p>
      ))}
    </section>
  );
}
```

Here, we've created a new component called `Instructions`. We'll pass the title of the instructions and the steps to this component. This way, we can reuse this component for "Cooking Instructions," "Baking Instructions," "Prep Instructions," or a "Pre-cook Checklist"—anything that has steps.

Now think about the ingredients. In the Recipe component, we're only displaying the ingredient names, but each ingredient in the data for the recipe has an amount and measurement as well. We'll create a component called Ingredient for this:

```
// ./src/components/Ingredient.js

import React from "react";

export default function Ingredient({ amount, measurement, name }) {
  return (
    <li>
      {amount} {measurement} {name}
    </li>
  );
}
```

Here, we assume each ingredient has an amount, a measurement, and a name. We destructure those values from our props object and display them each in independent classed span elements.

Using the Ingredient component, we can construct an IngredientsList component that can be used any time we need to display a list of ingredients:

```
// ./src/components/IngredientsList.js

import React from "react";
import Ingredient from "./Ingredient";

export default function IngredientsList({ list }) {
  return (
    <ul className="ingredients">
      {list.map((ingredient, i) => (
        <Ingredient key={i} {...ingredient} />
      ))}
    </ul>
  );
}
```

In this file, we first import the Ingredient component because we're going to use it for each ingredient. The ingredients are passed to this component as an array in a property called list. Each ingredient in the list array will be mapped to the Ingredient component. The JSX spread operator is used to pass all the data to the Ingredient component as props.

Using spread operator:

```
<Ingredient {...ingredient} />
```

is another way of expressing:

```
<Ingredient
  amount={ingredient.amount}
  measurement={ingredient.measurement}
  name={ingredient.name}
/>
```

So, given an ingredient with these fields:

```
let ingredient = {
  amount: 1,
  measurement: "cup",
  name: "sugar"
};
```

We get:

```
<Ingredient amount={1} measurement="cup" name="sugar" />
```

Now that we have components for ingredients and instructions, we can compose recipes using these components:

```
// ./src/components/Recipe.js

import React from "react";
import IngredientsList from "./IngredientsList";
import Instructions from "./Instructions";

function Recipe({ name, ingredients, steps }) {
  return (
    <section id={name.toLowerCase().replace(/ /g, "-")}>
      <h1>{name}</h1>
      <IngredientsList list={ingredients} />
      <Instructions title="Cooking Instructions" steps={steps} />
    </section>
  );
}

export default Recipe;
```

First, we import the components we're going to use: IngredientsList and Instructions. Now we can use them to create the Recipe component. Instead of a bunch of complicated code building out the entire recipe in one place, we've expressed our recipe more declaratively by composing smaller components. Not only is the code nice and simple, but it also reads well. This shows us that a recipe should display the name of the recipe, a list of ingredients, and some cooking instructions. We've abstracted away what it means to display ingredients and instructions into smaller, simple components.

In a modular approach, the Menu component would look pretty similar. The key difference is that it would live in its own file, import the modules it needs to use, and export itself:

```
// ./src/components/Menu.js

import React from "react";
import Recipe from "./Recipe";

function Menu({ recipes }) {
  return (
    <article>
      <header>
        <h1>Delicious Recipes</h1>
      </header>
      <div className="recipes">
        {recipes.map((recipe, i) => (
          <Recipe key={i} {...recipe} />
        ))}
      </div>
    </article>
  );
}

export default Menu;
```

We still need to use ReactDOM to render the `Menu` component. The main file for the project is *index.js*. This will be responsible for rendering the component to the DOM.

Let's create this file:

```
// ./src/index.js

import React from "react";
import { render } from "react-dom";
import Menu from "./components/Menu";
import data from "./data/recipes.json";

render(<Menu recipes={data} />, document.getElementById("root"));
```

The first four statements import the necessary modules for our app to work. Instead of loading `react` and `react-dom` via the `script` tag, we import them so webpack can add them to our bundle. We also need the `Menu` component and a sample data array that has been moved to a separate module. It still contains two recipes: Baked Salmon and Fish Tacos.

All of our imported variables are local to the *index.js* file. When we render the `Menu` component, we pass the array of recipe data to this component as a property.

The data is being pulled from the *recipes.json* file. This is the same data we used earlier in the chapter, but now it's following valid JSON formatting rules:

```
// ./src/data/recipes.json

[
  {
```

```
    "name": "Baked Salmon",
    "ingredients": [
      { "name": "Salmon", "amount": 1, "measurement": "lb" },
      { "name": "Pine Nuts", "amount": 1, "measurement": "cup" },
      { "name": "Butter Lettuce", "amount": 2, "measurement": "cups" },
      { "name": "Yellow Squash", "amount": 1, "measurement": "med" },
      { "name": "Olive Oil", "amount": 0.5, "measurement": "cup" },
      { "name": "Garlic", "amount": 3, "measurement": "cloves" }
    ],
    "steps": [
      "Preheat the oven to 350 degrees.",
      "Spread the olive oil around a glass baking dish.",
      "Add the yellow squash and place in the oven for 30 mins.",
      "Add the salmon, garlic, and pine nuts to the dish.",
      "Bake for 15 minutes.",
      "Remove from oven. Add the lettuce and serve."
    ]
  },
  {
    "name": "Fish Tacos",
    "ingredients": [
      { "name": "Whitefish", "amount": 1, "measurement": "lb" },
      { "name": "Cheese", "amount": 1, "measurement": "cup" },
      { "name": "Iceberg Lettuce", "amount": 2, "measurement": "cups" },
      { "name": "Tomatoes", "amount": 2, "measurement": "large" },
      { "name": "Tortillas", "amount": 3, "measurement": "med" }
    ],
    "steps": [
      "Cook the fish on the grill until cooked through.",
      "Place the fish on the 3 tortillas.",
      "Top them with lettuce, tomatoes, and cheese."
    ]
  }
]
```

Now that we've pulled our code apart into separate modules and files, let's create a build process with webpack that will put everything back together into a single file. You may be thinking, "Wait, we just did all of that work to break everything apart, and now we're going to use a tool to put it back together? Why on Earth…?" Splitting projects into separate files typically makes larger projects easier to manage because team members can work on separate components without overlap. It also means that files can be easier to test.

## 3. Creating the webpack build

In order to create a static build process with webpack, we'll need to install a few things. Everything we need can be installed with npm:

```
npm install --save-dev webpack webpack-cli
```

Remember that we've already installed React and ReactDOM.

For this modular Recipes app to work, we're going to need to tell webpack how to bundle our source code into a single file. As of version 4.0.0, webpack does not require a configuration file to bundle a project. If we don't include a config file, webpack will run the defaults to package our code. Using a config file, though, means we'll be able to customize our setup. Plus, this shows us some of the magic of webpack instead of hiding it away. The default webpack configuration file is always *webpack.config.js*.

The starting file for our Recipes app is *index.js*. It imports React, ReactDOM, and the *Menu.js* file. This is what we want to run in the browser first. Wherever webpack finds an `import` statement, it will find the associated module in the filesystem and include it in the bundle. *index.js* imports *Menu.js*, *Menu.js* imports *Recipe.js*, *Recipe.js* imports *Instructions.js* and *IngredientsList.js*, and *IngredientsList.js* imports *Ingredient.js*. Webpack will follow this import tree and include all of these necessary modules in our bundle. Traversal through all these files creates what's called a *dependency graph*. A dependency is just something our app needs, like a component file, a library file like React, or an image. Picture each file we need as a circle on the graph, with webpack drawing all the lines between the circles to create the graph. That graph is the bundle.

**Import Statements**

We're using `import` statements, which are not presently supported by most browsers or by Node.js. The reason `import` statements work is that Babel will convert them into `require('module/ path');` statements in our final code. The `require` function is how CommonJS modules are typically loaded.

As webpack builds our bundle, we need to tell it to transform JSX to React elements.

The *webpack.config.js* file is just another module that exports a JavaScript literal object that describes the actions webpack should take. The configuration file should be saved to the root folder of the project, right next to the *index.js* file:

```
// ./webpack.config.js

var path = require("path");

module.exports = {
  entry: "./src/index.js",
  output: {
    path: path.join(__dirname, "dist", "assets"),
    filename: "bundle.js"
  }
};
```

First, we tell webpack that our client entry file is *./src/index.js*. It will automatically build the dependency graph based on `import` statements starting in that file. Next, we specify that we want to output a bundled JavaScript file to *./dist/bundle.js*. This is where webpack will place the final packaged JavaScript.

Next, let's install the necessary Babel dependencies. We'll need `babel-loader` and `@babel/core`:

```
npm install babel-loader @babel/core --save-dev
```

The next set of instructions for webpack consists of a list of loaders to run on specified modules. This will be added to the config file under the `module` field:

```
module.exports = {
  entry: "./src/index.js",
  output: {
    path: path.join(__dirname, "dist", "assets"),
    filename: "bundle.js"
  },
  module: {
    rules: [{ test: /\.js$/, exclude: /node_modules/, loader: "babel-loader" }]
  }
};
```

The rules field is an array because there are many types of loaders you can incorporate with webpack. In this example, we're only incorporating the `babel-loader`. Each loader is a JavaScript object. The `test` field is a regular expression that matches the file path of each module that the loader should operate on. In this case, we're running the `babel-loader` on all imported JavaScript files except those found in the *node_modules* folder.

At this point, we need to specify presets for running Babel. When we set a preset, we tell Babel which transforms to perform. In other words, we can say, "Hey Babel. If you see some ESNext syntax here, go ahead and transform that code into syntax we're sure the browser understands. If you see some JSX, transform that too." Start by installing the presets:

```
npm install @babel/preset-env @babel/preset-react --save-dev
```

Then create one more file at the root of the project: `.babelrc`:

```
{
  "presets": ["@babel/preset-env", "@babel/preset-react"]
}
```

All right! We've created something pretty cool: a project that resembles a real React app! Let's go ahead and run webpack to make sure this works.

Webpack is run statically. Typically, bundles are created before the app is deployed to the server. You can run it from the command line using npx:

```
npx webpack --mode development
```

Webpack will either succeed and create a bundle or fail and show you an error. Most errors have to do with broken import references. When debugging webpack errors, look closely at the filenames and file paths used in `import` statements.

You can also add an npm script to your *package.json* file to create a shortcut:

```
"scripts": {
  "build": "webpack --mode production"
},
```

Then you can run the shortcut to generate the bundle:

```
npm run build
```

## Loading the Bundle

We have a bundle, so now what? We exported the bundle to the *dist* folder. This folder contains the files we want to run on the web server. The *dist* folder is where the *index.html* file should be placed. This file needs to include a target `div` element where the React `Menu` component will be mounted. It also requires a single `script` tag that will load our bundled JavaScript:

```
// ./dist/index.html

<!DOCTYPE html>
<html>
  <head>
    <meta charset="utf-8" />
    <title>React Recipes App</title>
  </head>
  <body>
    <div id="root"></div>
    <script src="bundle.js"></script>
  </body>
</html>
```

This is the home page for your app. It will load everything it needs from one file, one HTTP request: *bundle.js*. You'll need to deploy these files to your web server or build a web server application that will serve these files with something like Node.js or Ruby on Rails.

## Source Mapping

Bundling our code into a single file can cause some setbacks when it comes time to debug the application in the browser. We can eliminate this problem by providing a *source map*. A source map is a file that maps a bundle to the original source files. With webpack, all we have to do is add a couple lines to our *webpack.config.js* file.

```
//webpack.config.js with source mapping

module.exports = {
  ...
  devtool: "#source-map" // Add this option for source mapping
};
```

Setting the `devtool` property to `'#source-map'` tells webpack that you want to use source mapping. The next time you run webpack, you'll see that two output files are generated and added to the *dist* folder: the original *bundle.js* and *bundle.js.map*.

The source map is going to let you debug using your original source files. In the Sources tab of your browser's developer tools, you should find a folder named *webpack://*. Inside of this folder, you'll see all the source files in your bundle, as shown in Figure 5-4.

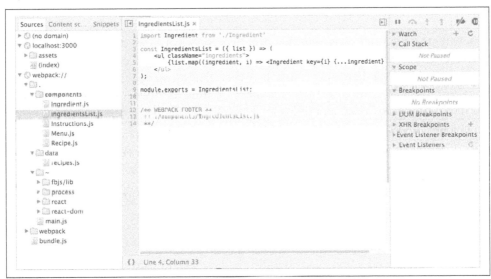

*Figure 5-4. Sources panel of Chrome Developer Tools*

You can debug from these files using the browser step-through debugger. Clicking on any line number adds a breakpoint. Refreshing the browser will pause JavaScript processing when any breakpoints are reached in your source file. You can inspect scoped variables in the Scope panel or add variables to watch in the Watch panel.

## Create React App

A pretty amazing tool to have at your disposal as a React developer is Create React App, a command-line tool that autogenerates a React project. Create React App was inspired by the Ember CLI project (*https://ember-cli.com*), and it lets developers get started with React projects quickly without the manual configuration of webpack, Babel, ESLint, and associated tools.

To get started with Create React App, install the package globally:

```
npm install -g create-react-app
```

Then, use the command and the name of the folder where you'd like the app to be created:

```
create-react-app my-project
```

> **npx**
>
> You can also use npx to run Create React App without the need for a global install. Simply run `npx create-react-app my-project`.

This will create a React project in that directory with just three dependencies: React, ReactDOM, and `react-scripts`. `react-scripts` was also created by Facebook and is where the real magic happens. It installs Babel, ESLint, webpack, and more so that you don't have to configure them manually. Within the generated project folder, you'll also find a *src* folder containing an *App.js* file. Here, you can edit the root component and import other component files.

From within the *my-react-project* folder, you can run `npm start`. If you prefer, you can also run `yarn start`. This will start your application on port 3000.

You can run tests with `npm test` or `yarn test`. This runs all of the test files in the project in an interactive mode.

You can also run the `npm run build` command. Using yarn, run `yarn build`.

This will create a production-ready bundle that has been transformed and minified.

Create React App is a great tool for beginners and experienced React developers alike. As the tool evolves, more functionality will likely be added, so you can keep an eye on the changes on GitHub (*https://github.com/facebook/create-react-app*). Another way to get started with React without having to worry about setting up your own customized webpack build is to use CodeSandbox. CodeSandbox is an IDE that runs online at *https://codesandbox.io*.

In this chapter, we leveled up our React skills by learning about JSX. We created components. We broke those components into a project structure, and we learned more about Babel and webpack. Now we're ready to take our knowledge of components to the next level. It's time to talk about Hooks.

# CHAPTER 6

# React State Management

Data is what makes our React components come to life. The user interface for recipes that we built in the last chapter is useless without the array of recipes. It's the recipes and the ingredients along with clear instructions that makes such an app worthwhile. Our user interfaces are tools that creators will use to generate content. In order to build the best tools possible for our content creators, we'll need to know how to effectively manipulate and change data.

In the last chapter, we constructed a *component tree*: a hierarchy of components that data was able to flow through as properties. Properties are half of the picture. State is the other half. The *state* of a React application is driven by data that has the ability to change. Introducing state to the recipe application could make it possible for chefs to create new recipes, modify existing recipes, and remove old ones.

State and properties have a relationship with each other. When we work with React applications, we gracefully compose components that are tied together based on this relationship. When the state of a component tree changes, so do the properties. The new data flows through the tree, causing specific leaves and branches to render to reflect the new content.

In this chapter, we're going to bring applications to life by introducing state. We'll learn to create stateful components and how state can be sent down a component tree and user interactions back up the component tree. We'll learn techniques for collecting form data from users. And we'll take a look at the various ways in which we can separate concerns within our applications by introducing stateful context providers.

# Building a Star Rating Component

We would all be eating terrible food and watching terrible movies without the five-star rating system. If we plan on letting users drive the content on our website, we'll need a way to know if that content is any good or not. That makes the StarRating component one of the most important React components you'll ever build (see Figure 6-1).

3 of 5 stars

*Figure 6-1. StarRating component*

The StarRating component will allow users to rate content based on a specific number of stars. Content that's no good gets one star. Highly recommended content gets five stars. Users can set the rating for specific content by clicking on a specific star. First, we'll need a star, and we can get one from react-icons:

```
npm i react-icons
```

react-icons is an npm library that contains hundreds of SVG icons that are distributed as React components. By installing it, we just installed several popular icon libraries that contain hundreds of common SVG icons. You can browse all the icons in the library (*https://react-icons.netlify.com*). We're going to use the star icon from the Font Awesome collection:

```
import React from "react";
import { FaStar } from "react-icons/fa";

export default function StarRating() {
  return [
    <FaStar color="red" />,
    <FaStar color="red" />,
    <FaStar color="red" />,
    <FaStar color="grey" />,
    <FaStar color="grey" />
  ];
}
```

Here, we've created a StarRating component that renders five SVG stars that we've imported from react-icons. The first three stars are filled in with red, and the last two are grey. We render the stars first because seeing them gives us a roadmap for what we'll have to build. A selected star should be filled in with red, and a star that's not selected should be greyed out. Let's create a component that automatically files the stars based upon the selected property:

```
const Star = ({ selected = false }) => (
  <FaStar color={selected ? "red" : "grey"} />
);
```

The Star component renders an individual star and uses the selected property to fill it with the appropriate color. If the selected property is not passed to this component, we'll assume that the star should not be selected and by default will be filled in with grey.

The 5-star rating system is pretty popular, but a 10-star rating system is far more detailed. We should allow developers to select the total number of stars they wish to use when they add this component to their app. This can be accomplished by adding a totalStars property to the StarRating component:

```
const createArray = length => [...Array(length)];

export default function StarRating({ totalStars = 5 }) {
  return createArray(totalStars).map((n, i) => <Star key={i} />);
}
```

Here, we added the createArray function from Chapter 2. All we have to do is supply the length of the array that we want to create and we get a new array at that length. We use this function with the totalStars property to create an array of a specific length. Once we have an array, we can map over it and render Star components. By default, totalStars is equal to 5, which means this component will render 5 grey stars, as shown in Figure 6-2.

*Figure 6-2. Five stars are displayed*

# The useState Hook

It's time to make the StarRating component clickable, which will allow our users to change the rating. Since the rating is a value that will change, we'll store and change that value using React state. We incorporate state into a function component using a React feature called *Hooks*. *Hooks* contain reusable code logic that is separate from the component tree. They allow us to *hook* up functionality to our components. React ships with several built-in hooks we can use out of the box. In this case, we want to

add state to our React component, so the first hook we'll work with is React's
useState hook. This hook is already available in the react package; we simply need
to import it:

```
import React, { useState } from "react";
import { FaStar } from "react-icons/fa";
```

The stars the user has selected represents the rating. We'll create a state variable called
selectedStars, which will hold the user's rating. We'll create this variable by adding
the useState hook directly to the StarRating component:

```
export default function StarRating({ totalStars = 5 }) {
  const [selectedStars] = useState(3);
  return (
    <>
      {createArray(totalStars).map((n, i) => (
        <Star key={i} selected={selectedStars > i} />
      ))}
      <p>
        {selectedStars} of {totalStars} stars
      </p>
    </>
  );
}
```

We just *hooked* this component up with state. The useState hook is a function that
we can invoke to return an array. The first value of that array is the state variable we
want to use. In this case, that variable is selectedStars, or the number of stars the
StarRating will color red. useState returns an array. We can take advantage of array
destructuring, which allows us to name our state variable whatever we like. The value
we send to the useState function is the default value for the state variable. In this
case, selectedStars will initially be set to 3, as shown in Figure 6-3.

*Figure 6-3. Three of five stars are selected*

In order to collect a different rating from the user, we'll need to allow them to click on
any of our stars. This means we'll need to make the stars clickable by adding an
onClick handler to the FaStar component:

```
const Star = ({ selected = false, onSelect = f => f }) => (
  <FaStar color={selected ? "red" : "grey"} onClick={onSelect} />
);
```

Here, we modified the star to contain an `onSelect` property. Check it out: this property is a function. When a user clicks on the `FaStar` component, we'll invoke this function, which can notify its parent that a star has been clicked. The default value for this function is `f => f`. This is simply a fake function that does nothing; it just returns whatever argument was sent to it. However, if we do not set a default function and the `onSelect` property is not defined, an error will occur when we click the `FaStar` component because the value for `onSelect` must be a function. Even though `f => f` does nothing, it is a function, which means it can be invoked without causing errors. If an `onSelect` property is not defined, no problem. React will simply invoke the fake function and nothing will happen.

Now that our `Star` component is clickable, we'll use it to change the state of the `Star Rating`:

```
export default function StarRating({ totalStars = 5 }) {
  const [selectedStars, setSelectedStars] = useState(0);
  return (
    <>
      {createArray(totalStars).map((n, i) => (
        <Star
          key={i}
          selected={selectedStars > i}
          onSelect={() => setSelectedStars(i + 1)}
        />
      ))}
      <p>
        {selectedStars} of {totalStars} stars
      </p>
    </>
  );
}
```

In order to change the state of the `StarRating` component, we'll need a function that can modify the value of `selectedStars`. The second item in the array that's returned by the `useState` hook is a function that can be used to change the state value. Again, by destructuring this array, we can name that function whatever we like. In this case, we're calling it `setSelectedStars`, because that's what it does: it sets the value of `selectedStars`.

The most important thing to remember about Hooks is that they can cause the component they're hooked into to rerender. Every time we invoke the `setSelectedStars` function to change the value of `selectedStars`, the `StarRating` function component will be reinvoked by the hook, and it will render again, this time with a new value for `selectedStars`. This is why Hooks are such a killer feature. When data within the hook changes, they have the power to rerender the component they're hooked into with new data.

The StarRating component will be rerendered every time a user clicks a Star. When the user clicks the Star, the onSelect property of that star is invoked. When the onSelect property is invoked, we'll invoke the setSelectedStars function and send it the number of the star that was just selected. We can use the i variable from the map function to help us calculate that number. When the map function renders the first Star, the value for i is 0. This means that we need to add 1 to this value to get the correct number of stars. When setSelectedStars is invoked, the StarRating component is invoked with a the value for selectedStars, as shown in Figure 6-4.

Figure 6-4. Hooks in React developer tools

The React developer tools will show you which Hooks are incorporated with specific components. When we render the StarRating component in the browser, we can view debugging information about that component by selecting it in the developer tools. In the column on the right, we can see that the StarRating component incorporates a state Hook that has a value of 2. As we interact with the app, we can watch the state value change and the component tree rerender with the corresponding number of stars selected.

# React State the "Old Way"

In previous versions of React, before v16.8.0, the only way to add state to a component was to use a class component. This required not only a lot of syntax, but it also made it more difficult to reuse functionality across components. Hooks were designed to solve problems presented with class components by providing a solution to incorporate functionality into function components.

The following code is a class component. This was the original StarRating component that was printed in the first edition of this book:

```
import React, { Component } from "react";

export default class StarRating extends Component {
  constructor(props) {
    super(props);
    this.state = {
      starsSelected: 0
    };
    this.change = this.change.bind(this);
  }

  change(starsSelected) {
    this.setState({ starsSelected });
  }

  render() {
    const { totalStars } = this.props;
    const { starsSelected } = this.state;
    return (
      <div>
        {[...Array(totalStars)].map((n, i) => (
          <Star
            key={i}
            selected={i < starsSelected}
            onClick={() => this.change(i + 1)}
          />
        ))}
        <p>
          {starsSelected} of {totalStars} stars
        </p>
      </div>
    );
  }
}
```

This class component does the same thing as our function component with noticeably more code. Additionally, it introduces more confusion thorough the use of the this keyword and function binding.

As of today, this code still works. We're no longer covering class components in this book because they're no longer needed. Function components and Hooks are the future of React, and we're not looking back. There could come a day where class components are officially deprecated, and this code will no longer be supported.

## Refactoring for Advanced Reusability

Right now, the Star component is ready for production. You can use it across several applications when you need to obtain a rating from a user. However, if we were to ship this component to npm so that anyone in the world could use it to obtain ratings from users, we may want to consider handling a couple more use cases.

First, let's consider the `style` property. This property allows you to add CSS styles to elements. It is highly possible that a future developer, even yourself, could come across the need to modify the style of your entire container. They may attempt to do something like this:

```
export default function App() {
  return <StarRating style={{ backgroundColor: "lightblue" }} />;
}
```

All React elements have style properties. A lot of components also have style properties. So attempting to modify the style for the entire component seems sensible.

All we need to do is collect those styles and pass them down to the `StarRating` container. Currently, the `StarRating` does not have a single container because we are using a React fragment. To make this work, we'll have to upgrade from a fragment to a `div` element and pass the styles to that `div`:

```
export default function StarRating({ style = {}, totalStars = 5 }) {
  const [selectedStars, setSelectedStars] = useState(0);
  return (
    <div style={{ padding: "5px", ...style }}>
      {createArray(totalStars).map((n, i) => (
        <Star
          key={i}
          selected={selectedStars > i}
          onSelect={() => setSelectedStars(i + 1)}
        />
      ))}
      <p>
        {selectedStars} of {totalStars} stars
      </p>
    </div>
  );
}
```

In the code above, we replaced the fragment with a div element and then applied styles to that div element. By default we assign that div a padding of 5px, and then we use the spread operator to apply the rest of the properties from the style object to the div style.

Additionally, we may find developers who attempt to implement other common properties properties to the entire star rating:

```
export default function App() {
  return (
    <StarRating
      style={{ backgroundColor: "lightblue" }}
      onDoubleClick={e => alert("double click")}
    />
  );
}
```

In this sample, the user is trying to add a double-click method to the entire StarRating component. If we feel it is necessary, we can also pass this method along with any other properties down to our containing div:

```
export default function StarRating({ style = {}, totalStars - 5, ...props }) {
  const [selectedStars, setSelectedStars] = useState(0);
  return (
    <div style={{ padding: 5, ...style }} {...props}>
    ...
    </div>
  );
}
```

The first step is to collect any and all properties that the user may be attempting to add to the StarRating. We gather these properties using the spread opera-tor: ...props. Next, we'll pass all of these remaining properties down to the div ele-ment: {...props}.

By doing this, we make two assumptions. First, we are assuming that users will add only those properties that are supported by the div element. Second, we are assuming that our user can't add malicious properties to the component.

This is not a blanket rule to apply to all of your components. In fact, it's only a good idea to add this level of support in certain situations. The real point is that it's impor-tant to think about how the consumers of your component may try to use it in the future.

# State in Component Trees

It's not a great idea to use state in every single component. Having state data distributed throughout too many of your components will make it harder to track down bugs and make changes within your application. This occurs because it's hard to keep track of where the state values live within your component tree. It's easier to understand your application's state, or state for a specific feature, if you manage it from one location. There are several approaches to this methodology, and the first one we'll analyze is storing state at the root of the component tree and passing it down to child components via props.

Let's build a small application that can be used to save a list of colors. We'll call the app the "Color Organizer", and it will allow users to associate a list of colors with a custom title and rating. To get started, a sample dataset may look like the following:

```
[
  {
    "id": "0175d1f0-a8c6-41bf-8d02-df5734d829a4",
    "title": "ocean at dusk",
    "color": "#00c4e2",
    "rating": 5
  },
  {
    "id": "83c7ba2f-7392-4d7d-9e23-35adbe186046",
    "title": "lawn",
    "color": "#26ac56",
    "rating": 3
  },
  {
    "id": "a11e3995-b0bd-4d58-8c48-5e49ae7f7f23",
    "title": "bright red",
    "color": "#ff0000",
    "rating": 0
  }
]
```

The *color-data.json* file contains an array of three colors. Each color has an id, title, color, and rating. First, we'll create a UI consisting of React components that will be used to display this data in a browser. Then we'll allow the users to add new colors as well as rate and remove colors from the list.

## Sending State Down a Component Tree

In this iteration, we'll store state in the root of the Color Organizer, the App component, and pass the colors down to child components to handle the rendering. The App component will be the only component within our application that holds state. We'll add the list of colors to the App with the useState hook:

```
import React, { useState } from "react";
import colorData from "./color-data.json";
import ColorList from "./ColorList.js";

export default function App() {
  const [colors] = useState(colorData);
  return <ColorList colors={colors} />;
}
```

The App component sits at the root of our tree. Adding useState to this component hooks it up with state management for colors. In this example, the colorData is the array of sample colors from above. The App component uses the colorData as the initial state for colors. From there, the colors are passed down to a component called the ColorList:

```
import React from "react";
import Color from "./Color";

export default function ColorList({ colors = [] }) {
  if(!colors.length) return <div>No Colors Listed.</div>;
  return (
    <div>
      {
        colors.map(color => <Color key={color.id} {...color} />)
      }
    </div>
  );
}
```

The ColorList receives the colors from the App component as props. If the list is empty, this component will display a message to our users. When we have a color array, we can map over it and pass the details about each color farther down the tree to the Color component:

```
export default function Color({ title, color, rating }) {
  return (
    <section>
      <h1>{title}</h1>
      <div style={{ height: 50, backgroundColor: color }} />
      <StarRating selectedStars={rating} />
    </section>
  );
}
```

The Color component expects three properties: title, color, and rating. These values are found in each color object and were passed to this component using the spread operator <Color {...color} />. This takes each field from the color object and passes it to the Color component as a property with the same name as the object key. The Color component displays these values. The title is rendered inside of an h1 element. The color value is displayed as the backgroundColor for a div element.

The `rating` is passed farther down the tree to the `StarRating` component, which will display the rating visually as selected stars:

```
export default function StarRating({ totalStars = 5, selectedStars = 0 }) {
  return (
    <>
      {createArray(totalStars).map((n, i) => (
        <Star
          key={i}
          selected={selectedStars > i}
        />
      ))}
      <p>
        {selectedStars} of {totalStars} stars
      </p>
    </>
  );
}
```

This `StarRating` component has been modified. We've turned it into a pure component. A pure component is a function component that does not contain state and will render the same user interface given the same props. We made this component a pure component because the state for color ratings are stored in the `colors` array at the root of the component tree. Remember that the goal of this iteration is to store state in a single location and not have it distributed through many different components within the tree.

 It is possible for the `StarRating` component to hold its own state and receive state from a parent component via props. This is typically necessary when distributing components for wider use by the community. We demonstrate this technique in the next chapter when we cover the `useEffect` hook.

At this point, we've finished passing state down the component tree from the `App` component all the way to each `Star` component that's filled red to visually represent the `rating` for each color. If we render the app based on the *color-data.json* file that was listed previously, we should see our colors in the browser, as shown in Figure 6-5.

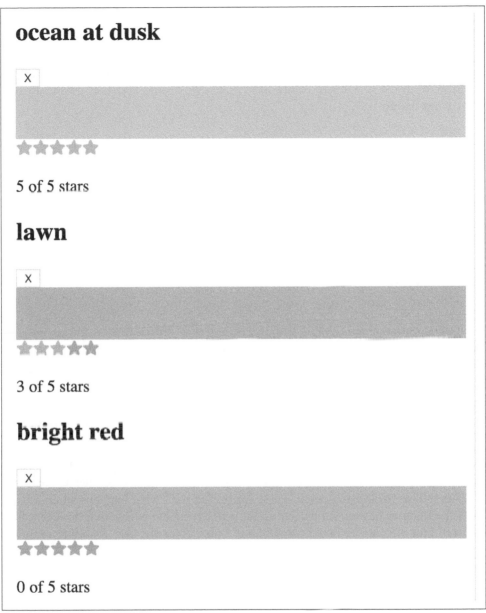

# ocean at dusk

X

★★★★★

5 of 5 stars

# lawn

X

★★★★★

3 of 5 stars

# bright red

X

★★★★★

0 of 5 stars

*Figure 6-5. Color Organizer rendered in the browser*

## Sending Interactions Back up a Component Tree

So far, we've rendered a representation of the `colors` array as UI by composing React components and passing data down the tree from parent component to child component via props. What happens if we want to remove a color from the list or change the rating of a color in our list? The `colors` are stored in state at the root of our tree. We'll need to collect interactions from child components and send them back up the tree to the root component where we can change the state.

For instance, let's say we wanted to add a Remove button next to each color's title that would allow users to remove colors from state. We would add that button to the `Color` component:

```
import { FaTrash } from "react-icons/fa";

export default function Color({ id, title, color, rating, onRemove = f => f }) {
  return (
    <section>
      <h1>{title}</h1>
      <button onClick={() => onRemove(id)}>
        <FaTrash />
      </button>
      <div style={{ height: 50, backgroundColor: color }} />
      <StarRating selectedStars={rating} />
    </section>
  );
}
```

Here, we've modified the color by adding a button that will allow users to remove colors. First, we imported a trash can icon from `react-icons`. Next, we wrapped the `FaTrash` icon in a button. Adding an `onClick` handler to this button allows us to invoke the `onRemove` function property, which has been added to our list of properties along with the `id`. When a user clicks the Remove button, we'll invoke `removeColor` and pass it the `id` of the color that we want to remove. That is why the `id` value has also been gathered from the `Color` component's properties.

This solution is great because we keep the `Color` component pure. It doesn't have state and can easily be reused in a different part of the app or another application altogether. The `Color` component is not concerned with what happens when a user clicks the Remove button. All it cares about is notifying the parent that this event has occurred and passing the information about which color the user wishes to remove. It's now the parent's responsibility to handle this event:

```
export default function ColorList({ colors = [], onRemoveColor = f => f }) {
  if (!colors.length) return <div>No Colors Listed. (Add a Color)</div>;

  return (
    colors.map(color => (
        <Color key={color.id} {...color} onRemove={onRemoveColor} />
      )
    }
  </div>
  );
}
```

The `Color` component's parent is the `ColorList`. This component also doesn't have access to state. Instead of removing the color, it simply passes the event up to its parent. It accomplishes this by adding an `onRemoveColor` function property. If a `Color` component invokes the `onRemove` property, the `ColorList` will in turn invoke its `onRemoveColor` property and send the responsibility for removing the color up to its parent. The color's `id` is still being passed to the `onRemoveColor` function.

The parent of the `ColorList` is the `App`. This component is the component that has been hooked up with state. This is where we can capture the color `id` and remove the color in state:

```
export default function App() {
  const [colors, setColors] = useState(colorData);
  return (
    <ColorList
      colors={colors}
      onRemoveColor={id => {
        const newColors = colors.filter(color => color.id !== id);
        setColors(newColors);
      }}
    />
  );
}
```

First, we add a variable for `setColors`. Remember that the second argument in the array returned by `useState` is a function we can use to modify the state. When the `ColorList` raises an `onRemoveColor` event, we capture the `id` of the color to remove from the arguments and use it to filter the list of colors to exclude the color the user wants to remove. Next, we change the state. We use the `setColors` function to change change the array of colors to the newly filtered array.

Changing the state of the `colors` array causes the `App` component to be rerendered with the new list of colors. Those new colors are passed to the `ColorList` component, which is also rerendered. It will render `Color` components for the remaining colors and our UI will reflect the changes we've made by rendering one less color.

If we want to rate the `colors` that are stored in the `App` components state, we'll have to repeat the process with an `onRate` event. First, we'll collect the new rating from the individual star that was clicked and pass that value to the parent of the `StarRating`:

```
export default function StarRating({
  totalStars = 5,
  selectedStars = 0,
  onRate = f => f
}) {
  return (
    <>
      {createArray(totalStars).map((n, i) => (
        <Star
```

```
            key={i}
            selected={selectedStars > i}
            onSelect={() => onRate(i + 1)}
        />
      ))}
    </>
  );
}
```

Then, we'll grab the rating from the onRate handler we added to the StarRating component. We'll then pass the new rating along with the id of the color to be rated up to the Color component's parent via another onRate function property:

```
export default function Color({
  id,
  title,
  color,
  rating,
  onRemove = f => f,
  onRate = f => f
}) {
  return (
    <section>
      <h1>{title}</h1>
      <button onClick={() => onRemove(id)}>
        <FaTrash />
      </button>
      <div style={{ height: 50, backgroundColor: color }} />
      <StarRating
        selectedStars={rating}
        onRate={rating => onRate(id, rating)}
      />
    </section>
  );
}
```

In the ColorList component, we'll have to capture the onRate event from individual color components and pass them up to its parent via the onRateColor function property:

```
export default function ColorList({
  colors = [],
  onRemoveColor = f => f,
  onRateColor = f => f
}) {
  if (!colors.length) return <div>No Colors Listed. (Add a Color)</div>;
  return (
    <div className="color-list">
      {
        colors.map(color => (
          <Color
            key={color.id}
```

```
        {...color}
        onRemove={onRemoveColor}
        onRate={onRateColor}
      />
    )
  }
  </div>
  );
}
```

Finally, after passing the event up through all of these components, we'll arrive at the App, where state is stored and the new rating can be saved:

```
export default function App() {
  const [colors, setColors] = useState(colorData);
  return (
    <ColorList
      colors={colors}
      onRateColor={(id, rating) => {
        const newColors = colors.map(color =>
          color.id === id ? { ...color, rating } : color
        );
        setColors(newColors);
      }}
      onRemoveColor={id => {
        const newColors = colors.filter(color => color.id !== id);
        setColors(newColors);
      }}
    />
  );
}
```

The `App` component will change color ratings when the `ColorList` invokes the `onRateColor` property with the `id` of the color to rate and the new rating. We'll use those values to construct an array of new colors by mapping over the existing colors and changing the rating for the color that matches the `id` property. Once we send the `newColors` to the `setColors` function, the state value for `colors` will change and the App component will be invoked with a new value for the `colors` array.

Once the state of our `colors` array changes, the UI tree is rendered with the new data. The new rating is reflected back to the user via red stars. Just as we passed data down a component tree via props, interactions can be passed back up the tree along with data via function properties.

# Building Forms

For a lot of us, being a web developer means collecting large amounts of information from users with forms. If this sounds like your job, then you'll be building a lot of form components with React. All of the HTML form elements that are available to the DOM are also available as React elements, which means that you may already know how to render a form with JSX:

```
<form>
  <input type="text" placeholder="color title..." required />
  <input type="color" required />
  <button>ADD</button>
</form>
```

This `form` element has three child elements: two `input` elements and a `button`. The first `input` element is a text input that will be used to collect the `title` value for new colors. The second `input` element is an HTML color input that will allow users to pick a `color` from a color wheel. We'll be using basic HTML form validation, so we've marked both inputs as `required`. The ADD button will be used to add a new color.

## Using Refs

When it's time to build a form component in React, there are several patterns available to you. One of these patterns involves accessing the DOM node directly using a React feature called refs. In React, a ref is an object that stores values for the lifetime of a component. There are several use cases that involve using refs. In this section, we'll look at how we can access a DOM node directly with a ref.

React provides us with a `useRef` hook that we can use to create a *ref*. We'll use this hook when building the `AddColorForm` component:

```
import React, { useRef } from "react";

export default function AddColorForm({ onNewColor = f => f }) {
  const txtTitle = useRef();
  const hexColor = useRef();

  const submit = e => { ... }

  return (...)
}
```

First, when creating this component, we'll also create two refs using the `useRef` hook. The `txtTitle` ref will be used to reference the text input we've added to the form to collect the color title. The `hexColor` ref will be used to access hexadecimal color values from the HTML color input. We can set the values for these refs directly in JSX using the `ref` property:

```
return (
  <form onSubmit={submit}>
    <input ref={txtTitle} type="text" placeholder="color title..." required />
    <input ref={hexColor} type="color" required />
    <button>ADD</button>
  </form>
```

```
    );
  }
```

Here, we set the value for the `txtTitle` and `hexColor` refs by adding the `ref` attribute to these input elements in JSX. This creates a `current` field on our ref object that references the DOM element directly. This provides us access to the DOM element, which means we can capture its value. When the user submits this form by clicking the ADD button, we'll invoke the `submit` function:

```
const submit = e => {
  e.preventDefault();
  const title = txtTitle.current.value;
  const color - hexColor.current.value;
  onNewColor(title, color);
  txtTitle.current.value = "";
  hexColor.current.value = "";
};
```

When we submit HTML forms, by default, they send a POST request to the current URL with the values of the form elements stored in the body. We don't want to do that. This is why the first line of code in the `submit` function is `e.preventDefault()`, which prevents the browser from trying to submit the form with a POST request.

Next, we capture the current values for each of our form elements using their refs. These values are then passed up to this component's parent via the `onNewColor` function property. Both the title and the hexadecimal value for the new color are passed as function arguments. Finally, we reset the `value` attribute for both inputs to clear the data and prepare the form to collect another color.

Did you notice the subtle paradigm shift that has occurred by using refs? We're mutating the `value` attribute of DOM nodes directly by setting them equal to `""` empty strings. This is imperative code. The `AddColorForm` is now what we call an *uncontrolled component* because it uses the DOM to save the form values. Sometimes using uncontrolled component can get you out of problems. For instance, you may want to share access to a form and its values with code outside of React. However, a controlled component is a better approach.

## Controlled Components

In a *controlled component*, the from values are managed by React and not the DOM. They do not require us to use refs. They do not require us to write imperative code. Adding features like robust form validation is much easier when working with a controlled component. Let's modify the `AddColorForm` by giving it control over the form's state:

```
import React, { useState } from "react";

export default function AddColorForm({ onNewColor = f => f }) {
  const [title, setTitle] = useState("");
  const [color, setColor] = useState("#000000");

  const submit = e => { ... };

  return ( ... );
}
```

First, instead of using refs, we're going to save the values for the `title` and `color` using React state. We'll create variables for `title` and `color`. Additionally, we'll define the functions that can be used to change state: `setTitle` and `setColor`.

Now that the component controls the values for `title` and `color`, we can display them inside of the form input elements by setting the `value` attribute. Once we set the `value` attribute of an input element, we'll no longer be able to change with the form. The only way to change the value at this point would be to change the state variable every time the user types a new character in the input element. That's exactly what we'll do:

```
<form onSubmit={submit}>
  <input
    value={title}
    onChange={event => setTitle(event.target.value)}
    type="text"
    placeholder="color title..."
    required
  />
  <input
    value={color}
    onChange={event => setColor(event.target.value)}
    type="color"
    required
  />
  <button>ADD</button>
</form>
}
```

This controlled component now sets the value of both `input` elements using the `title` and `color` from state. Whenever these elements raise an `onChange` event, we can access the new value using the `event` argument. The `event.target` is a reference to the DOM element, so we can obtain the current value of that element with `event.target.value`. When the `title` changes, we'll invoke `setTitle` to change the title value in state. Changing that value will cause this component to rerender, and we can now display the new value for `title` inside the `input` element. Changing the color works exactly the same way.

When it's time to submit the form, we can simply pass the state values for `title` and color to the onNewColor function property as arguments when we invoke it. The `set Title` and `setColor` functions can be used to reset the values after the new color has been passed to the parent component:

```
const submit = e => {
  e.preventDefault();
  onNewColor(title, color);
  setTitle("");
  setColor("");
};
```

It's called a controlled component because React controls the state of the form. It's worth pointing out that controlled form components are rerendered, a lot. Think about it: every new character typed in the `title` field causes the `AddColorForm` to rerender. Using the color wheel in the color picker causes this component to rerender way more than the `title` field because the color value repeatedly changes as the user drags the mouse around the color wheel. This is OK—React is designed to handle this type of workload. Hopefully, knowing that controlled components are rerendered frequently will prevent you from adding some long and expensive process to this component. At the very least, this knowledge will come in handy when you're trying to optimize your React components.

## Creating Custom Hooks

When you have a large form with a lot of `input` elements, you may be tempted to copy and paste these two lines of code:

```
value={title}
onChange={event => setTitle(event.target.value)}
```

It might seem like you're working faster by simply copying and pasting these properties into every form element while tweaking the variable names along the way. However, whenever you copy and paste code, you should hear a tiny little alarm sound in your head. Copying and pasting code suggests that there's something redundant enough to abstract away in a function.

We can package the details necessary to create controlled form components into a custom hook. We could create our own `useInput` hook where we can abstract away the redundancy involved with creating controlled form inputs:

```
import { useState } from "react";

export const useInput = initialValue => {
  const [value, setValue] = useState(initialValue);
  return [
    { value, onChange: e => setValue(e.target.value) },
    () => setValue(initialValue)
```

```
    ];
  };
```

This is a custom hook. It doesn't take a lot of code. Inside of this hook, we're still using the `useState` hook to create a state `value`. Next, we return an array. The first value of the array is the object that contains the same properties we were tempted to copy and paste: the `value` from state along with an onChange function property that changes that value in state. The second value in the array is a function that can be reused to reset the `value` back to its initial value. We can use our hook inside of the `AddColorForm`:

```
import React from "react";
import { useInput } from "./hooks";

export default function AddColorForm({ onNewColor = f => f }) {
  const [titleProps, resetTitle] = useInput("");
  const [colorProps, resetColor] = useInput("#000000");

  const submit = event => { ... }

  return ( ... )
}
```

The `useState` hook is encapsulated within our `useInput` hook. We can obtain the properties for both the title and the color by destructuring them from the first value of the returned array. The second value of this array contains a function we can use to reset the `value` property back to its initial value, an empty string. The `titleProps` and `colorProps` are ready to be spread into their corresponding input elements:

```
return (
  <form onSubmit={submit}>
    <input
      {...titleProps}
      type="text"
      placeholder="color title..."
      required
    />
    <input {...colorProps} type="color" required />
    <button>ADD</button>
  </form>
);
}
```

Spreading these properties from our custom hook is much more fun than pasting them. Now both the title and the color inputs are receiving properties for their value and onChange events. We've used our hook to create controlled form inputs without worrying about the underlying implementation details. The only other change we need to make is when this form is submitted:

```
const submit = event => {
  event.preventDefault();
  onNewColor(titleProps.value, colorProps.value);
  resetTitle();
  resetColor();
};
```

Within the `submit` function, we need to be sure to grab the `value` for both the title and the color from their properties. Finally, we can use the custom reset functions that were returned from the `useInput` hook.

Hooks are designed to be used inside of React components. We can compose hooks within other hooks because eventually the customized hook will be used inside of a component. Changing the state within this hook still causes the `AddColorForm` to rerender with new values for `titleProps` or `colorProps`.

## Adding Colors to State

Both the controlled form component and the uncontrolled from component pass the values for `title` and `color` to the parent component via the `onNewColor` function. The parent doesn't care whether we used a controlled component or an uncontrolled component; it only wants the values for the new color.

Let's add the `AddColorForm`, whichever one you choose, to the the `App` component. When the `onNewColor` property is invoked, we'll save the new color in state:

```
import React, { useState } from "react";
import colorData from "./color-data.json";
import ColorList from "./ColorList.js";
import AddColorForm from "./AddColorForm";
import { v4 } from "uuid";

export default function App() {
  const [colors, setColors] = useState(colorData);
  return (
    <>
      <AddColorForm
        onNewColor={(title, color) => {
          const newColors = [
            ...colors,
            {
              id: v4(),
              rating: 0,
              title,
              color
            }
          ];
          setColors(newColors);
        }}
      />
```

```
        <ColorList .../>
      </>
    );
  }
```

When a new color is added, the `onNewColor` property is invoked. The `title` and hex-adecimal value for the new `color` are passed to this function as arguments. We use these arguments to create a new array of colors. First, we spread the current `colors` from state into the new array. Then we add an entirely new color object using the `title` and `color` values. Additionally, we set the `rating` of the new color to 0 because it has not yet been rated. We also use the `v4` function found in the `uuid` package to generate a new unique `id` for the color. Once we have an array of colors that contains our new color, we save it to state by invoking `setColors`. This causes the `App` component to rerender with a new array of `colors`. That new array will be used to update the UI. We'll see the new color at bottom of the list.

With this change, we've completed the first iteration of the Color Organizer. Users can now add new colors to the list, remove colors from the list, and rate any existing color on that list.

## React Context

Storing state in one location at the root of our tree was an important pattern that helped us all be more successful with early versions of React. Learning to pass state both down and up a component tree via properties is a necessary right of passage for any React developer—it's something we should all know how to do. However, as React evolved and our component trees got larger, following this principle slowly became more unrealistic. It's hard for many developers to maintain state in a single location at the root of a component tree for a complex application. Passing state down and up the tree through dozens of components is tedious and bug ridden.

The UI elements that most of us work on are complex. The root of the tree is often very far from the leaves. This puts data the application depends on many layers away from the components that use the data. Every component must receive props that they only pass to their children. This will bloat our code and make our UI harder to scale.

Passing state data through every component as props until it reaches the component that needs to use it is like taking the train from San Francisco to DC. On the train, you'll pass through every state, but you won't get off until you reach your destination (see Figure 6-6).

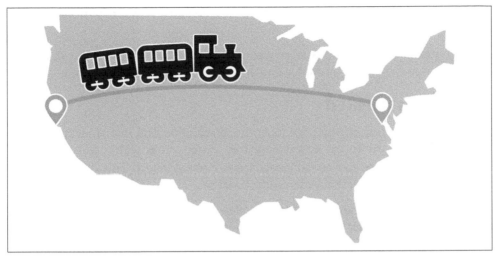

*Figure 6-6. Train from San Francisco to DC*

It's obviously more efficient to fly from San Francisco to DC. This way, you don't have to pass through every state—you simply fly over them (Figure 6-7).

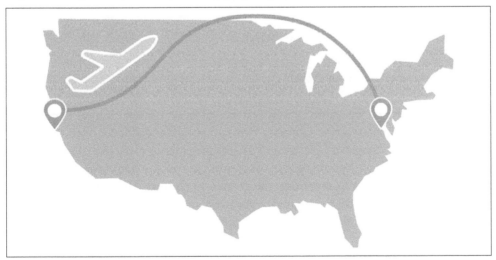

*Figure 6-7. Flight from San Francisco to DC*

In React, *context* is like jet-setting for your data. You can place data in React context by creating a *context provider*. A context provider is a React component you can wrap around your entire component tree or specific sections of your component tree. The context provider is the departing airport where your data boards the plane. It's also the airline hub. All flights depart from that airport to different destinations. Each destination is a *context consumer*. The context consumer is the React component that retrieves the data from context. This is the destination airport where your data lands, deplanes, and goes to work.

Using context still allows to us store state data in a single location, but it doesn't require us to pass that data through a bunch of components that don't need it.

## Placing Colors in Context

In order to use context in React, we must first place some data in a context provider and add that provider to our component tree. React comes with a function called createContext that we can use to create a new context object. This object contains two components: a context Provider and a Consumer.

Let's place the default colors found in the *color-data.json* file into context. We'll add context to the *index.js* file, the entry point of our application:

```
import React, { createContext } from "react";
import colors from "./color-data";
import { render } from "react-dom";
import App from "./App";

export const ColorContext = createContext();

render(
  <ColorContext.Provider value={{ colors }}>
    <App />
  </ColorContext.Provider>,
  document.getElementById("root")
);
```

Using createContext, we created a new instance of React context that we named ColorContext. The color context contains two components: ColorContext.Provider and ColorContext.Consumer. We need to use the provider to place the colors in state. We add data to context by setting the value property of the Provider. In this scenario, we added an object containing the colors to context. Since we wrapped the entire App component with the provider, the array of colors will made available to any context consumers found in our entire component tree. It's important to notice that we've also exported the ColorContext from this location. This is necessary because we will need to access the ColorContext.Consumer when we want to obtain the colors from context.

A context `Provider` doesn't always have to wrap an entire application. It's not only OK to wrap specific sections components with a context `Provider`, it can make your application more efficient. The `Provider` will only provide context values to its children.

It's OK to use multiple context providers. In fact, you may be using context providers in your React app already without even knowing it. Many npm packages designed to work with React use context behind the scenes.

Now that we're providing the `colors` value in context, the `App` component no longer needs to hold state and pass it down to its children as props. We've made the `App` component a "flyover" component. The `Provider` is the `App` component's parent, and it's providing the `colors` in context. The `ColorList` is the `App` component's child, and it can obtain the `colors` directly on its own. So the app doesn't need to touch the colors at all, which is great because the `App` component itself has nothing to do with colors. That responsibility has been delegated farther down the tree.

We can remove a lot of lines of code from the `App` component. It only needs to render the `AddColorForm` and the `ColorList`. It no longer has to worry about the data:

```
import React from "react";
import ColorList from "./ColorList.js";
import AddColorForm from "./AddColorForm";

export default function App() {
  return (
    <>
      <AddColorForm />
      <ColorList />
    </>
  );
}
```

## Retrieving Colors with useContext

The addition of Hooks makes working with context a joy. The `useContext` hook is used to obtain values from context, and it obtains those values we need from the context `Consumer`. The `ColorList` component no longer needs to obtain the array of `col ors` from its properties. It can access them directly via the `useContext` hook:

```
import React, { useContext } from "react";
import { ColorContext } from "./";
import Color from "./Color";

export default function ColorList() {
  const { colors } = useContext(ColorContext);
  if (!colors.length) return <div>No Colors Listed. (Add a Color)</div>;
  return (
```

```
    <div className="color-list">
      {
        colors.map(color => <Color key={color.id} {...color} />)
      }
    </div>
  );
}
```

Here, we've modified the ColorList component and removed the colors=[] property because the colors are being retrieved from context. The useContext hook
requires the context instance to obtain values from it. The ColorContext instance is
being imported from the *index.js* file where we create the context and add the provider to our component tree. The ColorList can now construct a user interface based
on the data that has been provided in context.

### Using Context Consumer

The Consumer is accessed within the useContext hook, which
means that we no longer have to work directly with the consumer
component. Before Hooks, we would have to obtain the colors
from context using a pattern called *render props* within the context
consumer. Render props are passed as arguments to a child function. The following example is how you would use the consumer to
obtain the colors from context:

```
export default function ColorList() {
  return (
    <ColorContext.Consumer>
      {context => {
      if (!context.colors.length)
      return <div>No Colors Listed. (Add a Color)</div>;
        return (
          <div className="color-list">
            {
              context.colors.map(color =>
  <Color key={color.id} {...color} />)
            }
          </div>
        )
      }}
    </ColorContext.Consumer>
  )
}
```

# Stateful Context Providers

The context provider can place an object into context, but it can't mutate the values in context on its own. It needs some help from a parent component. The trick is to create a stateful component that renders a context provider. When the state of the stateful component changes, it will rerender the context provider with new context data. Any of the context providers' children will also be rerendered with the new context data.

The stateful component that renders the context provider is our *custom provider*. That is: that's the component that will be used when it's time to wrap our App with the provider. In a brand-new file, let's create a `ColorProvider`:

```
import React, { createContext, useState } from "react";
import colorData from "./color-data.json";

const ColorContext = createContext();

export default function ColorProvider ({ children }) {
  const [colors, setColors] = useState(colorData);
  return (
    <ColorContext.Provider value={{ colors, setColors }}>
      {children}
    </ColorContext.Provider>
  );
};
```

The `ColorProvider` is a component that renders the `ColorContext.Provider`. Within this component, we've created a state variable for `colors` using the `useState` hook. The initial data for `colors` is still being populated from *color-data.json*. Next, the `ColorProvider` adds the `colors` from state to context using the `value` property of the `ColorContext.Provider`. Any children rendered within the `ColorProvider` will be wrapped by the `ColorContext.Provider` and will have access to the `colors` array from context.

You may have noticed that the `setColors` function is also being added to context. This gives context consumers the ability to change the value for colors. Whenever `setColors` is invoked, the `colors` array will change. This will cause the `ColorProvider` to rerender, and our UI will update itself to display the new `colors` array.

Adding `setColors` to context may not be the best idea. It invites other developers and you to make mistakes later on down the road when using it. There are only three options when it comes to changing the value of the `colors` array: users can add colors, remove colors, or rate colors. It's a better idea to add functions for each of these operations to context. This way, you don't expose the `setColors` function to consumers; you only expose functions for the changes they're allowed to make:

```
export default function ColorProvider ({ children }) {
  const [colors, setColors] = useState(colorData);

  const addColor = (title, color) =>
    setColors([
      ...colors,
      {
        id: v4(),
        rating: 0,
        title,
        color
      }
    ]);

  const rateColor = (id, rating) =>
    setColors(
      colors.map(color => (color.id === id ? { ...color, rating } : color))
    );

  const removeColor = id => setColors(colors.filter(color => color.id !== id));

  return (
    <ColorContext.Provider value={{ colors, addColor, removeColor, rateColor }}>
      {children}
    </ColorContext.Provider>
  );
};
```

That looks better. We added functions to context for all of the operations that can be made on the colors array. Now, any component within our tree can consume these operations and make changes to colors using simple functions that we can document.

## Custom Hooks with Context

There's one more killer change we can make. The introduction of Hooks has made it so that we don't have to expose context to consumer components at all. Let's face it: context can be confusing for team members who aren't reading this book. We can make everything much easier for them by wrapping context in a custom hook. Instead of exposing the `ColorContext` instance, we can create a hook called `useCol ors` that returns the colors from context:

```
import React, { createContext, useState, useContext } from "react";
import colorData from "./color-data.json";
import { v4 } from "uuid";

const ColorContext = createContext();
export const useColors = () => useContext(ColorContext);
```

This one simple change has a huge impact on architecture. We've wrapped all of the functionality necessary to render and work with stateful colors in a single JavaScript module. Context is contained to this module yet exposed through a hook. This works because we return context using the `useContext` hook, which has access to the Color Context locally in this file. It's now appropriate to rename this module color-hooks.js and distribute this functionality for wider use by the community.

Consuming colors using the `ColorProvider` and the `useColors` hook is a joyous event. This is why we program. Let's take this hook out for a spin in the current Color Organizer app. First, we need to wrap our `App` component with the custom `ColorProvider`. We can do this in the *index.js* file:

```
import React from "react";
import { ColorProvider } from "./color-hooks.js";
import { render } from "react-dom";
import App from "./App";

render(
  <ColorProvider>
    <App />
  </ColorProvider>,
  document.getElementById("root")
);
```

Now, any component that's a child of the `App` can obtain the `colors` from the `useColors` hook. The `ColorList` component needs to access the `colors` array to render the colors on the screen:

```
import React from "react";
import Color from "./Color";
import { useColors } from "./color-hooks";

export default function ColorList() {
  const { colors } = useColors();
  return ( ... );
}
```

We've removed any references to context from this component. Everything it needs is now being provided from our hook. The `Color` component could use our hook to obtain the functions for rating and removing colors directly:

```
import React from "react";
import StarRating from "./StarRating";
import { useColors } from "./color-hooks";

export default function Color({ id, title, color, rating }) {
  const { rateColor, removeColor } = useColors();
  return (
    <section>
      <h1>{title}</h1>
      <button onClick={() => removeColor(id)}>X</button>
      <div style={{ height: 50, backgroundColor: color }} />
      <StarRating
```

```
        selectedStars={rating}
        onRate={rating => rateColor(id, rating)}
      />
    </section>
  );
}
```

Now, the `Color` component no longer needs to pass events to the parent via function props. It has access to the `rateColor` and `removeColor` functions in context. They're easily obtained through the `useColors` hook. This is a lot of fun, but we're not finished yet. The `AddColorForm` can also benefit from the `useColors` hook:

```
import React from "react";
import { useInput } from "./hooks";
import { useColors } from "./color-hooks";

export default function AddColorForm() {
  const [titleProps, resetTitle] = useInput("");
  const [colorProps, resetColor] = useInput("#000000");
  const { addColor } = useColors();

  const submit = e => {
    e.preventDefault();
    addColor(titleProps.value, colorProps.value);
    resetTitle();
    resetColor();
  };

  return ( ... );
}
```

The `AddColorForm` component can add colors directly with the `addColor` function. When colors are added, rated, or removed, the state of the `colors` value in context will change. When this change happens, the children of the `ColorProvider` are rerendered with new context data. All of this is happening through a simple hook.

Hooks provide software developers with the stimulation they need to stay motivated and enjoy frontend programming. This is primarily because they're an awesome tool for separating concerns. Now, React components only need to concern themselves with rendering other React components and keeping the user interface up to date. React Hooks can concern themselves with the logic required to make the app work. Both the UI and Hooks can be developed separately, tested separately, and even deployed separately. This is all very good news for React.

We've only scratched the surface of what can be accomplished with Hooks. In the next chapter, we'll dive a little deeper.

# CHAPTER 7

# Enhancing Components with Hooks

Rendering is the heartbeat of a React application. When something changes (props, state), the component tree rerenders, reflecting the latest data as a user interface. So far, useState has been our workhorse for describing how our components should be rendering. But we can do more. There are more Hooks that define rules about why and when rendering should happen. There are more Hooks that enhance rendering performance. There are always more Hooks to help us out.

In the last chapter, we introduced useState, useRef, and useContext, and we saw that we could compose these Hooks into our own custom Hooks: useInput and use Colors. There's more where that came from, though. React comes with more Hooks out of the box. In this chapter, we're going to take a closer look at useEffect, use LayoutEffect, and useReducer. All of these are vital when building applications. We'll also look at useCallback and useMemo, which can help optimize our components for performance.

## Introducing useEffect

We now have a good sense of what happens when we render a component. A component is simply a function that renders a user interface. Renders occur when the app first loads and when props and state values change. But what happens when we need to do something after a render? Let's take a closer look.

Consider a simple component, the Checkbox. We're using useState to set a checked value and a function to change the value of checked: setChecked. A user can check and uncheck the box, but how might we alert the user that the box has been checked? Let's try this with an alert, as it's a great way to block the thread:

```
import React, { useState } from "react";

function Checkbox() {
  const [checked, setChecked] = useState(false);

  alert(`checked: ${checked.toString()}`);

  return (
    <>
      <input
        type="checkbox"
        value={checked}
        onChange={() => setChecked(checked => !checked)}
      />
      {checked ? "checked" : "not checked"}
    </>
  );
};
```

We've added the alert before the render to block the render. The component will not render until the user clicks the OK button on the alert box. Because the alert is blocking, we don't see the next state of the checkbox rendered until clicking OK.

That isn't the goal, so maybe we should place the alert after the return?

```
function Checkbox {
  const [checked, setChecked] = useState(false);

  return (
    <>
      <input
        type="checkbox"
        value={checked}
        onChange={() => setChecked(checked => !checked)}
      />
      {checked ? "checked" : "not checked"}
    </>
  );

  alert(`checked: ${checked.toString()}`);
};
```

Scratch that. We can't call alert after the render because the code will never be reached. To ensure that we see the alert as expected, we can use useEffect. Placing the alert inside of the useEffect function means that the function will be called after the render, as a side effect:

```
function Checkbox {
  const [checked, setChecked] = useState(false);

  useEffect(() => {
    alert(`checked: ${checked.toString()}`);
```

```
  });

  return (
    <>
      <input
        type="checkbox"
        value={checked}
        onChange={() => setChecked(checked => !checked)}
      />
      {checked ? "checked" : "not checked"}
    </>
  );
};
```

We use useEffect when a render needs to cause side effects. Think of a side effect as something that a function does that isn't part of the return. The function is the Check box. The Checkbox function renders UI. But we might want the component to do more than that. Those things we want the component to do other than return UI are called *effects*.

An alert, a console.log, or an interaction with a browser or native API is not part of the render. It's not part of the return. In a React app, though, the render affects the results of one of these events. We can use useEffect to wait for the render, then provide the values to an alert or a console.log:

```
useEffect(() => {
  console.log(checked ? "Yes, checked" : "No, not checked");
});
```

Similarly, we could check in with the value of checked on render and then set that to a value in localStorage:

```
useEffect(() => {
  localStorage.setItem("checkbox-value", checked);
});
```

We might also use useEffect to focus on a specific text input that has been added to the DOM. React will render the output, then call useEffect to focus the element:

```
useEffect(() => {
  txtInputRef.current.focus();
});
```

On render, the txtInputRef will have a value. We can access that value in the effect to apply the focus. Every time we render, useEffect has access to the latest values from that render: props, state, refs, etc.

Think of useEffect as being a function that happens after a render. When a render fires, we can access the current state values within our component and use them to do something else. Then, once we render again, the whole thing starts over. New values, new renders, new effects.

# The Dependency Array

useEffect is designed to work in conjunction with other stateful Hooks like useState and the heretofore unmentioned useReducer, which we promise to discuss later in the chapter. React will rerender the component tree when the state changes. As we've learned, useEffect will be called after these renders.

Consider the following, where the App component has two separate state values:

```
import React, { useState, useEffect } from "react";
import "./App.css";

function App() {
  const [val, set] = useState("");
  const [phrase, setPhrase] = useState("example phrase");

  const createPhrase = () => {
    setPhrase(val);
    set("");
  };

  useEffect(() => {
    console.log(`typing "${val}"`);
  });

  useEffect(() => {
    console.log(`saved phrase: "${phrase}"`);
  });

  return (
    <>
      <label>Favorite phrase:</label>
      <input
        value={val}
        placeholder={phrase}
        onChange={e => set(e.target.value)}
      />
      <button onClick={createPhrase}>send</button>
    </>
  );
}
```

val is a state variable that represents the value of the input field. The val changes every time the value of the input field changes. It causes the component to render every time the user types a new character. When the user clicks the Send button, the val of the text area is saved as the phrase, and the val is reset to "", which empties the text field.

This works as expected, but the useEffect hook is invoked more times than it should be. After every render, both useEffect Hooks are called:

---

```
typing ""                                   // First Render
saved phrase: "example phrase"              // First Render
typing "S"                                  // Second Render
saved phrase: "example phrase"              // Second Render
typing "Sh"                                 // Third Render
saved phrase: "example phrase"              // Third Render
typing "Shr"                                // Fourth Render
saved phrase: "example phrase"              // Fourth Render
typing "Shre"                               // Fifth Render
saved phrase: "example phrase"              // Fifth Render
typing "Shred"                              // Sixth Render
saved phrase: "example phrase"              // Sixth Render
```

We don't want every effect to be invoked on every render. We need to associate useEffect hooks with specific data changes. To solve this problem, we can incorporate the dependency array. The dependency array can be used to control when an effect is invoked:

```
useEffect(() => {
  console.log(`typing "${val}"`);
}, [val]);

useEffect(() => {
  console.log(`saved phrase: "${phrase}"`);
}, [phrase]);
```

We've added the dependency array to both effects to control when they're invoked. The first effect is only invoked when the val value has changed. The second effect is only invoked when the phrase value has changed. Now, when we run the app and take a look at the console, we'll see more efficient updates occurring:

```
typing ""                                   // First Render
saved phrase: "example phrase"              // First Render
typing "S"                                  // Second Render
typing "Sh"                                 // Third Render
typing "Shr"                                // Fourth Render
typing "Shre"                               // Fifth Render
typing "Shred"                              // Sixth Render
typing ""                                   // Seventh Render
saved phrase: "Shred"                       // Seventh Render
```

Changing the val value by typing into the input only causes the first effect to fire. When we click the button, the phrase is saved and the val is reset to "".

It's an array after all, so it's possible to check multiple values in the dependency array. Let's say we wanted to run a specific effect any time either the val or phrase has changed:

```
useEffect(() => {
  console.log("either val or phrase has changed");
}, [val, phrase]);
```

If either of those values changes, the effect will be called again. It's also possible to supply an empty array as the second argument to a useEffect function. An empty dependency array causes the effect to be invoked only once after the initial render:

```
useEffect(() => {
  console.log("only once after initial render");
}, []);
```

Since there are no dependencies in the array, the effect is invoked for the initial render. No dependencies means no changes, so the effect will never be invoked again. Effects that are only invoked on the first render are extremely useful for initialization:

```
useEffect(() => {
  welcomeChime.play();
}, []);
```

If you return a function from the effect, the function will be invoked when the component is removed from the tree:

```
useEffect(() => {
  welcomeChime.play();
  return () => goodbyeChime.play();
}, []);
```

This means that you can use useEffect for setup and teardown. The empty array means that the welcome chime will play once on first render. Then, we'll return a function as a cleanup function to play a goodbye chime when the component is removed from the tree.

This pattern is useful in many situations. Perhaps we'll subscribe to a news feed on first render. Then we'll unsubscribe from the news feed with the cleanup function. More specifically, we'll start by creating a state value for posts and a function to change that value, called setPosts. Then we'll create a function, addPosts, that will take in the newest post and add it to the array. Then we can use useEffect to subscribe to the news feed and play the chime. Plus, we can return the cleanup functions, unsubscribing and playing the goodbye chime:

```
const [posts, setPosts] = useState([]);
const addPost = post => setPosts(allPosts => [post, ...allPosts]);

useEffect(() => {
  newsFeed.subscribe(addPost);
  welcomeChime.play();
  return () => {
    newsFeed.unsubscribe(addPost);
    goodbyeChime.play();
  };
}, []);
```

This is a lot going on in useEffect, though. We might want to use a separate useEffect for the news feed events and another useEffect for the chime events:

```
useEffect(() => {
  newsFeed.subscribe(addPost);
  return () => newsFeed.unsubscribe(addPost);
}, []);

useEffect(() => {
  welcomeChime.play();
  return () => goodbyeChime.play();
}, []);
```

Splitting functionality into multiple useEffect calls is typically a good idea. But let's enhance this even further. What we're trying to create here is functionality for subscribing to a news feed that plays different jazzy sounds for subscribing, unsubscribing, and whenever there's a new post. Everyone loves lots of loud sounds right? This is a case for a custom hook. Maybe we should call it useJazzyNews:

```
const useJazzyNews = () => {
  const [posts, setPosts] = useState([]);
  const addPost = post => setPosts(allPosts => [post, ...allPosts]);

  useEffect(() => {
    newsFeed.subscribe(addPost);
    return () => newsFeed.unsubscribe(addPost);
  }, []);

  useEffect(() => {
    welcomeChime.play();
    return () => goodbyeChime.play();
  }, []);

  return posts;
};
```

Our custom hook contains all of the functionality to handle a jazzy news feed, which means that we can easily share this functionality with our components. In a new component called NewsFeed, we'll use the custom hook:

```
function NewsFeed({ url }) {
  const posts = useJazzyNews();

  return (
    <>
      <h1>{posts.length} articles</h1>
      {posts.map(post => (
        <Post key={post.id} {...post} />
      ))}
    </>
  );
}
```

# Deep Checking Dependencies

So far, the dependencies we've added to the array have been strings. JavaScript primitives like strings, booleans, numbers, etc., are comparable. A string would equal a string as expected:

```
if ("gnar" === "gnar") {
  console.log("gnarly!!");
}
```

However, when we start to compare objects, arrays, and functions, the comparison is different. For example, if we compared two arrays:

```
if ([1, 2, 3] !== [1, 2, 3]) {
  console.log("but they are the same");
}
```

These arrays [1,2,3] and [1,2,3] are not equal, even though they look identical in length and in entries. This is because they are two different instances of a similar-looking array. If we create a variable to hold this array value and then compare, we'll see the expected output:

```
const array = [1, 2, 3];
if (array === array) {
  console.log("because it's the exact same instance");
}
```

In JavaScript, arrays, objects, and functions are the same only when they're the exact same instance. So how does this relate to the useEffect dependency array? To demonstrate this, we're going to need a component we can force to render as much as we want. Let's build a hook that causes a component to render whenever a key is pressed:

```
const useAnyKeyToRender = () => {
  const [, forceRender] = useState();

  useEffect(() => {
    window.addEventListener("keydown", forceRender);
    return () => window.removeEventListener("keydown", forceRender);
  }, []);
};
```

At minimum, all we need to do to force a render is invoke a state change function. We don't care about the state value. We only want the state function: forceRender. (That's why we added the comma using array destructuring. Remember, from Chapter 2?) When the component first renders, we'll listen for keydown events. When a key is pressed, we'll force the component to render by invoking forceRender. As we've done before, we'll return a cleanup function where we stop listening to keydown events. By adding this hook to a component, we can force it to rerender simply by pressing a key.

---

With the custom hook built, we can use it in the App component (and any other component for that matter! Hooks are cool.):

```
function App() {
  useAnyKeyToRender();

  useEffect(() => {
    console.log("fresh render");
  });

  return <h1>Open the console</h1>;
}
```

Every time we press a key, the App component is rendered. useEffect demonstrates this by logging "fresh render" to the console every time the App is rendered. Let's adjust useEffect in the App component to reference the word value. If word changes, we'll rerender:

```
const word = "gnar";
useEffect(() => {
  console.log("fresh render");
}, [word]);
```

Instead of calling useEffect on every keydown event, we would only call this after first render and any time the word value changes. It doesn't change, so subsequent rerenders don't occur. Adding a primitive or a number to the dependency array works as expected. The effect is invoked once.

What happens if instead of a single word, we use an array of words?

```
const words = ["sick", "powder", "day"];
useEffect(() => {
  console.log("fresh render");
}, [words]);
```

The variable words is an array. Because a new array is declared with each render, JavaScript assumes that words has changed, thus invoking the "fresh render" effect every time. The array is a new instance each time, and this registers as an update that should trigger a rerender.

Declaring words outside of the scope of the App would solve the problem:

```
const words = ["sick", "powder", "day"];

function App() {
  useAnyKeyToRender();
  useEffect(() => {
    console.log("fresh render");
  }, [words]);

  return <h1>component</h1>;
}
```

The dependency array in this case refers to one instance of words that's declared outside of the function. The "fresh render" effect does not get called again after the first render because words is the same instance as the last render. This is a good solution for this example, but it's not always possible (or advisable) to have a variable defined outside of the scope of the function. Sometimes the value passed to the dependency array requires variables in scope. For example, we might need to create the words array from a React property like children:

```
function WordCount({ children = "" }) {
  useAnyKeyToRender();

  const words = children.split(" ");

  useEffect(() => {
    console.log("fresh render");
  }, [words]);

  return (
    <>
      <p>{children}</p>
      <p>
        <strong>{words.length} - words</strong>
      </p>
    </>
  );
}
```

```
function App() {
  return <WordCount>You are not going to believe this but...</WordCount>;
}
```

The App component contains some words that are children of the WordCount component. The WordCount component takes in children as a property. Then we set words in the component equal to an array of those words that we've called .split on. We would hope that the component will rerender only if words changes, but as soon as we press a key, we see the dreaded "fresh render" words appearing in the console.

Let's replace that feeling of dread with one of calm, because the React team has provided us a way to avoid these extra renders. They wouldn't hang us out to dry like that. The solution to this problem is, as you might expect, another hook: useMemo.

useMemo invokes a function to calculate a memoized value. In computer science in general, memoization is a technique that's used to improve performance. In a memoized function, the result of a function call is saved and cached. Then, when the function is called again with the same inputs, the cached value is returned. In React, useMemo allows us to compare the cached value against itself to see if it has actually changed.

---

The way `useMemo` works is that we pass it a function that's used to calculate and create a memoized value. `useMemo` will only recalculate that value when one of the dependencies has changed. First, let's import the `useMemo` hook:

```
import React, { useEffect, useMemo } from "react";
```

Then we'll use the function to set `words`:

```
const words = useMemo(() => {
  const words = children.split(" ");
  return words;
}, []);

useEffect(() => {
  console.log("fresh render");
}, [words]);
```

`useMemo` invokes the function sent to it and sets `words` to the return value of that function. Like `useEffect`, `useMemo` relies on a dependency array:

```
const words = useMemo(() => children.split(" "));
```

When we don't include the dependency array with `useMemo`, the words are calculated with every render. The dependency array controls when the callback function should be invoked. The second argument sent to the `useMemo` function is the dependency array and should contain the `children` value:

```
function WordCount({ children = "" }) {
  useAnyKeyToRender();

  const words = useMemo(() => children.split(" "), [children]);

  useEffect(() => {
    console.log("fresh render");
  }, [words]);

  return (...);
}
```

The `words` array depends on the `children` property. If `children` changes, we should calculate a new value for `words` that reflects that change. At that point, `useMemo` will calculate a new value for `words` when the component initially renders and if the `children` property changes.

The `useMemo` hook is a great function to understand when you're creating React applications.

`useCallback` can be used like `useMemo`, but it memoizes functions instead of values. For example:

```
const fn = () => {
  console.log("hello");
```

```
    console.log("world");
  };

  useEffect(() => {
    console.log("fresh render");
    fn();
  }, [fn]);
```

fn is a function that logs "Hello" then "World." It is a dependency of useEffect, but just like words, JavaScript assumes fn is different every render. Therefore, it triggers the effect every render. This yields a "fresh render" for every key press. It's not ideal.

Start by wrapping the function with useCallback:

```
  const fn = useCallback(() => {
    console.log("hello");
    console.log("world");
  }, []);

  useEffect(() => {
    console.log("fresh render");
    fn();
  }, [fn]);
```

useCallback memoizes the function value for fn. Just like useMemo and useEffect, it also expects a dependency array as the second argument. In this case, we create the memoized callback once because the dependency array is empty.

Now that we have an understanding of the uses and differences between useMemo and useCallback, let's improve our useJazzyNews hook. Every time there's a new post, we'll call newPostChime.play(). In this hook, posts are an array, so we'll need to use useMemo to memoize the value:

```
  const useJazzyNews = () => {
    const [_posts, setPosts] = useState([]);
    const addPost = post => setPosts(allPosts => [post, ...allPosts]);

    const posts = useMemo(() => _posts, [_posts]);

    useEffect(() => {
      newPostChime.play();
    }, [posts]);

    useEffect(() => {
      newsFeed.subscribe(addPost);
      return () => newsFeed.unsubscribe(addPost);
    }, []);

    useEffect(() => {
      welcomeChime.play();
      return () => goodbyeChime.play();
    }, []);
```

```
      return posts;
   };
```

Now, the useJazzyNews hook plays a chime every time there's a new post. We made this happen with a few changes to the hook. First, `const [posts, setPosts]` was renamed to `const [_posts, setPosts]`. We'll calculate a new value for `posts` every time `_posts` change.

Next, we added the effect that plays the chime every time the `post` array changes. We're listening to the news feed for new posts. When a new post is added, this hook is reinvoked with `_posts` reflecting that new post. Then, a new value for `post` is memoized because `_posts` have changed. Then the chime plays because this effect is dependent on `posts`. It only plays when the posts change, and the list of posts only changes when a new one is added.

Later in the chapter, we'll discuss the React Profiler, a browser extension for testing performance and rendering of React components. There, we'll dig into more detail about when to use `useMemo` and `useCallback`. (Spoiler alert: sparingly!)

## When to useLayoutEffect

We understand that the render always comes before `useEffect`. The render happens first, then all effects run in order with full access to all of the values from the render. A quick look at the React docs will point out that there's another type of effect hook: `useLayoutEffect`.

useLayoutEffect is called at a specific moment in the render cycle. The series of events is as follows:

1. Render
2. `useLayoutEffect` is called
3. Browser paint: the time when the component's elements are actually added to the DOM
4. `useEffect` is called

This can be observed by adding some simple console messages:

```
import React, { useEffect, useLayoutEffect } from "react";

function App() {
  useEffect(() => console.log("useEffect"));
  useLayoutEffect(() => console.log("useLayoutEffect"));
  return <div>ready</div>;
}
```

In the App component, useEffect is the first hook, followed by useLayoutEffect. We see that useLayoutEffect is invoked before useEffect:

```
useLayoutEffect
useEffect
```

useLayoutEffect is invoked after the render but before the browser paints the change. In most circumstances, useEffect is the right tool for the job, but if your effect is essential to the browser paint (the appearance or placement of the UI elements on the screen), you may want to use useLayoutEffect. For instance, you may want to obtain the width and height of an element when the window is resized:

```
function useWindowSize {
  const [width, setWidth] = useState(0);
  const [height, setHeight] = useState(0);

  const resize = () => {
    setWidth(window.innerWidth);
    setHeight(window.innerHeight);
  };

  useLayoutEffect(() => {
    window.addEventListener("resize", resize);
    resize();
    return () => window.removeEventListener("resize", resize);
  }, []);

  return [width, height];
};
```

The width and height of the window is information that your component may need before the browser paints. useLayoutEffect is used to calculate the window's width and height before the paint. Another example of when to use useLayoutEffect is when tracking the position of the mouse:

```
function useMousePosition {
  const [x, setX] = useState(0);
  const [y, setY] = useState(0);

  const setPosition = ({ x, y }) => {
    setX(x);
    setY(y);
  };

  useLayoutEffect(() => {
    window.addEventListener("mousemove", setPosition);
    return () => window.removeEventListener("mousemove", setPosition);
  }, []);

  return [x, y];
};
```

It's highly likely that the x and y position of the mouse will be used when painting the screen. useLayoutEffect is available to help calculate those positions accurately before the paint.

## Rules to Follow with Hooks

As you're working with Hooks, there are a few guidelines to keep in mind that can help avoid bugs and unusual behavior:

*Hooks only run in the scope of a component*
Hooks should only be called from React components. They can also be added to custom Hooks, which are eventually added to components. Hooks are not regular JavaScript—they're a React pattern, but they're starting to be modeled and incorporated in other libraries.

*It's a good idea to break functionality out into multiple Hooks*
In our earlier example with the Jazzy News component, we split everything related to subscriptions into one effect and everything related to sound effects into another effect. This immediately made the code easier to read, but there was another benefit to doing this. Since Hooks are invoked in order, it's a good idea to keep them small. Once invoked, React saves the values of Hooks in an array so the values can be tracked. Consider the following component:

```
function Counter() {
  const [count, setCount] = useState(0);
  const [checked, toggle] = useState(false);

  useEffect(() => {
    ...
  }, [checked]);

  useEffect(() => {
    ...
  }, []);

  useEffect(() => {
    ...
  }, [count]);

  return ( ... )
}
```

The order of Hook calls is the same for each and every render:

```
[count, checked, DependencyArray, DependencyArray, DependencyArray]
```

*Hooks should only be called at the top level*

Hooks should be used at the top level of a React function. They cannot be placed into conditional statements, loops, or nested functions. Let's adjust the counter:

```
function Counter() {
  const [count, setCount] = useState(0);

  if (count > 5) {
    const [checked, toggle] = useState(false);
  }

  useEffect(() => {
    ...
  });

  if (count > 5) {
    useEffect(() => {
      ...
    });
  }

  useEffect(() => {
    ...
  });

  return ( ... )
}
```

When we use `useState` within the `if` statement, we're saying that the hook should only be called when the `count` value is greater than 5. That will throw off the array values. Sometimes the array will be: `[count, checked, DependencyAr ray, 0, DependencyArray]`. Other times: `[count, DependencyArray, 1]`. The index of the effect in that array matters to React. It's how values are saved.

Wait, so are we saying that we can never use conditional logic in React applications anymore? Of course not! We just have to organize these conditionals differently. We can nest `if` statements, loops, and other conditionals within the hook:

```
function Counter() {
  const [count, setCount] = useState(0);
  const [checked, toggle] =
  useState(
  count => (count < 5)
  ? undefined
  : !c,
  (count < 5) ? undefined
  );

  useEffect(() => {
```

```
    ...
  });

  useEffect(() => {
    if (count < 5) return;
    ...
  });

  useEffect(() => {
    ...
  });

  return ( ... )
}
```

Here, the value for `checked` is based on the condition that the `count` is greater than 5. When `count` is less than 5, the value for `checked` is `undefined`. Nesting this conditional inside the hook means that the hook remains on the top level, but the result is similar. The second effect enforces the same rules. If the `count` is less than 5, the return statement will prevent the effect from continuing to execute. This keeps the hook values array intact: [`countValue`, `checkedValue`, `DependencyArray`, `DependencyArray`, `DependencyArray`].

Like conditional logic, you need to nest asynchronous behavior inside of a hook. `useEffect` takes a function as the first argument, not a promise. So you can't use an async function as the first argument: `useEffect(async () => {})`. You can, however, create an async function inside of the nested function like this:

```
useEffect(() => {
  const fn = async () => {
    await SomePromise();
  };
  fn();
});
```

We created a variable, `fn`, to handle the async/await, then we called the function as the return. You can give this function a name, or you can use async effects as an anonymous function:

```
useEffect(() => {
  (async () => {
    await SomePromise();
  })();
});
```

If you follow these rules, you can avoid some common gotchas with React Hooks. If you're using Create React App, there's an ESLint plug-in included called eslint-plugin-react-hooks that provides warning hints if you're in violation of these rules.

## Improving Code with useReducer

Consider the `Checkbox` component. This component is a perfect example of a component that holds simple state. The box is either checked or not checked. `checked` is the state value, and `setChecked` is a function that will be used to change the state. When the component first renders, the value of `checked` will be `false`:

```
function Checkbox() {
  const [checked, setChecked] = useState(false);

  return (
    <>
      <input
        type="checkbox"
        value={checked}
        onChange={() => setChecked(checked => !checked)}
      />
      {checked ? "checked" : "not checked"}
    </>
  );
}
```

This works well, but one area of this function could be cause for alarm:

```
onChange={() => setChecked(checked => !checked)}
```

Look at it closely. It feels OK at first glance, but are we stirring up trouble here? We're sending a function that takes in the current value of `checked` and returns the opposite, `!checked`. This is probably more complex than it needs to be. Developers could easily send the wrong information and break the whole thing. Instead of handling it this way, why not provide a function as a toggle?

Let's add a function called `toggle` that will do the same thing: call `setChecked` and return the opposite of the current value of `checked`:

```
function Checkbox() {
  const [checked, setChecked] = useState(false);

  function toggle() {
    setChecked(checked => !checked);
  }

  return (
    <>
      <input type="checkbox" value={checked} onChange={toggle} />
      {checked ? "checked" : "not checked"}
    </>
  );
}
```

This is better. onChange is set to a predictable value: the toggle function. We know what that function is going to do every time, everywhere it's used. We can still take this one step farther to yield even more predictable results each time we use the check box component. Remember the function we sent to setChecked in the toggle function?

```
setChecked(checked => !checked);
```

We're going to refer to this function, checked => !checked, by a different name now: a *reducer*. A reducer function's most simple definition is that it takes in the current state and returns a new state. If checked is false, it should return the opposite, true. Instead of hardcoding this behavior into onChange events, we can abstract the logic into a reducer function that will always produce the same results. Instead of useState in the component, we'll use useReducer:

```
function Checkbox() {
  const [checked, toggle] = useReducer(checked => !checked, false);

  return (
    <>
      <input type="checkbox" value={checked} onChange={toggle} />
      {checked ? "checked" : "not checked"}
    </>
  );
}
```

useReducer takes in the reducer function and the initial state, false. Then, we'll set the onChange function to setChecked, which will call the reducer function.

Our earlier reducer, checked => !checked, is a prime example of this. If the same input is provided to a function, the same output should be expected. This concept originates with Array.reduce in JavaScript. reduce fundamentally does the same thing as a reducer: it takes in a function (to reduce all of the values into a single value) and an initial value and returns one value.

Array.reduce takes in a reducer function and an initial value. For each value in the numbers array, the reducer is called until one value is returned:

```
const numbers = [28, 34, 67, 68];

numbers.reduce((number, nextNumber) => number + nextNumber, 0); // 197
```

The reducer sent to Array.reduce takes in two arguments. You can also send multiple arguments to a reducer function:

```
function Numbers() {
  const [number, setNumber] = useReducer(
    (number, newNumber) => number + newNumber,
    0
  );
```

```
    return <h1 onClick={() => setNumber(30)}>{number}</h1>;
  }
```

Every time we click on the h1, we'll add 30 to the total.

## useReducer to Handle Complex State

useReducer can help us handle state updates more predictably as state becomes more complex. Consider an object that contains user data:

```
const firstUser = {
  id: "0391-3233-3201",
  firstName: "Bill",
  lastName: "Wilson",
  city: "Missoula",
  state: "Montana",
  email: "bwilson@mtnwilsons.com",
  admin: false
};
```

Then we have a component called User that sets the firstUser as the initial state, and the component displays the appropriate data:

```
function User() {
  const [user, setUser] = useState(firstUser);

  return (
    <div>
      <h1>
        {user.firstName} {user.lastName} - {user.admin ? "Admin" : "User"}
      </h1>
      <p>Email: {user.email}</p>
      <p>
        Location: {user.city}, {user.state}
      </p>
      <button>Make Admin</button>
    </div>
  );
}
```

A common error when managing state is to overwrite the state:

```
<button
  onClick={() => {
    setUser({ admin: true });
  }}
>
  Make Admin
</button>
```

Doing this would overwrite state from `firstUser` and replace it with just what we sent to the `setUser` function: `{admin: true}`. This can be fixed by spreading the current values from user, then overwriting the `admin` value:

```
<button
  onClick={() => {
    setUser({ ...user, admin: true });
  }}
>
  Make Admin
</button>
```

This will take the initial state and push in the new key/values: `{admin: true}`. We need to rewrite this logic in every `onClick`, making it prone to error (we might forget to do this when we come back to the app tomorrow):

```
function User() {
  const [user, setUser] = useReducer(
    (user, newDetails) => ({ ...user, ...newDetails }),
    firstUser
  );
  ...
}
```

Then we'll send the new state value, `newDetails`, to the reducer, and it will be pushed into the object:

```
<button
  onClick={() => {
    setUser({ admin: true });
  }}
>
  Make Admin
</button>
```

This pattern is useful when state has multiple subvalues or when the next state depends on a previous state. Teach everyone to spread, they'll spread for a day. Teach everyone to `useReducer` and they'll spread for life.

---

## Legacy setState and useReducer

In previous versions of React, we used a function called `setState` to update state. Initial state would be assigned in the constructor as an object:

```
class User extends React.Component {
  constructor(props) {
    super(props);
    this.state = {
      id: "0391-3233-3201",
      firstName: "Bill",
      lastName: "Wilson",
```

---

```
          city: "Missoula",
          state: "Montana",
          email: "bwilson@mtnwilsons.com",
          admin: false
      };
    }
  }

  <button onSubmit={() =>
         {this.setState({admin: true });}}
  Make Admin
  </button>
```

The older incarnation of `setState` merged state values. The same is true of `useReducer`:

```
const [state, setState] = useReducer(
       (state, newState) =>
             ({...state, ...newState}),
       initialState);

<button onSubmit={() =>
       {setState({admin: true });}}
Make Admin
</button>
</div>);
```

If you like this pattern, you can use `legacy-set-state` npm or `useReducer`.

The past few examples are simple applications for a reducer. In the next chapter, we'll dig deeper into reducer design patterns that can be used to simplify state management in your apps.

## Improving Component Performance

In a React application, components are rendered...usually a lot. Improving performance includes preventing unnecessary renders and reducing the time a render takes to propagate. React comes with tools to help us prevent unnecessary renders: `memo`, `useMemo`, and `useCallback`. We looked at `useMemo` and `useCallback` earlier in the chapter, but in this section, we'll go into more detail about how to use these Hooks to make your websites perform better.

The `memo` function is used to create pure components. As discussed in Chapter 3, we know that, given the same parameters, a pure function will always return the same result. A pure component works the same way. In React, a pure component is a component that always renders the same output, given the same properties.

Let's create a component called `Cat`:

```
const Cat = ({ name }) => {
  console.log(`rendering ${name}`);
  return <p>{name}</p>;
};
```

Cat is a pure component. The output is always a paragraph that displays the name property. If the name provided as a property is the same, the output will be the same:

```
function App() {
  const [cats, setCats] = useState(["Biscuit", "Jungle", "Outlaw"]);
  return (
    <>
      {cats.map((name, i) => (
        <Cat key={i} name={name} />
      ))}
      <button onClick={() => setCats([...cats, prompt("Name a cat")])}>
        Add a Cat
      </button>
    </>
  );
}
```

This app uses the Cat component. After the initial render, the console reads:

```
rendering Biscuit
rendering Jungle
rendering Outlaw
```

When the "Add a Cat" button is clicked, the user is prompted to add a cat.

If we add a cat named "Ripple," we see that all Cat components are rerendered:

```
rendering Biscuit
rendering Jungle
rendering Outlaw
rendering Ripple
```

This code works because prompt is blocking. This is just an example. Don't use prompt in a real app.

Every time we add a cat, every Cat component is rendered, but the Cat component is a pure component. Nothing changes about the output given the same prop, so there shouldn't be a render for each of these. We don't want to rerender a pure component if the properties haven't changed. The memo function can be used to create a component that will only render when its properties change. Start by importing it from the React library and use it to wrap the current Cat component:

```
import React, { useState, memo } from "react";
```

```
const Cat = ({ name }) => {
  console.log(`rendering ${name}`);
  return <p>{name}</p>;
};

const PureCat = memo(Cat);
```

Here, we've created a new component called PureCat. PureCat will only cause the Cat to render when the properties change. Then we can replace the Cat component with PureCat in the App component:

```
cats.map((name, i) => <PureCat key={i} name={name} />);
```

Now, every time we add a new cat name, like "Pancake," we see only one render in the console:

```
rendering Pancake
```

Because the names of the other cats have not changed, we don't render those Cat components. This is working well for a name property, but what if we introduce a function property to the Cat component?

```
const Cat = memo(({ name, meow = f => f }) => {
  console.log(`rendering ${name}`);
  return <p onClick={() => meow(name)}>{name}</p>;
});
```

Every time a cat is clicked on, we can use this property to log a meow to the console:

```
<PureCat key={i} name={name} meow={name => console.log(`${name} has meowed`)} />
```

When we add this change, PureCat no longer works as expected. It's always rendering every Cat component even though the name property remains the same. This is because of the added meow property. Unfortunately, every time we define the meow property as a function, it's always new function. To React, the meow property has changed, and the component is rerendered.

The memo function will allow us to define more specific rules around when this component should rerender:

```
const RenderCatOnce = memo(Cat, () => true);
const AlwaysRenderCat = memo(Cat, () => false);
```

The second argument sent to the memo function is a *predicate*. A predicate is a function that only returns true or false. This function decides whether to rerender a cat or not. When it returns false, the Cat is rerendered. When this function returns true, the Cat will not be rerendered. No matter what, the Cat is always rendered at least once. This is why, with RenderCatOnce, it will render once and then never again. Typically, this function is used to check actual values:

```
const PureCat = memo(
  Cat,
```

```
  (prevProps, nextProps) => prevProps.name === nextProps.name
);
```

We can use the second argument to compare properties and decide if Cat should be
rerendered. The predicate receives the previous properties and the next properties.
These objects are used to compare the name property. If the name changes, the component will be re-rendered. If the name is the same, it will be rerendered regardless of
what React thinks about the meow property.

## shouldComponentUpdate and PureComponent

The concepts we're discussing are not new to React. The memo function is a new solution to a common problem. In previous versions of React, there was a method called
shouldComponentUpdate. If present in the component, it was used to let React know
under which circumstances the component should update. shouldComponentUpdate
described which props or state would need to change for the component to rerender.
Once shouldComponentUpdate was part of the React library, it was embraced as a useful feature by many. So useful that the React team decided to create an alternate way
of creating a component as a class. A class component would look like this:

```
class Cat extends React.Component {
  render() {
    return (
      {name} is a good cat!
    )
  }
}
```

A PureComponent would look like this:

```
class Cat extends React.PureComponent {
  render() {
    return (
      {name} is a good cat!
    )
  }
}
```

PureComponent is the same as React.memo, but PureComponent is only for class components; React.memo is only for function components.

useCallback and useMemo can be used to memoize object and function properties.
Let's use useCallback in the Cat component:

```
const PureCat = memo(Cat);
function App() {
  const meow = useCallback(name => console.log(`${name} has meowed`, []);
  return <PureCat name="Biscuit" meow={meow} />
}
```

In this case, we did not provide a property-checking predicate to memo(Cat). Instead, we used useCallback to ensure that the meow function had not changed. Using these functions can be helpful when dealing with too many rerenders in your component tree.

# When to Refactor

The last Hooks we discussed, useMemo and useCallback, along with the memo function, are commonly overused. React is designed to be fast. It's designed to have components render a lot. The process of optimizing for performance began when you decided to use React in the first place. It's fast. Any further refactoring should be a last step.

There are trade-offs to refactoring. Using useCallback and useMemo everywhere because it seems like a good idea might actually make your app less performant. You're adding more lines of code and developer hours to your application. When you refactor for performance, it's important to have a goal. Perhaps you want to stop the screen from freezing or flickering. Maybe you know there are some costly functions that are slowing the speed of your app unreasonably.

The React Profiler can be used to measure the performance of each of your components. The profiler ships with the React Developer Tools that you've likely installed already (available for Chrome (*https://oreil.ly/1UNct*) and Firefox (*https://oreil.ly/0NYbR*)).

Always make sure your app works and you're satisfied with the codebase before refactoring. Over-refactoring, or refactoring before your app works, can introduce weird bugs that are hard to spot, and it might not be worth your time and focus to introduce these optimizations.

In the last two chapters, we've introduced many of the Hooks that ship with React. You've seen use cases for each hook, and you've created your own custom Hooks by composing other Hooks. Next, we'll build on these foundational skills by incorporating additional libraries and advanced patterns.

# CHAPTER 8

# Incorporating Data

Data is the lifeblood of our applications. It flows like water, and it nourishes our components with value. The user interface components we've composed are vessels for data. We fill our applications with data from the internet. We collect, create, and send new data to the internet. The value of our applications is not the components themselves—it's the data that flows through those components

When we talk about data, it may sound a little like we're talking about water or food. *The cloud* is the abundantly endless source from which we send and receive data. It's the internet. It's the networks, services, systems, and databases where we manipulate and store zettabytes of data. The cloud *hydrates* our clients with the latest and freshest data from the source. We work with this data locally and even store it locally. But when our local data becomes out of sync with the source, it loses its freshness and is said to be *stale*.

These are the challenges we face as developers working with data. We need to keep our applications hydrated with fresh data from the cloud. In this chapter, we're going to take a look at various techniques for loading and working with data from the source.

## Requesting Data

In the movie Star Wars, the droid C-3P0 is a protocol droid. His specialty, of course, is communication. He speaks over six million languages. Surely, C-3P0 knows how to send an HTTP request, because the Hyper Text Transfer Protocol is one of the most popular ways to transmit data to and from the internet.

HTTP provides the backbone for our internet communication. Every time we load *http://www.google.com* into our browser, we're asking Google to send us a search form. The files necessary for us to search are transmitted to the browser over HTTP.

When we interact with Google by searching for "cat photos," we're asking Google to find us cat photos. Google responds with data, and images are transferred to our browser over HTTP.

In JavaScript, the most popular way to make an HTTP request is to use fetch. If we wanted to ask GitHub for information about Moon Highway, we could do so by sending a fetch request:

```
fetch(`https://api.github.com/users/moonhighway`)
  .then(response => response.json())
  .then(console.log)
  .catch(console.error);
```

The fetch function returns a promise. Here, we're making an asynchronous request to a specific URL: *https://api.github.com/users/moonhighway*. It takes time for that request to traverse the internet and respond with information. When it does, that information is passed to a callback using the .then(callback) method. The GitHub API will respond with JSON data, but that data is contained in the body of the HTTP response, so we call response.json() to obtain that data and parse it as JSON. Once obtained, we log that data to the console. If anything goes wrong, we'll pass the error to the console.error method.

GitHub will respond to this request with a JSON object:

```
{
  "login": "MoonHighway",
  "id": 5952087,
  "node_id": "MDEyOk9yZ2FuaXphdGlvbjU5NTIwODc=",
  "avatar_url": "https://avatars0.githubusercontent.com/u/5952087?v=4",
  "bio": "Web Development classroom training materials.",

  ...

}
```

On GitHub, basic information about user accounts is made available by their API. Go ahead, try searching for yourself: *https://api.github.com/users/<YOUR_GIT-HUB_USER_NAME>*.

Another way of working with promises is to use async/await. Since fetch returns a promise, we can await a fetch request inside of an async function:

```
async function requestGithubUser(githubLogin) {
  try {
    const response = await fetch(
      `https://api.github.com/users/${githubLogin}`
    );
    const userData = await response.json();
    console.log(userData);
  } catch (error) {
    console.error(error);
```

```
    }
  }
```

This code achieves the exact same results as the previous fetch request that was made by chaining `.then` functions on to the request. When we `await` a promise, the next line of code will not be executed until the promise has resolved. This format gives us a nice way to work with promises in code. We'll be using both approaches for the remainder of this chapter.

## Sending Data with a Request

A lot of requests require us to upload data with the request. For instance, we need to collect information about a user in order to create an account, or we may need new information about a user to update their account.

Typically, we use a POST request when we're creating data and a PUT request when we're modifying it. The second argument of the `fetch` function allows us to pass an object of options that `fetch` can use when creating our HTTP request:

```
fetch("/create/user", {
  method: "POST",
  body: JSON.stringify({ username, password, bio })
});
```

This fetch is using the POST method to create a new user. The `username`, `password`, and user's `bio` are being passed as string content in the body of the request.

## Uploading Files with fetch

Uploading files requires a different type of HTTP request: a `multipart-formdata` request. This type of request tells the server that a file or multiple files are located in the body of the request. To make this request in JavaScript, all we have to do is pass a `FormData` object in the body of our request:

```
const formData = new FormData();
formData.append("username", "moontahoe");
formData.append("fullname", "Alex Banks");
forData.append("avatar", imgFile);

fetch("/create/user", {
  method: "POST",
  body: formData
});
```

This time, when we create a user, we're passing the `username`, `fullname`, and `avatar` image along with the request as a `formData` object. Although these values are hardcoded here, we could easily collect them from a form.

## Authorized Requests

Sometimes, we need to be authorized to make requests. Authorization is typically required to obtain personal or sensitive data. Additionally, authorization is almost always required for users to take action on the server with POST, PUT, or DELETE requests.

Users typically identify themselves with each request by adding a unique token to the request that a service can use to identify the user. This token is usually added as the `Authorization` header. On GitHub, you can see your personal account information if you send a token along with your request:

```
fetch(`https://api.github.com/users/${login}`, {
  method: "GET",
  headers: {
    Authorization: `Bearer ${token}`
  }
});
```

Tokens are typically obtained when a user signs into a service by providing their username and password. Tokens can also be obtained from third parties like GitHub or Facebook using with an open standard protocol called OAuth.

GitHub allows you to generate a Personal User token. You can generate one by logging in to GitHub and navigating to: Settings > Developer Settings > Personal Access Tokens. From here, you can create tokens with specific read/write rules and then use those tokens to obtain personal information from the GitHub API. If you generate a Personal Access Token and send it along with the fetch request, GitHub will provide additional private information about your account.

Fetching data from within a React component requires us to orchestrate the `useState` and `useEffect` hooks. The `useState` hook is used to store the response in state, and the `useEffect` hook is used to make the fetch request. For example, if we wanted to display information about a GitHub user in a component, we could use the following code:

```
import React, { useState, useEffect } from "react";

function GitHubUser({ login }) {
  const [data, setData] = useState();

  useEffect(() => {
    if (!login) return;
    fetch(`https://api.github.com/users/${login}`)
      .then(response => response.json())
      .then(setData)
      .catch(console.error);
  }, [login]);
```

```
  if (data)
    return <pre>{JSON.stringify(data, null, 2)}</pre>;

  return null;
}

export default function App() {
  return <GitHubUser login="moonhighway" />;
}
```

In this code, our App renders a GitHubUser component and displays JSON data about moonhighway. On the first render, GitHubUser sets up a state variable for data using the useState hook. Then, because data is initially null, the component returns null. Returning null from a component tells React to render nothing. It doesn't cause an error; we'll just see a black screen.

After the component is rendered, the useEffect hook is invoked. This is where we make the fetch request. When we get a response, we obtain and parse the data in that response as JSON. Now we can pass that JSON object to the setData function, which causes our component to render once again, but this time it will have data. This useEffect hook will not be invoked again unless the value for login changes. When it does, we'll need to request more information about a different user from GitHub.

When there is data, we're rendering it as a JSON string in a pre element. The JSON.stringify method takes three arguments: the JSON data to convert to a string, a replacer function that can be used to replace properties of the JSON object, and the number of spaces to use when formatting the data. In this case, we sent null as the replacer because we don't want to replace anything. The 2 represents the number of spaces to be used when formatting the code. This will indent the JSON string two spaces. Using the pre element honors whitespace, so readable JSON is what is finally rendered.

## Saving Data Locally

We can save data locally to the browser using the Web Storage API. Data can be saved by either using the window.localStorage or window.sessionStorage objects. The sessionStorage API only saves data for the user's session. Closing the tabs or restarting the browser will clear any data saved to sessionStorage. On the other hand, localStorage will save data indefinitely until you remove it.

JSON data should be saved in browser storage as a string. This means converting an object into a JSON string before saving it and parsing that string into JSON while loading it. Some function to handle saving and loading JSON data to the browser could look like:

```
const loadJSON = key =>
  key && JSON.parse(localStorage.getItem(key));
```

```
const saveJSON = (key, data) =>
  localStorage.setItem(key, JSON.stringify(data));
```

The loadJSON function loads an item from localStorage using the key. The local Storage.getItem function is used to load the data. If the item is there, it's then parsed into JSON before being returned. If it's not there, the loadJSON function will return null.

The saveJSON function will save some data to localStorage using a unique key identifier. The localStorage.setItem function can be used to save data to the browser. Before saving the data, we'll need to convert it to a JSON string.

Loading data from web storage, saving data to web storage, stringifying data, and parsing JSON strings are all synchronous tasks. Both the loadJSON and saveJSON functions are synchronous. So be careful—calling these functions too often with too much data can lead to performance issues. It's typically a good idea to throttle or debounce these functions for the sake of performance.

We could save the user's data that we received from our GitHub request. Then the next time that same user is requested, we could use the data saved to localStorage instead of sending another request to GitHub. We'll add the following code to the GitHubUser component:

```
const [data, setData] = useState(loadJSON(`user:${login}`));
useEffect(() => {
  if (!data) return;
  if (data.login === login) return;
  const { name, avatar_url, location } = data;
  saveJSON(`user:${login}`, {
    name,
    login,
    avatar_url,
    location
  });
}, [data]);
```

The loadJSON function is synchronous, so we can use it when we invoke useState to set the initial value for data. If there was user data saved to the browser under user:moonhighway, we'll initially set the data using that value. Otherwise, data will initially be null.

When data changes here after it has been loaded from GitHub, we'll invoke saveJSON to save only those user details that we need: name, login, avatar_url, and location. No need to save the rest of the user object when we're not using it. We also skip saving the data when that object is empty, !data. Also, if the current login and data.login are equal to each other, then we already have saved data for that user. We'll skip the step of saving that data again.

---

Here's a look at the entire `GitHubUser` component that uses `localStorage` to save data in the browser:

```
import React, { useState, useEffect } from "react";

const loadJSON = key =>
  key && JSON.parse(localStorage.getItem(key));
const saveJSON = (key, data) =>
  localStorage.setItem(key, JSON.stringify(data));

function GitHubUser({ login }) {
  const [data, setData] = useState(
    loadJSON(`user:${login}`)
  );

  useEffect(() => {
    if (!data) return;
    if (data.login === login) return;
    const { name, avatar_url, location } = data;
    saveJSON(`user:${login}`, {
      name,
      login,
      avatar_url,
      location
    });
  }, [data]);

  useEffect(() => {
    if (!login) return;
    if (data && data.login === login) return;
    fetch(`https://api.github.com/users/${login}`)
      .then(response => response.json())
      .then(setData)
      .catch(console.error);
  }, [login]);

  if (data)
    return <pre>{JSON.stringify(data, null, 2)}</pre>;

  return null;
}
```

Notice the `GitHubUser` component now has two `useEffect` hooks. The first hook is used to save the data to the browser. It's invoked whenever the value for `data` changes. The second hook is used to request more data from GitHub. The fetch request is not sent when there's already data saved locally for that user. This is handled by the second `if` statement in the second `useEffect` hook: `if (data && data.login === login) return;`. If there is `data` and the `login` for that data matches the `login` property, then there's no need to send an additional request to GitHub. We'll just use the local data.

The first time we run the application, if the `login` is set to `moonhighway`, the following object will be rendered to the page:

```
{
  "login": "MoonHighway",
  "id": 5952087,
  "node_id": "MDEyOk9yZ2FuaXphdGlvbjU5NTIwODc=",
  "avatar_url": "https://avatars0.githubusercontent.com/u/5952087?v=4",
  "gravatar_id": "",
  "url": "https://api.github.com/users/MoonHighway",
  "html_url": "https://github.com/MoonHighway",

  ...

}
```

This is the response from GitHub. We can tell because this object contains a lot of extra information about the user that we don't need. The first time we run this page we'll see this lengthy response. But the second time we run the page, the response is much shorter:

```
{
  "name": "Moon Highway",
  "login": "moonhighway",
  "avatar_url": "https://avatars0.githubusercontent.com/u/5952087?v=4",
  "location": "Tahoe City, CA"
}
```

This time, the data we saved locally for `moonhighway` is being rendered to the browser. Since we only needed four fields of data, we only saved four fields of data. We'll always see this smaller offline object until we clear the storage:

```
localStorage.clear();
```

Both `sessionStorage` and `localStorage` are essential weapons for web developers. We can work with this local data when we're offline, and they allow us to increase the performance of our applications by sending fewer network requests. However, we must know when to use them. Implementing offline storage adds complexity to our applications, and it can make them tough to work with in development. Additionally, we don't need to work with web storage to cache data. If we're simply looking for a performance bump, we could try letting HTTP handle caching. Our browser will automatically cache content if we add `Cache-Control: max-age=<EXP_DATE>` to our headers. The `EXP_DATE` defines the expiration date for the content.

## Handling Promise States

HTTP requests and promises both have three states: pending, success (fulfilled), and fail (rejected). A request is *pending* when we make the request and are waiting for a response. That response can only go one of two ways: success or fail. If a response is successful, it means we've successfully connected to the server and have received data. In the world of promises, a successful response means that the promise has been *resolved*. If something goes wrong during this process, we can say the HTTP request has failed or the promise has been *rejected*. In both cases, we'll receive an error explaining what happened.

We really need to handle all three of these states when we make HTTP requests. We can modify the GitHub user component to render more than just a successful response. We can add a "loading..." message when the request is pending, or we can render the error details if something goes wrong:

```
function GitHubUser({ login }) {
  const [data, setData] = useState();
  const [error, setError] = useState();
  const [loading, setLoading] = useState(false);

  useEffect(() => {
    if (!login) return;
    setLoading(true);
    fetch(`https://api.github.com/users/${login}`)
      .then(data => data.json())
      .then(setData)
      .then(() => setLoading(false))
      .catch(setError);
  }, [login]);

  if (loading) return <h1>loading...</h1>;
  if (error)
    return <pre>{JSON.stringify(error, null, 2)}</pre>;
  if (!data) return null;

  return (
    <div className="githubUser">
      <img
        src={data.avatar_url}
        alt={data.login}
        style={{ width: 200 }}
      />
      <div>
        <h1>{data.login}</h1>
        {data.name && <p>{data.name}</p>}
        {data.location && <p>{data.location}</p>}
      </div>
    </div>
  );
}
```

When this request is successful, Moon Highway's information is rendered for the user to see on the screen, as shown in Figure 8-1.

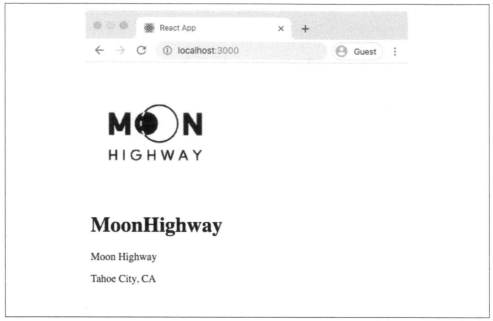

*Figure 8-1. Sample output*

If something goes wrong, we're simply displaying the error object as a JSON string. In production, we would do more with the error. Maybe we would track it, log it, or try to make another request. While in development, it's OK to render error details, which gives the developer instant feedback.

Finally, while the request is pending, we simply display a "loading…" message using an h1.

Sometimes an HTTP request can succeed with an error. This happens when the request was successful—successfully connected to a server and received a response—but the response body contains an error. Sometimes servers pass additional errors as successful responses.

Handling all three of these states bloats our code a little bit, but it's essential to do so on every request. Requests take time and a lot could go wrong. Because all requests—and promises—have these three states, it makes it possible to handle all HTTP requests with a reusable hook, or a component, or even a React feature called Suspense. We'll cover each of these approaches, but first, we must introduce the concept of render props.

# Render Props

*Render props* are exactly what they sound like: properties that are rendered. This can mean components that are sent as properties that are rendered when specific conditions are met, or it can mean function properties that return components that will be rendered. In the second case, when they're functions, data can be passed as arguments and used when rendering the returned component.

Render props are useful when maximizing reusability in asynchronous components. With this pattern, we can create components that abstract away complex mechanics or monotonous boilerplate that's necessary for application development.

Consider the task of displaying a list:

```
import React from "react";

const tahoe_peaks = [
  { name: "Freel Peak", elevation: 10891 },
  { name: "Monument Peak", elevation: 10067 },
  { name: "Pyramid Peak", elevation: 9983 },
  { name: "Mt. Tallac", elevation: 9735 }
];

export default function App() {
  return (
    <ul>
      {tahoe_peaks.map((peak, i) => (
        <li key={i}>
          {peak.name} - {peak.elevation.toLocaleString()}ft
        </li>
      ))}
    </ul>
  );
}
```

In this example, the four tallest peaks in Tahoe are rendered into an unordered list. This code makes sense, but mapping over an array to render each item individually does introduce some code complexity. Mapping over an array of items is also a pretty common task. We may find ourselves frequently repeating this pattern. We could create a `List` component that we can reuse as a solution whenever we need to render an unordered list.

In JavaScript, arrays either contain values or they're empty. When a list is empty, we need to display a message to our users. However, that message may change upon implementation. No worries—we can pass a component to render when the list is empty:

```
function List({ data = [], renderEmpty }) {
  if (!data.length) return renderEmpty;
  return <p>{data.length} items</p>;
```

```
    }

    export default function App() {
      return <List renderEmpty={<p>This list is empty</p>} />;
    }
```

The `List` component expects two properties: `data` and `renderEmpty`. The first argument, `data`, represents the array of items that are to be mapped over. Its default value is an empty array. The second argument, `renderEmpty`, is a component that will be rendered if the list is empty. So when `data.length` is `0`, the `List` component renders whatever was passed as the `renderEmpty` property by returning that property.

In this case, users would see the following message: `This list is empty`.

`renderEmpty` is a render prop because it contains a component to render when a particular condition has been met—in this case, when the list is empty or the `data` property has not been provided.

We can send this component an actual array of `data`:

```
    export default function App() {
      return (
        <List
          data={tahoe_peaks}
          renderEmpty={<p>This list is empty</p>}
        />
      );
    }
```

Doing so at this point only renders the number of items found within the array: 4 `items`.

We can also tell our `List` component what to render for each item found within the array. For example, we can send a `renderItem` property:

```
    export default function App() {
      return (
        <List
          data={tahoe_peaks}
          renderEmpty={<p>This list is empty</p>}
          renderItem={item => (
            <>
              {item.name} - {item.elevation.toLocaleString()}ft
            </>
          )}
        />
      );
    }
```

This time, the render prop is a function. The data (the item itself) is passed to this function as an argument so that it can be used when what to render for each Tahoe

Peak is decided. In this case, we render a React fragment that displays the item's name and elevation. If the array is tahoe_peaks, we expect the renderItem property to be invoked four times: once for each of the peaks in the array.

This approach allows us to abstract away the mechanics of mapping over arrays. Now the List component will handle the mapping; we just have to tell it what to render:

```
function List({ data = [], renderItem, renderEmpty }) {
  return !data.length ? (
    renderEmpty
  ) : (
    <ul>
      {data.map((item, i) => (
        <li key={i}>{renderItem(item)}</li>
      ))}
    </ul>
  );
}
```

When the data array is not empty, the List component renders an unordered list, <ul>. It maps over each item within the array using the .map method and renders a list item, <li>, for every value within the array. The List component makes sure each list item receives a unique key. Within each <li> element, the renderItem property is invoked and the item itself is passed to that function property as an argument. The result is an unordered list that displays the name and elevation of each of Tahoe's tallest peaks.

The good news is we have a reusable List component that we can use whenever we need to render an unordered list. The bad news is our component is a bit bare bones. There are better components we can use to handle this task.

# Virtualized Lists

If it's our job to develop a reusable component for rendering lists, there are many different use cases to consider and solutions to implement. One of the most important things to consider is what happens when the list is very large. Many of the data points we work with in production can feel infinite. A Google search yields pages and pages of results. Searching for a place to stay in Tahoe on Airbnb results in a list of houses and apartments that seems to never end. Production applications typically have a lot of data that needs to be rendered, but we can't render it all at once.

There's a limit to what the browser can render. Rendering takes time, processing power, and memory, all three of which have eventual limitations. This should be taken into consideration when developing a reusable list component. When the data array is very large, what should we do?

Even though our search for a place to stay may have yielded one thousand results, we cannot possibly look at all those results at the same time—there's not enough screen space for all the images, names, and prices. We might only be able to see about five results at a time. When scrolling, we can see more results, but we have to scroll down pretty far to see a thousand results. Rendering a thousand results in a scrollable layer is asking a lot of the phone.

Instead of rendering 1,000 results at a time, what if we only rendered 11? Remember that the user can only see about five results on one screen. So we render the five items the user can see and render six items off screen both above and below the visible window of items. Rendering items above and below the visible window will allow the user to scroll in both directions. We can see that in Figure 8-2.

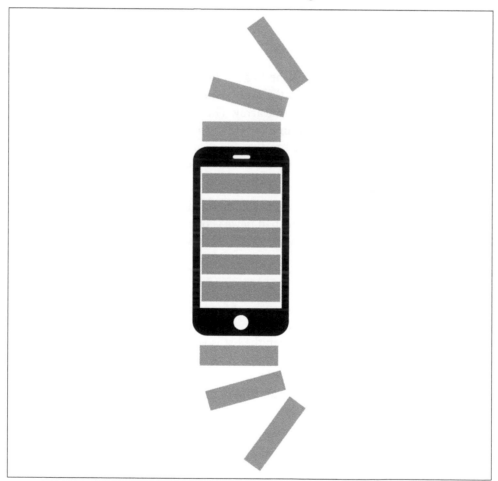

*Figure 8-2. Windowing with off-screen content*

As the user scrolls, we can unmount the results that have already been viewed as well as render new results off screen, ready for the user to reveal via the scroll. This resulting solution means that the browser will only render 11 elements at a time while the data for the rest of the elements is there waiting to be rendered. This technique is called *windowing* or *virtualization*. It allows us to scroll very large, sometimes infinite lists of data without crashing our browser.

There's a lot to consider when building a virtualized list component. Thankfully, we don't have to start from scratch; the community has already developed many virtualized list components for us to use. The most popular of these for the browser are react-window and react-virtualized. Virtualized lists are so important that React Native even ships with one: the FlatList. Most of us will not have to build virtualized list components, but we do need to know how to use them.

To implement a virtualized list, we're going to need a lot of data—in this case, fake data:

```
npm i faker
```

Installing faker will allow us to create a large array of fake data. For this example, we'll use fake users. We'll create five thousand fake users at random:

```
import faker from "faker";

const bigList = [...Array(5000)].map(() => ({
  name: faker.name.findName(),
  email: faker.internet.email(),
  avatar: faker.internet.avatar()
}));
```

The bigList variable was created by mapping over an array of five thousand empty values and replacing those empty values with information about a fake user. The name, email, and avatar for each user are generated at random using functions supplied by faker.

If we use the List component we created in the last section, it will render all five thousand users at the same time:

```
export default function App() {
  const renderItem = item => (
    <div style={{ display: "flex" }}>
      <img src={item.avatar} alt={item.name} width={50} />
      <p>
        {item.name} - {item.email}
      </p>
    </div>
  );

  return <List data={bigList} renderItem={renderItem} />;
}
```

This code creates a div element for each user. Within that div, an img element is rendered for that user's photo, and the user name and email are rendered with a paragraph element, as shown in Figure 8-3.

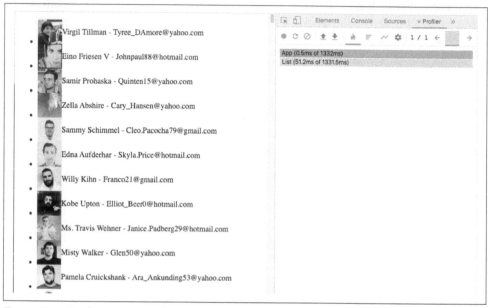

*Figure 8-3. Performance results*

The combination of React and modern browsers is already pretty amazing. We're most likely able to render all five thousand users, but it takes a while. In this example, it took 52ms to be exact. As the number of users in our list goes up, so does this time, until we eventually reach a tipping point.

Let's render the same fake user list using react-window:

```
npm i react-window
```

react-window is a library that has several components we can use to render virtualized lists. In this example, we'll use the FixSizeList component from react-window:

```
import React from "react";
import { FixedSizeList } from "react-window";
import faker from "faker";

const bigList = [...Array(5000)].map(() => ({
  name: faker.name.findName(),
  email: faker.internet.email(),
  avatar: faker.internet.avatar()
}));
```

```
export default function App() {
  const renderRow = ({ index, style }) => (
    <div style={{ ...style, ...{ display: "flex" } }}>
      <img
        src={bigList[index].avatar}
        alt={bigList[index].name}
        width={50}
      />
      <p>
        {bigList[index].name} - {bigList[index].email}
      </p>
    </div>
  );

  return (
    <FixedSizeList
      height={window.innerHeight}
      width={window.innerWidth - 20}
      itemCount={bigList.length}
      itemSize={50}
    >
      {renderRow}
    </FixedSizeList>
  );
}
```

FixedSizeList is slightly different from our List component. It requires the total number of items in the list along with the number of pixels each row requires as the itemSize property. Another big difference in this syntax is that the render prop is being passed to FixedSizeList as the children property. This render props pattern is used quite frequently.

So, let's see what happens when five thousand fake users are rendered with the Fix SizeList component (see Figure 8-4).

This time, not all of the users are being rendered at once. Only those rows that the user can see or easily scroll to are being rendered. Notice that it only takes 2.6ms for this initial render.

As you scroll down to reveal more users, the FixedSizeList is hard at work rendering more users off screen as well as removing users that have scrolled off screen. This component automatically handles scrolling in both directions. This component may render quite frequently, but the renders are fast. It also doesn't matter how many users are in our array: the FixedSizeList can handle it.

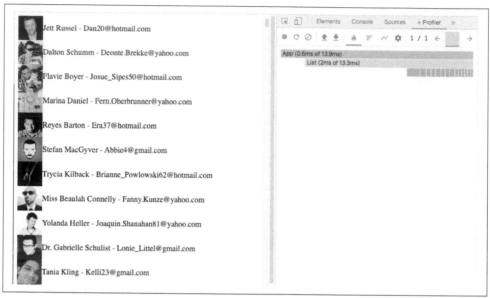

*Figure 8-4. 2.6ms for this render*

## Creating a Fetch Hook

We know that a request is either pending, successful, or failed. We can reuse the logic that's necessary for making a fetch request by creating a custom hook. We'll call this hook useFetch, and we can use it in components across our application whenever we need to make a fetch request:

```
import React, { useState, useEffect } from "react";

export function useFetch(uri) {
  const [data, setData] = useState();
  const [error, setError] = useState();
  const [loading, setLoading] = useState(true);

  useEffect(() => {
    if (!uri) return;
    fetch(uri)
      .then(data => data.json())
      .then(setData)
      .then(() => setLoading(false))
      .catch(setError);
  }, [uri]);

  return {
    loading,
    data,
    error
```

```
  };
}
```

This custom hook was created by composing the useState and useEffect hooks. The three states of a fetch request are represented in this hook: pending, success, and error. When the request is pending, the hook will return true for loading. When the request is successful and data is retrieved, it will be passed to the component from this hook. If something goes wrong, then this hook will return the error.

All three of these states are managed inside of the useEffect hook. This hook is invoked every time the value for uri changes. If there's no uri, the fetch request is not made. When there's a uri, the fetch request begins. If the request is successful, we pass the resulting JSON to the setData function, changing the state value for data. After that, we then change the state value for loading to false because the request was successful (i.e., it's no longer pending). Finally, if anything goes wrong, we catch it and pass it to setError, which changes the state value for error.

Now we can use this hook to make fetch requests within our components. Anytime the values for loading, data, or error change, this hook causes the GitHubUser component to rerender with those new values:

```
function GitHubUser({ login }) {
  const { loading, data, error } = useFetch(
    `https://api.github.com/users/${login}`
  );

  if (loading) return <h1>loading...</h1>;
  if (error)
    return <pre>{JSON.stringify(error, null, 2)}</pre>;

  return (
    <div className="githubUser">
      <img
        src={data.avatar_url}
        alt={data.login}
        style={{ width: 200 }}
      />
      <div>
        <h1>{data.login}</h1>
        {data.name && <p>{data.name}</p>}
        {data.location && <p>{data.location}</p>}
      </div>
    </div>
  );
}
```

Although the component now has less logic, it still handles all three states. Assuming we have a SearchForm component ready to collect search strings from the user, we can add the GitHubUser component to our main App component:

```
import React, { useState } from "react";
import GitHubUser from "./GitHubUser";
import SearchForm from "./SearchForm";

export default function App() {
  const [login, setLogin] = useState("moontahoe");

  return (
    <>
      <SearchForm value={login} onSearch={setLogin} />
      <GitHubUser login={login} />
    </>
  );
}
```

The main App component stores the username of the GitHub user in state. The only way to change this value is to use the search form to search for a new user. Whenever the value of login changes, the value sent to useFetch changes because it depends on the login property: *https://api.github.com/users/${login}*. This changes the uri within our hook and triggers a fetch request for the new user login. We've created a custom hook and used it to successfully create a small application that can be used to look up and display GitHub user details. We'll continue to use this hook as we iterate on this application.

## Creating a Fetch Component

Hooks typically allow us to reuse functionality across components. There are times when we find ourselves repeating the exact same pattern when it comes to rendering within our components. For example, the loading spinner we choose to render may be the exact same spinner we want to render across our entire application whenever a fetch request is pending. The way we handle errors with our fetch requests may also be consistent across our application.

Instead of replicating the exact same code in multiple components across our application, we can create one component to render consistent loading spinners and consistently handle all of our errors across our entire domain. Let's create a Fetch component:

```
function Fetch({
  uri,
  renderSuccess,
  loadingFallback = <p>loading...</p>,
  renderError = error => (
    <pre>{JSON.stringify(error, null, 2)}</pre>
  )
}) {
  const { loading, data, error } = useFetch(uri);
  if (loading) return loadingFallback;
  if (error) return renderError(error);
```

```
    if (data) return renderSuccess({ data });
  }
```

The custom hook, useFetch, is one layer of abstraction: it abstracts away the mechanics of making a fetch request. The Fetch component is an additional layer of abstraction: it abstracts away the mechanics of handling what to render. When the request is loading, the Fetch component will render whatever was passed to the optional loadingFallback property. When it's successful, the JSON response data is passed to the renderSuccess property. If there's an error, it's rendered using the optional ren derError property. The loadingFallback and renderError properties provide an optional layer of customization. However, when they're not supplied, they fall back to their default values.

With the Fetch component in our arsenal, we can really simplify the logic in our GitHubUser component:

```
import React from "react";
import Fetch from "./Fetch";

export default function GitHubUser({ login }) {
  return (
    <Fetch
      url={`https://api.github.com/users/${login}`}
      renderSuccess={UserDetails}
    />
  );
}

function UserDetails({ data }) {
  return (
    <div className="githubUser">
      <img
        src={data.avatar_url}
        alt={data.login}
        style={{ width: 200 }}
      />
      <div>
        <h1>{data.login}</h1>
        {data.name && <p>{data.name}</p>}
        {data.location && <p>{data.location}</p>}
      </div>
    </div>
  );
}
```

The GitHubUser component receives a login for a user to look up on GitHub. We use that login to construct the uri property we send to the fetch component. If successful, the UserDetails component is rendered. When the Fetch component is loading, the default "loading..." message will be displayed. If something goes wrong, the error details are automatically displayed.

We can provide custom values for these properties. Here's an example of how we can alternatively use our flexible component:

```
<Fetch
  uri={`https://api.github.com/users/${login}`}
  loadingFallback={<LoadingSpinner />}
  renderError={error => {
    // handle error
    return <p>Something went wrong... {error.message}</p>;
  }}
  renderSuccess={({ data }) => (
    <>
      <h1>Todo: Render UI for data</h1>
      <pre>{JSON.stringify(data, null, 2)}</pre>
    </>
  )}
/>
```

This time, the Fetch component will render our custom loading spinner. If something goes wrong, we hide the error details. When the request is successful, we've chosen to alternatively render the raw data along with a TODO message for ourselves.

Be careful: extra layers of abstraction, whether through hooks or components, can add complexity to our code. It's our job to reduce complexity wherever we can. However, in this case, we've reduced complexity by abstracting away reusable logic into a component and a hook.

## Handling Multiple Requests

Once we start making requests for data from the internet, we won't be able to stop. More often than not, we need to make several HTTP requests to obtain all the data required to hydrate our application. For example, we're currently asking GitHub to provide information about a user's account. We'll also need to obtain information about that user's repositories. Both of these data points are obtained by making separate HTTP requests.

GitHub users typically have many repositories. Information about a user's repositories is passed as an array of objects. We're going to create a special custom hook called useIterator that will allow us to iterate through any array of objects:

```
export const useIterator = (
  items = [],
  initialIndex = 0
) => {
  const [i, setIndex] = useState(initialIndex);

  const prev = () => {
    if (i === 0) return setIndex(items.length - 1);
    setIndex(i - 1);
```

```
  };

  const next = () => {
    if (i === items.length - 1) return setIndex(0);
    setIndex(i + 1);
  };

  return [items[i], prev, next];
};
```

This hook will allow us to cycle through any array. Because it returns items inside of an array, we can take advantage of array destructuring to give these values names that make sense:

```
const [letter, previous, next] = useIterator([
  "a",
  "b",
  "c"
]);
```

In this case, the initial letter is "b." If the user invokes next, the component will rerender, but this time, the value for letter will be "b." Invoke next two more times, and the value for letter will once again be "a" because this iterator circles back around to the first item in the array instead of letting the index go out of bounds.

The useIterator hook takes in an array of items and an initial index. The key value to this iterator hook is the index, i, which was created with the useState hook. i is used to identify the current item in the array. This hook returns the current item, item[i], as well as functions for iterating through that array: prev and next. Both the prev and next functions either decrement or increment the value of i by invoking setIndex. This action causes the hook to rerender with a new index.

## Memozing Values

The useIterator hook is pretty cool. But we can do even better by memoizing the value for item as well as the function for prev and next:

```
import React, { useCallback, useMemo } from "react";

export const useIterator = (
  items = [],
  initialValue = 0
) => {
  const [i, setIndex] = useState(initialValue);

  const prev = useCallback(() => {
    if (i === 0) return setIndex(items.length - 1);
    setIndex(i - 1);
  }, [i]);
```

```
const next = useCallback(() => {
  if (i === items.length - 1) return setIndex(0);
  setIndex(i + 1);
}, [i]);

const item = useMemo(() => items[i], [i]);

return [item || items[0], prev, next];
};
```

Here, both `prev` and `next` are created with the `useCallback` hook. This ensures that the function for `prev` will always be the same until the value for i changes. Likewise, the `item` value will always point to the same item object unless the value for i changes.

Memoizing these values does not give us huge performance gains, or at least not enough to justify the code complexity. However, when a consumer uses the `useItera tor` component, the memoized values will always point to the exact same object and function. This makes it easier on our consumers when they need to compare these values or use them in their own dependency arrays.

Now, we're going to create a repository menu component. Within this component, we'll use the `useIterator` hook to allow the users to cycle through their list of repositories:

```
< learning-react >
```

If they click the Next button, they'll see the name of the next repository. Likewise, if they click the Previous button, they'll see the name of the previous repository. `Repo Menu` is the component we'll create to provide this feature:

```
import React from "react";
import { useIterator } from "../hooks";

export function RepoMenu({
  repositories,
  onSelect = f => f
}) {
  const [{ name }, previous, next] = useIterator(
    repositories
  );

  useEffect(() => {
    if (!name) return;
    onSelect(name);
  }, [name]);

  return (
    <div style={{ display: "flex" }}>
      <button onClick={previous}>&lt;</button>
      <p>{name}</p>
```

```
        <button onClick={next}>&gt;</button>
      </div>
    );
  }
```

RepoMenu receives a list of `repositories` as a prop. It then destructures the `name` from the current repository object and the `previous` and `next` functions from `useIterator`. `&lt;` is an entity for "Less Than," and a less than sign, "<", is displayed. The same is true for `&gt;`, greater than. These are indicators for previous and next, and when the user clicks on either of these indicators, the component is rerendered with a new repository name. If the `name` changes, then the user has selected a different repository, so we invoke the `onSelect` function and pass the `name` of the new repository to that function as an argument.

Remember, array destructuring allows us to name the items whatever we want. Even though we named those functions `prev` and `next` within the hook, here, when we use the hook, we can change their names to `previous` and `next`.

Now we can create the `UserRepositories` component. This component should request a list of a GitHub user's repositories first, and once received, pass that list to the RepoMenu component:

```
import React from "react";
import Fetch from "./Fetch";
import RepoMenu from "./RepoMenu";

export default function UserRepositories({
  login,
  selectedRepo,
  onSelect = f => f
}) {
  return (
    <Fetch
      uri={`https://api.github.com/users/${login}/repos`}
      renderSuccess={({ data }) => (
        <RepoMenu
          repositories={data}
          selectedRepo={selectedRepo}
          onSelect={onSelect}
        />
      )}
    />
  );
}
```

The `UserRepositories` component requires a `login` to use in order to make the fetch request for a list of repositories. That `login` is used to create the URI and pass it to the `Fetch` component. Once the fetch has successfully resolved, we'll render the Repo Menu along with the list of repositories that was returned from the `Fetch` component

---

as data. When the user selects a different repository, we simply pass the name of that new repository along to the parent object:

```
function UserDetails({ data }) {
  return (
    <div className="githubUser">
      <img src={data.avatar_url} alt={data.login} style={{ width: 200 }} />
      <div>
        <h1>{data.login}</h1>
        {data.name && <p>{data.name}</p>}
        {data.location && <p>{data.location}</p>}
      </div>
      <UserRepositories
        login={data.login}
        onSelect={repoName => console.log(`${repoName} selected`)}
      />
    </div>
  );
```

Now we need to add our new component to the `UserDetails` component. When the `UserDetails` component is rendered, we'll also render that user's repository list. Assuming the `login` value is `eveporcello`, the rendered output for the above component would look something like Figure 8-5.

*Figure 8-5. Repository output*

In order to get information about Eve's account along with her list of repositories, we need to send two separate HTTP requests. A majority of our lives as React developers will be spent like this: making multiple requests for information and composing all of the information received into beautiful user interface applications. Making two requests for information is just the beginning. In the next section, we'll continue to make more requests of GitHub so we can see the README.md for the selected repository.

## Waterfall Requests

In the last section, we made two HTTP requests. The first request was for a user's details, then once we had those details, we made a second request for that user's repositories. These requests happen one at a time, one after the other.

The first request is made when we initially fetch the user's details:

```
<Fetch
  uri={`https://api.github.com/users/${login}`}
  renderSuccess={UserDetails}
/>
```

Once we have that user's details, the `UserDetails` component is rendered. It in turn renders `UserRepositories`, which then sends a fetch request for that user's repositories:

```
<Fetch
  uri={`https://api.github.com/users/${login}/repos`}
  renderSuccess={({ data }) => (
    <RepoMenu repositories={data} onSelect={onSelect} />
  )}
/>
```

We call these requests *waterfall* requests because they happen one right after the other —they're dependent on each other. If something goes wrong with the user details request, the request for that user's repositories is never made.

Let's add some more layers (water?) to this waterfall. First, we request the user's info, then their repository list, then, once we have their repository list, we make a request for the first repository's README.md file. As the user cycles through the list of repositories, we'll make additional requests for the associated README to each repository.

Repository README files are written using Markdown, which is a text format that can be easily rendered as HTML with the `ReactMarkdown` component. First, let's install `react-markdown`:

```
npm i react-markdown
```

Requesting the contents of a repository's README file also requires a waterfall of requests. First, we have to make a data request to the repository's README route: *https://api.github.com/repos/${login}/${repo}/readme*. GitHub will respond to this route with the details about a repository's README file but not the contents of that file. It does provide us with a download_url that we can use to request the contents of the README file. But to get the Markdown content, we'll have to make an additional request. Both of these requests can be made within a single async function:

```
const loadReadme = async (login, repo) => {
  const uri = `https://api.github.com/repos/${login}/${repo}/readme`;
  const { download_url } = await fetch(uri).then(res =>
    res.json()
  );
  const markdown = await fetch(download_url).then(res =>
    res.text()
  );

  console.log(`Markdown for ${repo}\n\n${markdown}`);
};
```

In order to find a repository README, we need the repository owner's login and the name of the repository. Those values are used to construct a unique URL: *https://api.github.com/repos/moonhighway/learning-react/readme*. When this request is successful, we destructure the download_url from its response. Now we can use this value to download the contents of the README; all we have to do is fetch the download_url. We'll parse this text as text—res.text()—rather than JSON because the body of the response is Markdown text.

Once we have the Markdown, let's render it by wrapping the loadReadme function inside of a React component:

```
import React, {
  useState,
  useEffect,
  useCallback
} from "react";
import ReactMarkdown from "react-markdown";

export default function RepositoryReadme({ repo, login }) {
  const [loading, setLoading] = useState(false);
  const [error, setError] = useState();
  const [markdown, setMarkdown] = useState("");

  const loadReadme = useCallback(async (login, repo) => {
    setLoading(true);
    const uri = `https://api.github.com/repos/${login}/${repo}/readme`;
    const { download_url } = await fetch(uri).then(res =>
      res.json()
    );
    const markdown = await fetch(download_url).then(res =>
      res.text()
    );
    setMarkdown(markdown);
    setLoading(false);
```

```
    }, []);

    useEffect(() => {
      if (!repo || !login) return;
      loadReadme(login, repo).catch(setError);
    }, [repo]);

    if (error)
      return <pre>{JSON.stringify(error, null, 2)}</pre>;
    if (loading) return <p>Loading...</p>;

    return <ReactMarkdown source={markdown} />;
  }
```

First, we add the `loadReadme` function to the component using the `useCallback` hook to memoize the function when the component initially renders. This function now changes the loading state to `true` before the fetch request and changes it back to `false` after the request. When the Markdown is received, it's saved in state using the `setMarkdown` function.

Next, we need to actually call `loadReadme`, so we add a `useEffect` hook to load the README file after the component initially renders. If for some reason the properties for `repo` and `login` are not present, the README will not be loaded. The dependency array in this hook contains `[repo]`. This is because we want to load another README if the value for `repo` changes. If anything goes wrong while loading the README, it will be caught and sent to the `setError` function.

Notice we have to handle the same three render states that we do for every fetch request: pending, success, and fail. Finally, when we have a successful response, the Markdown itself is rendered using the `ReactMarkdown` component.

All there is left to do is render the `RepositoryReadme` component inside of the `Repo Menu` component. As the user cycles through repositories using the `RepoMenu` component, the README for each repository will also be loaded and displayed:

```
  export function RepoMenu({ repositories, login }) {
    const [{ name }, previous, next] = useIterator(
      repositories
    );
    return (
      <>
        <div style={{ display: "flex" }}>
          <button onClick={previous}>&lt;</button>
          <p>{name}</p>
          <button onClick={next}>&gt;</button>
        </div>
        <RepositoryReadme login={login} repo={name} />
      </>
    );
  }
```

Now our application is really making multiple requests; initially, it makes four requests: one for the user's details, then one for that user's repository list, then one for information about the selected repository's README, and finally one more request for the text contents of the README. These are all waterfall requests because they happen one after another.

Additionally, as the user interacts with the application, more requests are made. Two waterfall requests are made to obtain the README file every time the user changes the current repository. All four initial waterfall requests are made every time the user searches for a different GitHub account.

## Throttling the Network Speed

All of these requests are visible from the Network tab under your developer tools. From this tab, you can see every request, and you can throttle your network speed to see how these requests unfold on slow networks. If you want to see how the waterfall requests happen one after another you can slow down your network speed and see the loading messages as they're rendered.

The Network tab is available under the developer tools of most major browsers. To throttle the network speed in Google Chrome, select the arrow next to the word "Online," as demonstrated in Figure 8-6.

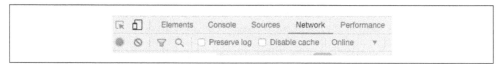

*Figure 8-6. Changing the speed of the network request*

This will open a menu where you can choose various speeds, as you can see in Figure 8-7.

*Figure 8-7. Selecting the speed of the network request*

Selecting "Fast 3G" or "Slow 3G" will significantly throttle your network requests.

Additionally, the Network tab displays a timeline for all of the HTTP requests. You can filter this timeline to only view "XHR" requests. This means it will only show the request made using `fetch` (Figure 8-8).

| Name | St... | Ty... | Initiator | Size | Ti... | Waterfall | ▲ |
|------|-------|-------|-----------|------|-------|-----------|---|
| ☐ eveporcello | 200 | fe... | hooks... | 1.... | 2.... | | |
| ☐ repos | 200 | fe... | hooks... | 1.... | 2.... | | |
| ☐ readme | 200 | fe... | Repo... | 2.... | 2.... | | |
| ☐ readme.md | 200 | fe... | Repo... | 1.... | 2.... | | |

*Figure 8-8. The waterfall of a request*

Here, we see that four requests were made one after the other. Notice that the loading graphic is titled "Waterfall." This shows that each request is made after the other is complete.

## Parallel Requests

Sometimes, it's possible to make an application faster by sending all requests at once. Instead of having each request occur one after another in a waterfall, we can send our requests in *parallel*, or at the same time.

The reason our application is currently making a waterfall of request is that the components are rendered inside of one another. GitHubUser eventually renders UserRepositories, which eventually renders RepositoryReadme. Requests are not made until each component has been rendered.

Making these requests in parallel is going to require a different approach. First, we'll need to remove the <RepositoryReadme /> from the RepoMenu's render function. This is a good move. The RepoMenu should only focus on the logistics of creating a menu of repositories that the user can cycle through. The RepositoryReadme component should be handed in a different component.

Next, we'll need to remove <RepoMenu /> from the renderSuccess property of User Repositories. Likewise, <UserRepositories /> needs to be removed from the User Details component.

Instead of nesting these components inside of one another, we'll place them all on the same level next to one another, all within the App component:

```
import React, { useState } from "react";
import SearchForm from "./SearchForm";
import GitHubUser from "./GitHubUser";
import UserRepositories from "./UserRepositories";
import RepositoryReadme from "./RepositoryReadme";

export default function App() {
  const [login, setLogin] = useState("moonhighway");
  const [repo, setRepo] = useState("learning-react");
  return (
    <>
      <SearchForm value={login} onSearch={setLogin} />
```

```
          <GitHubUser login={login} />
          <UserRepositories
            login={login}
            repo={repo}
            onSelect={setRepo}
          />
          <RepositoryReadme login={login} repo={repo} />
        </>
      );
    }
```

The GitHubUser, UserRepositories, and RepositoryReadme components all send HTTP requests to GitHub for data. Rendering them side-by-side on the same level will cause all of these requests to happen at the same time, in parallel.

Each component requires specific information in order to make the request. We need a login to obtain a GitHub user. We need a login to obtain a list of user repositories. The RepositoryReadme requires both a login and a repo to work properly. To make sure all of the components have what they need to make their requests, we initialize the app to display the details for the user "moonhighway" and the repository "learning-react."

If the user searches for another GitHubUser with the SearchForm, the value for login will change, which will trigger the useEffect hooks within our components, causing them to make additional requests for data. If the user cycles through the list of repositories, then the onSelect property for UserRepositories will be invoked, which causes the repo value to change. Changing the repo value will trigger the useEffect hook inside of the RepositoryReadme component, and a new README will be requested.

The RepoMenu component always starts with the first repository, no matter what. We have to see if there's a selectedRepo property. If there is, we need to use it to find the initial index for the repository to be displayed:

```
    export function RepoMenu({ repositories, selected, onSelect = f => f }) {
      const [{ name }, previous, next] = useIterator(
        repositories,
        selected ? repositories.findIndex(repo => repo.name === selected) : null
      );
      ...
    }
```

The second argument for the useIterator hook is the initial index to start with. If there's a selected property, then we'll search for the index of the selected repository by name. This is required to make sure the repository menu displays the correct repository initially. We also need to pass this selected property to this component from UserRepositories:

---

```
<Fetch
  uri={`https://api.github.com/users/${login}/repos`}
  renderSuccess={({ data }) => (
    <RepoMenu
      repositories={data}
      selected={repo}
      onSelect={onSelect}
    />
  )}
/>
```

Now that the repo property is being passed down to the RepoMenu, the menu should select the initial repository, which in our case is "learning-react."

If you take a look at the Network tab, you'll notice we've made three requests in parallel, as shown in Figure 8-9.

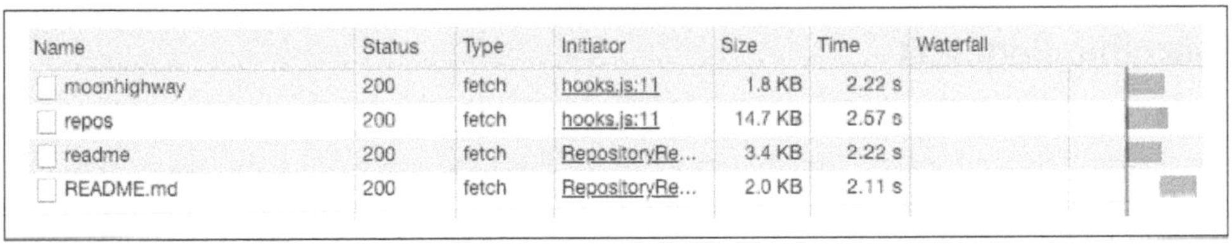

| Name | Status | Type | Initiator | Size | Time | Waterfall | |
|------|--------|------|-----------|------|------|-----------|---|
| moonhighway | 200 | fetch | hooks.js:11 | 1.8 KB | 2.22 s | | |
| repos | 200 | fetch | hooks.js:11 | 14.7 KB | 2.57 s | | |
| readme | 200 | fetch | RepositoryRe... | 3.4 KB | 2.22 s | | |
| README.md | 200 | fetch | RepositoryRe... | 2.0 KB | 2.11 s | | |

Figure 8-9. Creating a parallel request

So each component made its request at the same time. The RepoReadme component still has to make a waterfall request to obtain the contents of the README file. This is OK. It's hard to make every request right when your app initially renders. Parallel and waterfall requests can work in conjunction with each other.

## Waiting for Values

We currently initialize the values for login and repo to "moonhighway" and "learning-react." We may not always be able to guess which data to render first. When that's the case, we simply don't render the component until the data it requires is present:

```
export default function App() {
  const [login, setLogin] = useState();
  const [repo, setRepo] = useState();
  return (
    <>
      <SearchForm value={login} onSearch={setLogin} />
      {login && <GitHubUser login={login} />}
      {login && (
        <UserRepositories
          login={login}
          repo={repo}
          onSelect={setRepo}
```

```
        />
      )}
      {login && repo && (
        <RepositoryReadme login={login} repo={repo} />
      )}
    </>
  );
}
```

In this scenario, none of the components are rendered until their required props have values. Initially, the only component rendered is the SearchForm. Searching for a user will change the value for login, causing the UserRepositories component to render. When this component looks up the repositories, it will select the first repository in the list, causing setRepo to be invoked. Finally, we have a login and a repo, so the RepositoryReadme component will be rendered.

## Canceling Requests

Thinking about our application a little bit more, we realize that the user could empty the search field and search for no user at all. In this case, we would also want to make sure that the value for repo is also empty. Let's add a handleSearch method that makes sure the repo value changes when there's no value for login:

```
export default function App() {
  const [login, setLogin] = useState("moonhighway");
  const [repo, setRepo] = useState("learning-react");

  const handleSearch = login => {
    if (login) return setLogin(login);
    setLogin("");
    setRepo("");
  };

  if (!login)
    return (
      <SearchForm value={login} onSearch={handleSearch} />
    );

  return (
    <>
      <SearchForm value={login} onSearch={handleSearch} />
      <GitHubUser login={login} />
      <UserRepositories
        login={login}
        repo={repo}
        onSelect={setRepo}
      />
      <RepositoryReadme login={login} repo={repo} />
    </>
```

```
  );
}
```

We've added a handleSearch method. Now, when the user clears the search field and searches for an empty string, the repo value is also set to an empty string. If for some reason there's not a login, we only render one component: the SearchForm. When we have a value for login, we'll render all four components.

Now, technically our app has two screens. One screen only displays a search form. The other screen only shows when the search form contains a value, in which case, it shows all four components. We've set ourselves up to mount or unmount components based on user interactivity. Let's say we were looking at the details for "moonhighway." If the user empties the search field, then the GitHubUser, UserRepositories, and RepositoryReadme components are unmounted and will no longer be displayed. But what if these components were in the middle of loading data when they were unmounted?

You can try it out:

1. Throttle the network to "Slow 3G" to have enough time to cause problems

2. Change the value of the search field from "moonhighway" to "eveporcello"

3. While the data is loading, search for an empty string, ""

These steps will cause the GitHubUser, UserRepositories, and RepositoryReadme to become unmounted while they're in the middle of making fetch requests. Eventually, when there's a response to the fetch request, these components are no longer mounted. Attempting to change state values in an unmounted component will cause the error shown in Figure 8-10.

*Figure 8-10. Mounted error*

Whenever our users load data over a slow network, these errors can occur. But we can protect ourselves. First, we can create a hook that will tell us whether or not the current component is mounted:

```
export function useMountedRef() {
  const mounted = useRef(false);
  useEffect(() => {
    mounted.current = true;
    return () => (mounted.current = false);
```

```
  });
  return mounted;
}
```

The `useMountedRef` hook uses a ref. When the component unmounts, state is wiped clean, but refs are still available. The above `useEffect` doesn't have a dependency array; it's invoked every time a component renders and ensures that the value for the ref is `true`. Whenever the component unmounts, the function returned from `useEffect` is invoked, which changes the value of the ref to `false`.

Now we can use this hook inside of the `RepoReadme` component. This will allow us to make sure the component is mounted before applying any state updates:

```
const mounted = useMountedRef();

const loadReadme = useCallback(async (login, repo) => {
  setLoading(true);
  const uri = `https://api.github.com/repos/${login}/${repo}/readme`;
  const { download_url } = await fetch(uri).then(res =>
    res.json()
  );
  const markdown = await fetch(download_url).then(res =>
    res.text()
  );
  if (mounted.current) {
    setMarkdown(markdown);
    setLoading(false);
  }
}, []);
```

Now we have a ref that tells us whether or not the component is mounted. It will take time for both of these requests to finish. When they do, we check to make sure the component is still mounted before calling `setMarkdown` or `setLoading`.

Let's add the same logic to our `useFetch` hook:

```
const mounted = useMountedRef();

useEffect(() => {
  if (!uri) return;
  if (!mounted.current) return;
  setLoading(true);
  fetch(uri)
    .then(data => {
      if (!mounted.current) throw new Error("component is not mounted");
      return data;
    })
    .then(data => data.json())
    .then(setData)
    .then(() => setLoading(false))
    .catch(error => {
      if (!mounted.current) return;
```

```
    setError(error);
  });
```

The useFetch hook is used to make the rest of the fetch requests in our app. In this hook, we compose the fetch request using thenables, chainable .then() functions, instead of async/await. When the fetch is complete, we check to see if the component is mounted in the first .then callback. If the component is mounted, the data is returned and the rest of the .then functions are invoked. When the component is not mounted, the first .then function throws an error, preventing the rest of the .then functions from executing. Instead, the .catch function is invoked and the new error is passed to that function. The .catch function will check to see if the component is mounted before it tries to invoke setError.

We've successfully canceled our requests. We didn't stop the HTTP request itself from occurring, but we did protect the state calls we make after the request is resolved. It's always a good idea to test your app under slow network conditions. These bugs will be revealed and eliminated.

# Introducing GraphQL

Just like React, GraphQL was designed at Facebook. And, just like React is a declarative solution for composing user interfaces, GraphQL is a declarative solution for communicating with APIs. When we make parallel data requests, we're attempting to get all the data we need immediately at the same time. GraphQL was designed to do just that.

In order to get data from a GraphQL API, we still need to make an HTTP request to a specific URI. However, we also need to send a query along with the request. A GraphQL query is a declarative description of the data we're requesting. The service will parse this description and will package all the data we're asking for into a single response.

## GitHub GraphQL API

In order to use GraphQL in your React application, the backend service you're communicating with needs to be built following GraphQL specifications. Fortunately, GitHub also exposes a GraphQL API. Most GraphQL services provide a way to explore the GraphQL API. At GitHub, this is called the GraphQL Explorer (*https://devel oper.github.com/v4/explorer*). In order to use the Explorer, you must sign in with your GitHub account.

The left panel of the Explorer is where we draft our GraphQL query. Inside of this panel, we could add a query to obtain information about a single GitHub user:

```
query {
  user(login: "moontahoe") {
    id
    login
    name
    location
    avatarUrl
  }
}
```

This is a GraphQL query. We're asking for information about the GitHub user "moontahoe." Instead of getting all of the public information available about moontahoe, we only get the data we want: `id`, `login`, `avatarUrl`, `name`, and `location`. When we press the Play button on this page, we send this query as an HTTP POST request to *https://api.github.com/graphql*. All GitHub GraphQL queries are sent to this URI. GitHub will parse this query and return only the data we asked for:

```
{
  "data": {
    "user": {
      "id": "MDQ6VXNlcjU5NTIwODI=",
      "login": "MoonTahoe",
      "name": "Alex Banks",
      "location": "Tahoe City, CA",
      "avatarUrl": "https://github.com/moontahoe.png"
    }
  }
}
```

We can formalize this GraphQL query into a reusable operation named `findRepos`. Every time we want to find information about a user and their repositories, we could do so by sending a `login` variable to this query:

```
query findRepos($login: String!) {
  user(login: $login) {
    login
    name
    location
    avatar_url: avatarUrl
    repositories(first: 100) {
      totalCount
      nodes {
        name
      }
    }
  }
}
```

Now we've created a formal `findRepos` query that we can reuse simply by chaining the value of the `$login` variable. We set this variable using the Query Variables panel shown in Figure 8-11.

*Figure 8-11. GitHub GraphQL Explorer*

In addition to obtaining details about a user, we're also asking for that user's first hundred repositories. We're asking for the number of repositories returned by the query, the `totalCount`, along with the `name` of each repository. GraphQL only returns the data we ask for. In this case, we'll only get the `name` for each repository, nothing else.

There's one more change that we made to this query: we used an alias for the `avatar Url`. The GraphQL field to obtain a user's avatar is called `avatarUrl`, but we want that variable to be named `avatar_url`. The alias tells GitHub to rename that field in the data response.

GraphQL is a huge topic. We wrote a whole book about it: *Learning GraphQL*. We're only scratching the surface here, but GraphQL is increasingly becoming more of a requirement for any developer. In order to be a successful developer in the 21st century, it's important to understand the fundamentals of GraphQL.

## Making a GraphQL Request

A GraphQL request is an HTTP request that contains a query in the body of the request. You can use `fetch` to make a GraphQL request. There are also a number of libraries and frameworks that can handle the details of making these types of requests for you. In this next section, we'll see how we can hydrate our applications with GraphQL data using a library called `graphql-request`.

 GraphQL is not restricted to HTTP. It's a specification of how data requests should be made over a network. It can technically work with any network protocol. Additionally, GraphQL is language-agnostic.

First, let's install `graphql-request`:

```
npm i graphql-request
```

GitHub's GraphQL API requires identification to send requests from client applications. In order to complete this next sample, you must obtain a personal access token from GitHub, and this token must be sent with every request.

To obtain a personal access token for GraphQL requests, navigate to Settings > Developer Settings > Personal Access Tokens. On this form, you can create an access token that has specific rights. The token must have the following read access in order to make GraphQL requests:

- user
- public_repo
- repo
- repo_deployment
- repo:status
- read:repo_hook
- read:org
- read:public_key
- read:gpg_key

We can use `graphql-request` to make GraphQL requests from JavaScript:

```
import { GraphQLClient } from "graphql-request";

const query = `
  query findRepos($login:String!) {
    user(login:$login) {
      login
      name
      location
      avatar_url: avatarUrl
      repositories(first:100) {
        totalCount
```

```
          nodes {
            name
          }
        }
      }
    }
  }
`;

const client = new GraphQLClient(
  "https://api.github.com/graphql",
  {
    headers: {
      Authorization: `Bearer <PERSONAL_ACCESS_TOKEN>`
    }
  }
);

client
  .request(query, { login: "moontahoe" })
  .then(results => JSON.stringify(results, null, 2))
  .then(console.log)
  .catch(console.error);
```

We send this request using the GraphQLClient constructor from graphql-request. When we create the client, we use the URI for GitHub's GraphQL API: *https://api.github.com/graphql*. We also send some additional headers that contain our personal access token. This token identifies us and is required by GitHub when using their GraphQL API. We can now use the client to make our GraphQL requests.

In order to make a GraphQL request, we'll need a query. The query is simply a string that contains the GraphQL query from above. We send the query to the request function along with any variables that the query may require. In this case, the query requires a variable named $login, so we send an object that contains a value for $login in the login field.

Here, we're simply converting the resulting JSON to a string and logging it to the console:

```
{
  "user": {
    "id": "MDQ6VXNlcjU5NTIwODI=",
    "login": "MoonTahoe",
    "name": "Alex Banks",
    "location": "Tahoe City, CA",
    "avatar_url": "https://avatars0.githubusercontent.com/u/5952082?v-4",
    "repositories": {
      "totalCount": 52,
      "nodes": [
        {
          "name": "snowtooth"
        },
```

```
        {
          "name": "Memory"
        },
        {
          "name": "snowtooth-status"
        },

        ...

      ]
    }
  }
}
```

Just like `fetch`, `client.request` returns a promise. Getting this data inside of your React component will feel very similar to fetching data from a route:

```
export default function App() {
  const [login, setLogin] = useState("moontahoe");
  const [userData, setUserData] = useState();
  useEffect(() => {
    client
      .request(query, { login })
      .then(({ user }) => user)
      .then(setUserData)
      .catch(console.error);
  }, [client, query, login]);

  if (!userData) return <p>loading...</p>;

  return (
    <>
      <SearchForm value={login} onSearch={setLogin} />
      <UserDetails {...userData} />
      <p>{userData.repositories.totalCount} - repos</p>
      <List
        data={userData.repositories.nodes}
        renderItem={repo => <span>{repo.name}</span>}
      />
    </>
  );
}
```

We make the `client.request` inside of a `useEffect` hook. If the `client`, `query`, or `login` changes, the `useEffect` hook will make another request. Then we'll render the resulting JSON with React, as shown in Figure 8-12.

*Figure 8-12. GraphQL app*

This example doesn't put care into handling `loading` and `error` states, but we can apply everything we learned in the rest of this chapter to GraphQL. React doesn't really care how we get the data. As long as we understand how to work with asynchronous objects like promises within our components, we'll be ready for anything.

Loading data from the internet is an asynchronous task. When we request data, it takes some time for it to be delivered, and stuff can go wrong. Handling the `pending`, `success`, and `fail` states of a promise within a React component is an orchestration of stateful hooks with the `useEffect` hook.

We spent much of this chapter covering promises, `fetch`, and HTTP. This is because HTTP is still the most popular way to request data from the internet, and promises fit nicely with HTTP requests. Sometimes, you may work with a different protocol like WebSockets. No worries: this is accomplished by working with stateful hooks and `useEffect`.

Here's a brief example of how we can incorporate socket.io into a custom `useChat Room` hook:

```
const reducer = (messages, incomingMessage) => [
  messages,
  ...incomingMessage
];

export function useChatRoom(socket, messages = []) {
  const [status, setStatus] = useState(null);
  const [messages, appendMessage] = useReducer(
    reducer,
    messages
  );

  const send = message => socket.emit("message", message);

  useEffect(() => {
    socket.on("connection", () => setStatus("connected"));
    socket.on("disconnecting", () =>
      setStatus("disconnected")
    );
    socket.on("message", setStatus);
    return () => {
      socket.removeAllListeners("connect");
      socket.removeAllListeners("disconnect");
      socket.removeAllListeners("message");
    };
  }, []);

  return {
    status,
    messages,
    send
  };
}
```

This hook provides an array of chat messages, the websocket connection status, and a function that can be used to broadcast new messages to the socket. All of these values are affected by listeners that are defined in the useEffect hook. When the socket raises connection or disconnecting events, the value for status changes. When new messages are received, they're appended to the array of messages via the useReducer hook.

In this chapter, we've discussed some techniques for handling asynchronous data in applications. This is a hugely important topic, and in the next chapter, we'll show how Suspense might lead to future changes in this area.

# CHAPTER 9

# Suspense

This is the least important chapter in this book. At least, that's what we've been told by the React team. They didn't specifically say, "this is the least important chapter, don't write it." They've only issued a series of tweets warning educators and evangelists that much of their work in this area will very soon be outdated. All of this will change.

It could be said that the work the React team has done with Fiber, Suspense, and concurrent mode represents the future of web development. This work may change the way browsers interpret JavaScript. That sounds pretty important. We're saying that this is the least important chapter in this book because the community hype for Suspense is high; we need to say it to balance out your expectations. The APIs and patterns that make up Suspense are not the single overarching theory that defines how all things large and small should operate.

Suspense is a just a feature. You may not ever need to use it. It's being designed to solve specific problems that Facebook experiences working at scale. We don't all have the same problems as Facebook, so we may want to think twice before reaching for those tools as the solution to all our problems. They may unnecessarily introduce complexity where complexity is not needed. Plus, this is all going to change. Concurrent mode is an experimental feature, and the React team has issued stern warnings about trying to use it in production. In fact, most of these concepts involve using hooks. If you don't see yourself developing custom hooks on a daily basis, you'll probably never need to know about these features. Much of the mechanics involving Suspense can be abstracted away in hooks.

In light of these three paragraphs of downplay, the concepts covered in this chapter are exciting. If used correctly, they could someday help us create better user experiences. If you own or maintain a React library of hooks and/or components, you may find these concepts valuable. They'll help you fine-tune your custom hooks to allow for better feedback and prioritization.

In this chapter, we'll build another small app to demonstrate some of these features. We'll essentially rebuild the app from Chapter 8, but this time with a little more structure. For example, we'll be using a SiteLayout component:

```
export default function SiteLayout({
  children,
  menu = c => null
}) {
  return (
    <div className="site-container">
      <div>{menu}</div>
      <div>{children}</div>
    </div>
  );
}
```

SiteLayout will rendered within the App component to help us compose our UI:

```
export default function App() {
  return (
    <SiteLayout menu={<p>Menu</p>}>
      <>
        <Callout>Callout</Callout>
        <h1>Contents</h1>
        <p>This is the main part of the example layout</p>
      </>
    </SiteLayout>
  );
}
```

This component will be used to give our layout some style, as shown in Figure 9-1.

Specifically, it will allow us to clearly see where and when specific components are rendered.

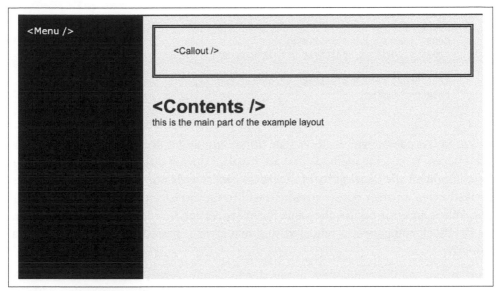

*Figure 9-1. Sample layout*

# Error Boundaries

Thus far, we haven't done the best job with handling errors. An error thrown anywhere in our component tree will take down the entire application. Larger component trees only further complicate our project and complicate debugging it. Sometimes, it can be hard to pinpoint where an error has occurred, especially when they occur within components that we didn't write.

Error boundaries are components that can be used to prevent errors from crashing the entire app. They also allow us to render sensible error messages in production. Because errors can be handled by a single component, they could potentially track errors within the application and report them to an issue management system.

Currently, the only way to make an error boundary component is to use a class component. Like most topics in this chapter, this too will eventually change. In the future, creating error boundaries could be possible with a hook or some other solution that doesn't require creating a class. For now, here's an example of an ErrorBoundary component:

```
import React, { Component } from "react";

export default class ErrorBoundary extends Component {
  state = { error: null };

  static getDerivedStateFromError(error) {
    return { error };
  }
}
```

```
    render() {
      const { error } = this.state;
      const { children, fallback } = this.props;

      if (error) return <fallback error={error} />;
      return children;
    }
  }
```

This is a class component. It stores state differently, and it doesn't use hooks. Instead, it has access to specific methods that are invoked during different times throughout the component life cycle. getDerivedStateFromError is one of those methods. It is invoked when an error occurs anywhere within the children during the render process. When an error occurs, the value for state.error is set. Where there's an error, the fallback component is rendered, and that error is passed to the component as a property.

Now we can use this component in our tree to capture errors and render a fallback component if they occur. For example, we could wrap our entire application with an error boundary:

```
function ErrorScreen({ error }) {
  //
  // Here you can handle or track the error before rendering the message
  //

  return (
    <div className="error">
      <h3>We are sorry... something went wrong</h3>
      <p>We cannot process your request at this moment.</p>
      <p>ERROR: {error.message}</p>
    </div>
  );
}

<ErrorBoundary fallback={ErrorScreen}>
  <App />
</ErrorBoundary>;
```

The ErrorScreen provides a gentle message for our users that an error has occurred. It renders some details about the error. It also gives us a place to potentially track errors that occur anywhere within our app. If an error does occur within the app, this component will be rendered instead of a black screen. We can make this component look nice with a little CSS:

```
.error {
  background-color: #efacac;
  border: double 4px darkred;
  color: darkred;
  padding: 1em;
}
```

To test this out we're going to create a component we can use to intentionally cause errors. BreakThings always throws an error:

```
const BreakThings = () => {
  throw new Error("We intentionally broke something");
};
```

Error boundaries can be composed. Sure, we wrapped the App component in an ErrorBoundary, but we can also wrap individual components within the App with Error:

```
return (
  <SiteLayout
    menu={
      <ErrorBoundary fallback={ErrorScreen}>
        <p>Site Layout Menu</p>
        <BreakThings />
      </ErrorBoundary>
    }
  >
    <ErrorBoundary fallback={ErrorScreen}>
      <Callout>Callout<BreakThings /></Callout>
    </ErrorBoundary>
    <ErrorBoundary fallback={ErrorScreen}>
      <h1>Contents</h1>
      <p>this is the main part of the example layout</p>
    </ErrorBoundary>
  </SiteLayout>
```

Each ErrorBoundary will render a fallback if an error occurs anywhere within their children. In this case, we used the BreakThings component in the menu and within the Callout. This would result in rendering the ErrorScreen twice, as we can see in Figure 9-2.

We can see that the ErrorBoundaries are rendered in place. Notice that the two errors that have occurred have been contained to their regions. The boundaries are like walls that prevent these errors from attacking the rest of the application. Despite intentionally throwing two errors, the contents are still rendered without issue.

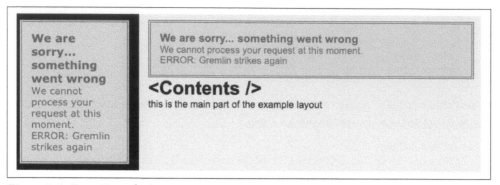

*Figure 9-2. ErrorBoundaries*

In Figure 9-3, we can observe what happens when we move the BreakThings compo-nent to only the contents.

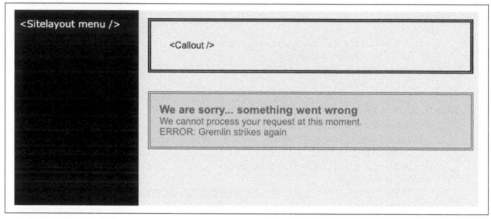

*Figure 9-3. Error*

Now we see the menu and the callout being rendered without issue, but the contents has rendered an error to notify the user that an error has occurred.

Inside of the render method in the ErrorBoundary class component, we can make the fallback property optional. When it's not included, we'll simply use our ErrorScreen component:

```
render() {
  const { error } = this.state;
  const { children } = this.props;

  if (error && !fallback) return <ErrorScreen error={error} />;
  if (error) return <fallback error={error} />;
```

```
      return children;
  }
```

This is a good solution for handling errors consistently across an application. Now, we just have to wrap specific parts of our component tree with an `ErrorBoundary` and let the component handle the rest:

```
<ErrorBoundary>
  <h1>&lt;Contents /&gt;</h1>
  <p>this is the main part of the example layout</p>
  <BreakThings />
</ErrorBoundary>
```

Error boundaries are not only a good idea—they're essential for retaining users in production, and they'll prevent some small bug in a relatively unimportant component from bringing down the entire application.

# Code Splitting

If the applications you're working on are small now, chances are they won't stay that way. A lot of the applications you work on will eventually contain massive codebases with hundreds, maybe even thousands, of components. Most of your users could be accessing your applications via their phones on potentially slow networks. They can't wait for the entire codebase of your application to successfully download before React completes its first render.

*Code splitting* provides us with a way to split our codebase into manageable chunks and then load those chunks as they're needed. To exemplify the power of code splitting, we'll add a user agreement screen to our application:

```
export default function Agreement({ onAgree = f => f }) {
  return (
    <div>
      <p>Terms...</p>
      <p>These are the terms and stuff. Do you agree?</p>
      <button onClick={onAgree}>I agree</button>
    </div>
  );
}
```

Next, we'll move the rest of our codebase from a component called `App` to a component called `Main`, and we'll place that component in its own file:

```
import React from "react";
import ErrorBoundary from "./ErrorBoundary";

const SiteLayout = ({ children, menu = c => null }) => {
  return (
    <div className="site-container">
      <div>{menu}</div>
```

```
      <div>{children}</div>
    </div>
  );
};

const Menu = () => (
  <ErrorBoundary>
    <p style={{ color: "white" }}>TODO: Build Menu</p>
  </ErrorBoundary>
);

const Callout = ({ children }) => (
  <ErrorBoundary>
    <div className="callout">{children}</div>
  </ErrorBoundary>
);

export default function Main() {
  return (
    <SiteLayout menu={<Menu />}>
      <Callout>Welcome to the site</Callout>
      <ErrorBoundary>
        <h1>TODO: Home Page</h1>
        <p>Complete the main contents for this home page</p>
      </ErrorBoundary>
    </SiteLayout>
  );
}
```

So Main is where the current site layout is rendered. Now we'll modify the App component to render the Agreement until the user agrees to it. When they agree, we'll unmount the Agreement component and render the Main website component:

```
import React, { useState } from "react";
import Agreement from "./Agreement";
import Main from "./Main";
import "./SiteLayout.css";

export default function App() {
  const [agree, setAgree] = useState(false);

  if (!agree)
    return <Agreement onAgree={() => setAgree(true)} />;

  return <Main />;
}
```

Initially, the only component that's rendered is the Agreement component. Once the user agrees, the value for agree changes to true, and the Main component is rendered. The issue is that all code for the Main component and all of its children is packaged into a single JavaScript file: the bundle. That means that users have to wait for this codebase to download completely before the `Agreement` component is initially rendered.

We can put off loading the main component until it has rendered by declaring it using `React.lazy` instead of initially importing it:

```
const Main = React.lazy(() => import("./Main"));
```

We're telling React to wait to load the codebase for the `Main` component until it's initially rendered. When it is rendered, it will be imported at that time using the `import` function.

Importing code during runtime is just like loading anything else from the internet. First, the request for the JavaScript code is pending. Then it's either successful, and a JavaScript file is returned, or it fails, causing an error to occur. Just like we need to notify a user that we're in the process of loading data, we'll need to let the user know that we're in the process of loading code.

## Introducing: The Suspense Component

Once again, we find ourselves in a situation where we're managing an asynchronous request. This time, we have the `Suspense` component to help us out. The `Suspense` component works much like the `ErrorBoundary` component. We wrap it around specific components in our tree. Instead of falling back to an error message when an error occurs, the `Suspense` component renders a loading message when lazy loading occurs.

We can modify the app to lazy load the `Main` component with the following code:

```
import React, { useState, Suspense, lazy } from "react";
import Agreement from "./Agreement";
import ClimbingBoxLoader from "react-spinners/ClimbingBoxLoader";

const Main = lazy(() => import("./Main"));

export default function App() {
  const [agree, setAgree] = useState(false);

  if (!agree)
    return <Agreement onAgree={() => setAgree(true)} />;

  return (
    <Suspense fallback={<ClimbingBoxLoader />}>
      <Main />
    </Suspense>
  );
}
```

Now the app initially only loads the codebase for React, the Agreement component, and the ClimbingBoxLoader. React will hold off on loading the Main component until the user agrees to the agreement.

The Main component has been wrapped in a Suspense component. As soon as the user agrees to the agreement, we start loading the codebase for the Main component. Because the request for this codebase is pending, the Suspense component will render the ClimbingBoxLoader in its place until the codebase has successfully loaded. Once that happens, the Suspense component will unmount the ClimbingBoxLoader and render the Main component.

 React Spinners is a library of animated loading spinners that indicate that something is loading or that the app is working. For the remainder of this chapter, we'll be sampling different loader components from this library. Make sure you install this library: npm i react-spinners.

What happens when the internet connection goes down before trying to load the Main component? Well, we'll have an error on our hands. We can handle that by wrapping our Suspense component within an ErrorBoundary:

```
<ErrorBoundary fallback={ErrorScreen}>
  <Suspense fallback={<ClimbingBoxLoader />}>
    <Main />
  </Suspense>
</ErrorBoundary>
```

The composition of these three components gives us a way to handle most asynchronous requests. We have a solution for pending: the Suspense component will render a loader animation while the request for the source code is pending. We have a solution for the failed state: if an error occurs while loading the Main component, it will be caught and handled by the ErrorBoundary. We even have a solution for success: if the request is successful, we'll render the Main component.

## Using Suspense with Data

In the last chapter, we built a useFetch hook and a Fetch component to help us handle the three states involved with making a GitHub request: pending, success, and fail. That was our solution. We think it was pretty cool. However, in the last section, we handled these three states by elegantly composing the ErrorBoundary and Suspense components. That was for lazy loading JavaScript source code, but we can use the same pattern to help us load data.

Let's say we have a Status component that's capable of rendering some sort of status message:

```
import React from "react";

const loadStatus = () => "success - ready";

function Status() {
  const status = loadStatus();
  return <h1>status: {status}</h1>;
}
```

This component invokes the loadStatus function to retrieve the current status message. We can render the Status component in our App component:

```
export default function App() {
  return (
    <ErrorBoundary>
      <Status />
    </ErrorBoundary>
  );
}
```

If we were to run this code as-is, we would see our successful status message, as shown in Figure 9-4.

*Figure 9-4. Success: everything works*

When we rendered the Status component within the App component, we were good React developers because we wrapped the Status component inside of an error boundary. Now if something goes wrong while loading the status, the ErrorBoundary will fall back to the default error screen. To demonstrate this, let's cause an error inside of the loadStatus function:

```
const loadStatus = () => {
  throw new Error("something went wrong");
};
```

Now when we run our application, we see the expected output. The `ErrorBoundary` caught our error and rendered a message to the user instead (Figure 9-5).

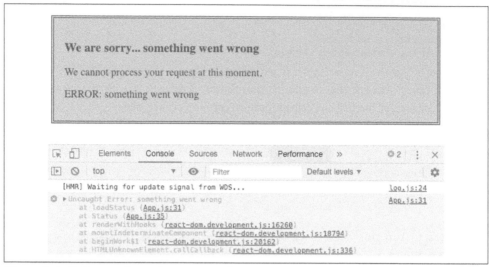

*Figure 9-5. Fail: error boundary triggered*

So far, everything is working as suspected. We've composed the `Status` component inside of an `ErrorBoundary`, and the combination of these two components is handling two of the three promise states: success or rejected. "Rejected" is the official promise term for a failed or error state.

We have two of the three states covered. What about the third state? Pending? That state can be triggered by throwing a promise:

```
const loadStatus = () => {
  throw new Promise(resolves => null);
};
```

If we throw a promise from the `loadStatus` function, we'll see a special type of error in the browser (Figure 9-6).

This error is telling us that a pending state was triggered, but there is no `Suspense` component configured somewhere higher in the tree. Whenever we throw a promise from a React app, we need a `Suspense` component to handle rendering a fallback:

```
export default function App() {
  return (
    <Suspense fallback={<GridLoader />}>
      <ErrorBoundary>
        <Status />
      </ErrorBoundary>
    </Suspense>
```

```
  );
}
```

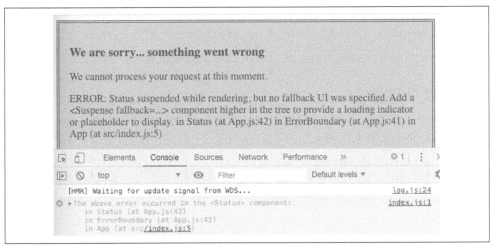

*Figure 9-6. Throw promise*

Now we have the right component composition to handle all three states. The load Status function is still throwing a promise, but there's now a Suspense component configured somewhere higher in the tree to handle it. When we throw the promise, we're telling React that we're waiting on a pending promise. React responds by rendering the fallback GridLoader component (Figure 9-7).

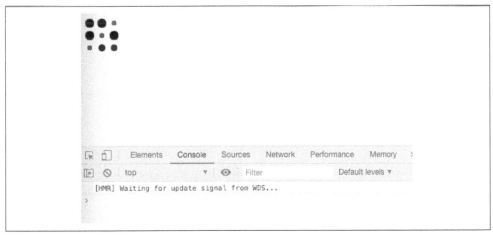

*Figure 9-7. GridLoader*

When `loadStatus` successfully returns a result, we'll render the `Status` component as planned. If something goes wrong (if `loadStatus` throws an error), we have it covered with an `ErrorBoundary`. When `loadStatus` throws a promise, we trigger the pending state, which is handled by the `Suspense` component.

This is a pretty cool pattern, but wait…what do you mean, "throw a promise"?

## Throwing Promises

In JavaScript, the `throw` keyword is technically for errors. You've probably used it many times in your own code:

```
throw new Error("inspecting errors");
```

This line of code causes an error. When this error goes unhandled, it crashes the whole app, as demonstrated in Figure 9-8.

*Figure 9-8. Throwing an error*

The error screen you see rendered in the browser is a development-mode feature of Create React App. Whenever you're in development mode, unhandled errors are caught and displayed directly on the screen. If you close this screen by clicking on the "X" in the upper right-hand corner, you'll see what your production users see when there's an error: nothing, a blank, white screen.

Unhandled errors are always visible in the console. All the red text we see in the console is information about the error we've thrown.

JavaScript is a pretty free-loving language. It lets us get away with a lot of stuff that we can't get away with when using traditional typed languages. For example, in Java-Script, we can throw any type:

```
throw "inspecting errors";
```

Here, we've thrown a string. The browser will tell us that something has gone uncaught, but it's not an error (Figure 9-9).

*Figure 9-9. GridLoader*

This time, when we threw a string, the Create React App error screen wasn't rendered inside the browser. React knows the difference between an error and a string.

JavaScript lets us throw any type, which means we can throw a promise:

```
throw new Promise(resolves => null);
```

Now the browser is telling us that something has gone uncaught. It's not an error, it's a promise, as shown in Figure 9-10.

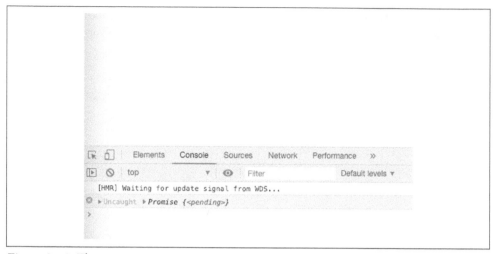

*Figure 9-10. Throwing a promise*

To throw a promise within the React component tree, we'll do so first in a loadStatus function:

```
const loadStatus = () => {
  console.log("load status");
  throw new Promise(resolves => setTimeout(resolves, 3000));
};
```

If we use this loadStatus function inside a React component, a promise is thrown, then somewhere farther up the tree is caught by the Suspense component. That's right: JavaScript allows us to throw any type, which also means that we can catch any type.

Consider the following example:

```
safe(loadStatus);

function safe(fn) {
  try {
    fn();
  } catch (error) {
    if (error instanceof Promise) {
      error.then(() => safe(fn));
    } else {
      throw error;
    }
  }
}
```

We're sending the loadStatus function a safe function, which makes safe a higher-order function. loadStatus becomes fn within the scope of the safe function. The safe function tries to invoke the fn that's passed as the argument. In this case, safe tries to invoke loadStatus. When it does, loadStatus throws a promise, an intentional delay of three seconds. That promise is immediately caught and becomes error within the scope of the catch block. We can check to see if the error is a promise, and in this case, it is. Now we can wait for that promise to resolve and then attempt to call safe again with the same loadStatus function.

What do we expect to happen when we invoke the safe function recursively with a function that creates a promise that causes a three-second delay? We get a delayed loop, as shown in Figure 9-11.

*Figure 9-11. An unfortunate loop*

The safe function is invoked, the promise is caught, we wait three seconds for the promise to resolve, then we call safe again with the same function, and the cycle starts all over again. Every three seconds, the string "load status" is printed to the console. How many times you watch that happen depends upon how patient you are.

We didn't make this endless recursive loop to test your patience; we made it to demonstrate a point. Watch what happens when we use this new loadStatus function in conjunction with our Status component from earlier:

```
const loadStatus = () => {
  console.log("load status");
  throw new Promise(resolves => setTimeout(resolves, 3000));
};

function Status() {
  const status = loadStatus();
  return <h1>status: {status}</h1>;
}

export default function App() {
  return (
    <Suspense fallback={<GridLoader />}>
      <ErrorBoundary>
        <Status />
      </ErrorBoundary>
    </Suspense>
  );
}
```

Because loadStatus is throwing a promise, the GridLoader animation renders on the screen. When you take a look at the console, the results are once again testing your patience (Figure 9-12).

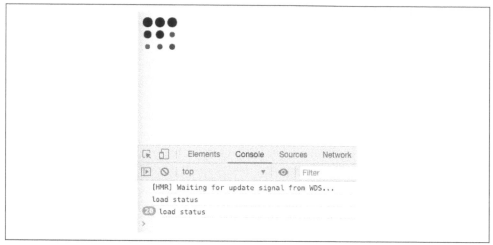

*Figure 9-12. Suspense recursion*

We see the same pattern as we did with the safe function. The Suspense component knows that a promise was thrown. It will render the fallback component. Then the Suspense component waits for the thrown promise to be resolved, just like the safe function did. Once resolved, the Suspense component rerenders the Status component. When Status renders again, it calls loadStatus and the whole process repeats itself. We see "load status" printed to the console, every three seconds, endlessly, forever.

An endless loop is typically not the desired output. It isn't for React, either. It's important to know that, when we throw a promise, it's caught by the Suspense component, and we enter into a pending state until the promise has been resolved.

## Building Suspenseful Data Sources

A Suspenseful data source needs to provide a function that handles all the states associated with loading data: pending, success, and error. The loadStatus function can only return or throw one type at a time. We need the loadStatus function to throw a promise when the data is loading, return a response when the data is successful, or throw an error if something goes wrong:

```
function loadStatus() {
  if (error) throw error;
  if (response) return response;
  throw promise;
}
```

We'll need a place to declare error, response, and promise. We also need to make sure that these variables are scoped appropriately and do not collide with other requests. The solution is to define loadStatus using a closure:

```
const loadStatus = (function() {
  let error, promise, response;

  return function() {
    if (error) throw error;
    if (response) return response;
    throw promise;
  };
})();
```

This is a closure. The scope of the error, promise, and response are closed off from any code outside of the function where they're defined. When we declare loadStatus, an anonymous function is declared and immediately invoked: fn() is the same as (fn)(). The value of loadStatus becomes the inner function that's returned. The loadStatus function now has access to error, promise, and response, but the rest of our JavaScript world does not.

Now all we need to do is handle the values for error, response, and promise. The promise will be pending for three seconds before it's successfully resolved. When the promise resolves, the value for response will be set to "success." We'll catch any errors or promise rejections and use them to set the error value:

```
const loadStatus = (function() {
  let error, response;
  const promise = new Promise(resolves =>
    setTimeout(resolves, 3000)
  )
    .then(() => (response = "success"))
    .catch(e => (error = e));
  return function() {
    if (error) throw error;
    if (response) return response;
    throw pending;
  };
})();
```

We created a promise that's pending for three seconds. If the loadStatus function is invoked at any point during that time, the promise itself will be thrown. After the three seconds, the promise is successfully resolved and response is assigned a value. If you invoke loadStatus now, it will return the response: "success." If something went wrong, then the loadStatus function would return the error.

The loadStatus function is our Suspenseful data source. It is capable of communicating its state with the Suspense architecture. The inner workings of loadStatus are hardcoded. It always resolves the same three-second delay promise. However, the mechanics of handling error, response, and promise are repeatable. We can wrap any promise with this technique to produce suspenseful data sources.

All we need to create a Suspenseful data source is a promise, so we can create a function that takes a promise as an argument and returns a Suspenseful data source. In this example, we call that function createResource:

```
const resource = createResource(promise);
const result = resource.read();
```

This code assumes that createResource(promise) will successfully create a resource object. This object has a read function, and we can invoke read as many times as we like. When the promise is resolved, read will return the resulting data. When the promise is pending, read will throw the promise. And if anything goes wrong, read will throw an error. This data source is ready to work with Suspense.

The createResource function looks a lot like our anonymous function from before:

```
function createResource(pending) {
  let error, response;
  pending.then(r => (response = r)).catch(e => (error = e));
  return {
    read() {
      if (error) throw error;
      if (response) return response;
      throw pending;
    }
  };
}
```

This function still closes off the values for error and response, but it allows consumers to pass in a promise as an argument called pending. When the pending promise is resolved, we capture the results with a .then function. If the promise is rejected, we'll catch the error and use it to assign a value to the error variable.

The createResource function returns a resource object. This object contains a function called read. If the promise is still pending, then error and response will be undefined. So read throws the promise. Invoking read when there's a value for error will cause that error to be thrown. Finally, invoking read when there's a response will yield whatever data was resolved by the promise. It doesn't matter how many times we call read—it will always accurately report on the state of our promise.

In order to test it out in a component, we'll need a promise, ideally one that sounds like the name of an '80s ski movie:

```
const threeSecondsToGnar = new Promise(resolves =>
  setTimeout(() => resolves({ gnar: "gnarly!" }), 3000)
);
```

The `threeSecondsToGnar` promise waits three seconds before resolving to an object that has a field and value for `gnar`. Let's use this promise to create a Suspenseful data resource and use that data resource in a small React application:

```
const resource = createResource(threeSecondsToGnar);

function Gnar() {
  const result = resource.read();
  return <h1>Gnar: {result.gnar}</h1>;
}

export default function App() {
  return (
    <Suspense fallback={<GridLoader />}>
      <ErrorBoundary>
        <Gnar />
      </ErrorBoundary>
    </Suspense>
  );
}
```

React components can render a lot. The `Gnar` component will be rendered several times before it actually returns a response. Each time `Gnar` is rendered, `resource.read()` is invoked. The first time `Gnar` is rendered, a promise is thrown. That promise is handled by the `Suspense` component and a `fallback` component will be rendered.

When the promise has resolved, the `Suspense` component will attempt to render `Gnar` again. `Gnar` will invoke `resource.read()` again, but this time, assuming everything went OK, `resource.read()` will successfully return `Gnar`, which is used to render the state of `Gnar` in an `h1` element. If something went wrong, `resource.read()` would have thrown an error, which would be handed by the `ErrorBoundary`.

As you can imagine, the `createResource` function can become quite robust. Our resource can attempt to handle errors. Maybe when there's a network error, the resource can wait a few seconds and automatically attempt to load the data again. Our resource could communicate with other resources. Maybe we can log the performance statistics behind all of our resources. The sky's the limit. As long as we have a function that we can use to read the current state of that resource, we can do whatever we like with the resource itself.

At present, this is how Suspense works. This is how we can use the `Suspense` component with any type of asynchronous resource. This could all change, and we expect it to change. However, whatever the finalized API for Suspense ends up being, it will be sure to handle three states: pending, success, and fail.

The look at these Suspense APIs has been kind of high-level, and this was intentional because this stuff is experimental. It's going to change. What's important to take away from this chapter is that React is always tinkering with ways to make React apps faster.

Behind the scenes of a lot of this work is the way that React itself works—specifically, its reconciliation algorithm called Fiber.

## Fiber

Throughout this book, we've talked about React components as being functions that return data as a UI. Every time this data changes (props, state, remote data, etc), we rely on React to rerender the component. If we click a star to rate a color, we assume that our UI will change, and we assume that it'll happen fast. We assume this because we trust React to make it happen. How exactly does this work though? To understand how React efficiently updates the DOM, let's take a closer look at how React works.

Consider that you're writing an article for your company blog. You want feedback, so you send the article to your coworker before you publish. They recommend a few quick changes, and now you need to incorporate those changes. You create a brand-new document, type out the entire article from scratch, and then add in the edits.

You're probably groaning at this unnecessary extra effort, but this is how a lot of libraries previously worked. To make an update, we'd get rid of everything, then start from scratch and rebuild the DOM during the update.

Now, you're writing another blog post and you send it to your coworker again. This time, you've modernized your article-writing process to use GitHub. Your coworker checks out a GitHub branch, makes the changes, and merges in the branch when they're finished. Faster and more efficient.

This process is similar to how React works. When a change occurs, React makes a copy of the component tree as a JavaScript object. It looks for the parts of the tree that need to change and changes only those parts. Once complete, the copy of the tree (known as the work-in-progress tree) replaces the existing tree. It's important to reiterate that it uses the parts of the tree that are already there. For example, if we had to update an item in the list from red to green:

```
<ul>
  <li>blue</li>
  <li>purple</li>
  <li>red</li>
</ul>
```

React would not get rid of the third li. Instead it would replace its children (red text) with green text. This is an efficient approach to updating and is the way that React has updated the DOM since its inception. There is a potential problem here, though. Updating the DOM is an expensive task because it's synchronous. We have to wait for all of the updates to be reconciled and then rendered before we can do other tasks on the main thread. In other words, we'd have to wait for React to recursively move through all of the updates, which could make the user experience seem unresponsive.

The React team's solution to this was a full rewrite of React's reconciliation algorithm, called Fiber. Fiber, released in version 16.0, rewrote the way that DOM updates worked by taking a more asynchronous approach. The first change with 16.0 was the separation of the renderer and the reconciler. A renderer is the part of the library that handles rendering, and the reconciler is the part of the library that manages updates when they occur.

Separating the renderer from the reconciler was a big deal. The reconciliation algorithm was kept in React Core (the package you install to use React), and each rendering target was made responsible for rendering. In other words, ReactDOM, React Native, React 360, and more would be responsible for the logic of rendering and could be plugged into React's core reconciliation algorithm.

Another huge shift with React Fiber was its changes to the reconciliation algorithm. Remember our expensive DOM updates that blocked the main thread? This lengthy block of updates is called *work*—with Fiber, React split the work into smaller units of work called *fibers*. A fiber is a JavaScript object that keeps track of what it's reconciling and where it is in the updating cycle.

Once a fiber (unit of work) is complete, React checks in with the main thread to make sure there's not anything important to do. If there is important work to do, React will give control to the main thread. When it's done with that important work, React will continue its update. If there's nothing critical to jump to on the main thread, React moves on to the next unit of work and renders those changes to the DOM.

To use the GitHub example from earlier, each fiber represents a commit on a branch, and when we check the branch back into the main branch, that represents the updated DOM tree. By breaking up the work of an update into chunks, Fiber allows priority tasks to jump the line for immediate handling by the main thread. The result is a user experience that feels more responsive.

If this was all Fiber did, it would be a success, but there's even more to it than that! In addition to the performance benefits of breaking work into smaller units, the rewrite also sets up exciting possibilities for the future. Fiber provides the infrastructure for prioritizing updates. In the longer term, the developer may even be able to tweak the defaults and decide which types of tasks should be given the highest priority. The process of prioritizing units of work is called *scheduling*; this concept underlies the experimental concurrent mode, which will eventually allow these units of work to be performed in parallel.

An understanding of Fiber is not vital to working with React in production, but the rewrite of its reconciliation algorithm provides interesting insight into how React works and how its contributors are thinking about the future.

# CHAPTER 10

# React Testing

In order to keep up with our competitors, we must move quickly while ensuring quality. One vital tool that allows us to do this is *unit testing*. Unit testing makes it possible to verify that every piece, or unit, of our application functions as intended.[1]

One benefit of practicing functional techniques is that they lend themselves to writing testable code. Pure functions are naturally testable. Immutability is easily testable. Composing applications out of small functions designed for specific tasks produces testable functions or units of code.

In this section, we'll demonstrate techniques that can be used to unit test React applications. This chapter will not only cover testing, but also tools that can be used to help evaluate and improve your code and your tests.

## ESLint

In most programming languages, code needs to be compiled before you can run anything. Programming languages have pretty strict rules about coding style and will not compile until the code is formatted appropriately. JavaScript does not have those rules and does not come with a compiler. We write code, cross our fingers, and run it in the browser to see if it works or not. The good news is that there are tools we can use to analyze our code and make us stick to specific formatting guidelines.

The process of analyzing JavaScript code is called *hinting* or *linting*. JSHint and JSLint are the original tools used to analyze JavaScript and provide feedback about formatting. ESLint (*http://eslint.org*) is the latest code linter that supports emerging

---

1 For a brief introduction to unit testing, see Martin Fowler's article, "Unit Testing" (*http://martinfowler.com/bliki/UnitTest.html*).

JavaScript syntax. Additionally, ESLint is pluggable. This means we can create and share plug-ins that can be added to ESLint configurations to extend its capabilities.

ESLint is supported out of the box with Create React App, and we've already seen lint warnings and errors appear in the console.

We'll be working with a plug-in called `eslint-plugin-react` (*https://oreil.ly/3yeXO*). This plug-in will analyze our JSX and React syntax in addition to our JavaScript.

Let's install `eslint` as a dev dependency. We can install `eslint` with npm:

```
npm install eslint --save-dev

# or

yarn add eslint --dev
```

Before we use ESLint, we'll need to define some configuration rules that we can agree to follow. We'll define these in a configuration file that's located in our project root. This file can be formatted as JSON or YAML. YAML (*http://yaml.org*) is a data serialization formation like JSON but with less syntax, making it a little easier for humans to read.

ESLint comes with a tool that helps us set up configuration. There are several companies that have created ESLint config files that we can use as a starting point, or we can create our own.

We can create an ESLint configuration by running `eslint --init` and answering some questions about our coding style:

```
npx eslint --init

How would you like to configure ESLint?
To check syntax and find problems

What type of modules does your project use?
JavaScript modules (import/export)

Which framework does your project use?
React

Does your project use TypeScript?
N

Where does your code run? (Press space to select, a to toggle all,
i to invert selection)
Browser

What format do you want your config file to be in?
JSON
```

```
Would you like to install them now with npm?
Y
```

After npx eslint --init runs, three things happen:

1. eslint-plugin-react is installed locally to the *./node_modules* folder.

2. These dependencies are automatically added to the *package.json* file.

3. A configuration file, *.eslintrc.json*, is created and added to the root of our project.

If we open *.eslintrc.json*, we'll see an object of settings:

```
{
  "env": {
    "browser": true,
    "es6": true
  },
  "extends": [
    "eslint:recommended",
    "plugin:react/recommended"
  ],
  "globals": {
    "Atomics": "readonly",
    "SharedArrayBuffer": "readonly"
  },
  "parserOptions": {
    "ecmaFeatures": {
      "jsx": true
    },
    "ecmaVersion": 2018,
    "sourceType": "module"
  },
  "plugins": ["react"],
  "rules": {}
}
```

Importantly, if we look at the extends key, we'll see that our --init command initalized defaults for eslint and react. This means that we don't have to manually configure all of the rules. Instead, those rules are provided to us.

Let's test our ESLint configuration and these rules by creating a *sample.js* file:

```
const gnar = "gnarly";

const info = ({
  file = __filename,
  dir = __dirname
}) => (
  <p>
    {dir}: {file}
  </p>
);
```

```
switch (gnar) {
  default:
    console.log("gnarly");
    break;
}
```

This file has some issues, but nothing that would cause errors in the browser. Technically, this code works just fine. Let's run ESLint on this file and see what feedback we get based on our customized rules:

```
npx eslint sample.js


3:7  error  'info' is assigned a value but never used  no-unused-vars
4:3  error  'file' is missing in props validation  react/prop-types
4:10 error  'filename' is not defined  no-undef
5:3  error  'dir' is missing in props validation  react/prop-types
5:9  error  'dirname' is not defined  no-undef
7:3  error  'React' must be in scope when using JSX  react/react-in-jsx-scope


✖ 6 problems (6 errors, 0 warnings)
```

ESLint has performed a static analysis of our code and is reporting some issues based on our configuration choices. There are errors about property validation, and ESLint also complains about __filename and __dirname because it does not automatically include Node.js globals. And finally, ESLint's default React warnings let us know that React must be in scope when using JSX.

The command eslint . will lint our entire directory. To do this, we'll most likely require that ESLint ignore some JavaScript files. The *.eslintignore* file is where we can add files or directories for ESLint to ignore:

```
dist/assets/
sample.js
```

This *.eslintignore* file tells ESLint to ignore our new *sample.js* file as well as anything in the *dist/assets* folder. If we don't ignore the *assets* folder, ESLint will analyze the client *bundle.js* file, and it will probably find a lot to complain about in that file.

Let's add a script to our *package.json* file for running ESLint:

```
{
  "scripts": {
    "lint": "eslint ."
  }
}
```

Now ESLint can be run any time we want with npm run lint, and it will analyze all of the files in our project except the ones we've ignored.

## ESLint Plug-Ins

There are a multitude of plug-ins that can be added to your ESLint configuration to help you as you're writing code. For a React project, you'll definitely want to install `eslint-plugin-react-hooks` (*https://reactjs.org/docs/hooks-rules.html*), a plug-in to enforce the rules of React Hooks. This package was released by the React team to help fix bugs related to Hooks usage.

Start by installing it:

```
npm install eslint-plugin-react-hooks --save-dev

# OR

yarn add eslint-plugin-react-hooks --dev
```

Then, open the *.eslintrc.json* file and add the following:

```
{
  "plugins": [
    // ...
    "react-hooks"
  ],
  "rules": {
    "react-hooks/rules-of-hooks": "error",
    "react-hooks/exhaustive-deps": "warn"
  }
}
```

This plug-in will check to ensure that functions that start with the word "use" (assumed to be a hook) are following the rules of Hooks.

Once this has been added, we'll write some sample code to test the plug-in. Adjust the code in *sample.js*. Even though this code won't run, we're testing to see if the plug-in is working appropriately:

```
function gnar() {
  const [nickname, setNickname] = useState(
    "dude"
  );
  return <h1>gnarly</h1>;
}
```

Several errors will pop up from this code, but most importantly, there's the error that lets us know we're trying to call `useState` in a function that isn't a component or a hook:

```
4:35 error React Hook "useState" is called in function "gnar" that is neither
a React function component nor a custom React Hook function
react-hooks/rules-of-hooks
```

These shoutouts will help us along the way as we learn the ins and outs of working with Hooks.

Another useful ESLint plug-in to incorporate into your projects is `eslint-plugin-jsx-a11y`. A11y is a numeronym, which means that there are 11 letters between the "a" and the "y" in accessibility. When we consider accessibility, we build tools, websites, and technologies that can be used by people with disabilities.

This plug-in will analyze your code and ensure that it's not breaking any accessibility rules. Accessibility should be an area of focus for all of us, and working with this plug-in will promote good practices when writing accessible React applications.

To install, we'll use npm or yarn again:

```
npm install eslint-plugin-jsx-a11y

// or

yarn add eslint-plugin-jsx-a11y
```

Then we'll add to our config, *.eslintrc.json*:

```
{
  "extends": [
    // ...
    "plugin:jsx-a11y/recommended"
  ],
  "plugins": [
    // ...
    "jsx-a11y"
  ]
}
```

Now let's test it. We'll adjust our *sample.js* file to include an image tag that has no alt property. In order for an image to pass a lint check, it must have an alt prop or an empty string if the image doesn't affect the user's understanding of the content:

```
function Image() {
  return <img src="/img.png" />;
}
```

If we run lint again with `npm run lint`, we'll see that there's a new error that's called by the `jsx/a11y` plug-in:

```
5:10 error img elements must have an alt prop, either with meaningful text,
or an empty string for decorative images
```

There are many other ESLint plug-ins you can use to statically analyze your code, and you could spend weeks tuning your ESLint config to perfection. If you're looking to take yours to the next level, there are many useful resources in the Awesome ESLint repository (*https://github.com/dustinspecker/awesome-eslint*).

---

# Prettier

Prettier is an opinionated code formatter you can use on a range of projects. The effect Prettier has had on the day-to-day work of web developers since its release has been pretty incredible. Based on historical records, arguing over syntax filled 87% of an average JavaScript developer's day, but now Prettier handles code formatting and defining the rules around what code syntax should be used per project. The time savings are significant. Also, if you've ever unleashed Prettier on a Markdown table, the quick, crisp formatting that occurs is a pretty incredible sight to behold.

ESLint used to be in charge of code formatting for many projects, but now there's a clear delineation of responsibilities. ESLint handles code-quality concerns. Prettier handles code formatting.

To make Prettier work with ESLint, we'll tinker with the configuration of our project a bit more. You can install Prettier globally to get started:

```
sudo npm install -g prettier
```

Now you can use Prettier anywhere on any project.

## Configuring Prettier by Project

To add a Prettier configuration file to your project, you can create a *.prettierrc* file. This file will describe the project defaults:

```
{
  "semi": true,
  "trailingComma": none,
  "singleQuote": false,
  "printWidth": 80
}
```

These are our preferred defaults, but of course, choose what makes most sense to you. For more Prettier formatting options, check out Prettier's documentation (*https://pret tier.io/docs/en/options.html*).

Let's replace what currently lives in our *sample.js* file with some code to format:

```
console.log("Prettier Test")
```

Now let's try running the Prettier CLI from the Terminal or Command Prompt:

```
prettier --check "sample.js"
```

Prettier runs the test and shows us the following message: `Code style issues found in the above file(s). Forgot to run Prettier?` To run it from the CLI, we can pass the `write` flag:

```
prettier --write "sample.js"
```

Once we do this, we'll see an output of a certain number of milliseconds that it took Prettier to format the file. If we open the file, we'll see that the content has changed based on the defaults supplied in the *.prettierrc* file. If you're thinking that this process seems laborious and could be sped up, you're right. Let's start automating!

First, we'll integrate ESLint and Prettier by installing a config tool and a plug-in:

```
npm install eslint-config-prettier eslint-plugin-prettier --save-dev
```

The config (`eslint-config-prettier`) turns off any ESLint rules that could conflict with Prettier. The plug-in (`eslint-plugin-prettier`) integrates Prettier rules into ESLint rules. In other words, when we run our `lint` script, Prettier will run, too.

We'll incorporate these tools into *.eslintrc.json*:

```
{
  "extends": [
    // ...
    "plugin:prettier/recommended"
  ],
  "plugins": [
    //,
  "prettier"],
  "rules": {
    // ...
    "prettier/prettier": "error"
  }
}
```

Make sure to break some formatting rules in your code to ensure that Prettier is working. For example, in *sample.js*:

```
console.log("Prettier Test");
```

Running the lint command `npm run lint` will yield the following output:

```
1:13 error Replace `'Prettier·Test')` with `"Prettier·Test");` prettier/prettier
```

All of the errors were found. Now you can run the Prettier write command and sweep the formatting for one file:

```
prettier --write "sample.js"
```

Or for all of the JavaScript files in certain folders:

```
prettier --write "src/*.js"
```

## Prettier in VSCode

If you're using VSCode, it's highly recommended that you set up Prettier in your editor. Configuration is fairly quick and will save you a lot of time as you're writing code.

You'll first want to install the VSCode extension for Prettier. Just follow this link (*https://oreil.ly/-7Zgz*) and click Install. Once installed, you can run Prettier with Control + Command + P on a Mac or Ctrl + Shift + P on a PC to manually format a file or highlighted bit of code. For even better results, you can format your code on Save. This involves adding some settings to VSCode.

To access these settings, select the Code menu, then Preferences, then Settings. (Or Command + comma on a Mac or Ctrl + comma on a PC, if you're in a hurry.) Then you can click on the small paper icon in the upper right-hand corner to open the VSCode settings as JSON. You'll want to add a few helpful keys here:

```
{
  "editor.formatOnSave": true
}
```

Now when you save any file, Prettier will format it based on the `.prettierrc` defaults! Pretty killer. You can also search Settings for Prettier options to set up defaults in your editor if you want to enforce formatting, even if your project doesn't contain a *.prettierrc* config file.

If you're using a different editor, Prettier likely supports that, too. For instructions specific to other code editors, check out the Editor Integration section of the docs (*https://prettier.io/docs/en/editors.html*).

# Typechecking for React Applications

When you're working with a larger application, you may want to incorporate type-checking to help pinpoint certain types of bugs. There are three main solutions for typechecking in React apps: the `prop-types` library, Flow, and TypeScript. In the next section, we'll take a closer look at how you might set up these tools to increase code quality.

## PropTypes

In the first edition of this book, PropTypes were part of the core React library and were the recommended way to add typechecking to your application. Today, due to the emergence of other solutions like Flow and TypeScript, the functionality has been moved to its own library to make React's bundle size smaller. Still, PropTypes are a widely used solution.

To add PropTypes to your app, install the `prop-types` library:

```
npm install prop-types --save-dev
```

We'll test this by creating a minimal `App` component that renders the name of a library:

```
import React from "react";
import ReactDOM from "react-dom";

function App({ name }) {
  return (
    <div>
      <h1>{name}</h1>
    </div>
  );
}

ReactDOM.render(
  <App name="React" />,
  document.getElementById("root")
);
```

Then we'll import the `prop-types` library and use `App.propTypes` to define which type each property should be:

```
import PropTypes from "prop-types";

function App({ name }) {
  return (
    <div>
      <h1>{name}</h1>
    </div>
  );
}

App.propTypes = {
  name: PropTypes.string
};
```

The `App` component has one property `name` and should always be a string. If an incorrect type value is passed as the name, an error will be thrown. For example, if we used a boolean:

```
ReactDOM.render(
  <App name="React" />,
  document.getElementById("root")
);
```

Our console would report a problem back to us:

```
Warning: Failed prop type: Invalid prop name of type boolean supplied to App,
expected string. in App
```

When a value of an incorrect type is provided for a property, the warning only appears in development mode. The warnings and broken renders won't appear in production.

Other types are available, of course, when validating properties. We could add a boolean for whether or not a technology was used at a company:

```
function App({ name, using }) {
  return (
    <div>
      <h1>{name}</h1>
      <p>
        {using ? "used here" : "not used here"}
      </p>
    </div>
  );
}

App.propTypes = {
  name: PropTypes.string,
  using: PropTypes.bool
};

ReactDOM.render(
  <App name="React" using={true} />,
  document.getElementById("root")
);
```

The longer list of type checks includes:

- PropTypes.array
- PropTypes.object
- PropTypes.bool
- PropTypes.func
- PropTypes.number
- PropTypes.string
- PropTypes.symbol

Additionally, if you want to ensure that a value was provided, you can chain .isRe
quired onto the end of any of these options. For example, if a string must be supplied, you'd use:

```
App.propTypes = {
  name: PropTypes.string.isRequired
};

ReactDOM.render(
  <App />,
  document.getElementById("root")
);
```

Then, if you fail to provide a value for this field, the following warning will appear in
the console:

```
index.js:1 Warning: Failed prop type: The prop name is marked as required in App,
but its value is undefined.
```

There also may be situations where you don't care what the value is, as long as a value is provided. In that case, you can use any. For example:

```
App.propTypes = {
  name: PropTypes.any.isRequired
};
```

This means that a boolean, string, number--anything--could be supplied. As long as name is not undefined, the typecheck will succeed.

In addition to the basic typechecks, there are a few other utilities that are useful for many real-world situations. Consider a component where there are two status options: Open and Closed:

```
function App({ status }) {
  return (
    <div>
      <h1>
        We're {status === "Open" ? "Open!" : "Closed!"}
      </h1>
    </div>
  );
}

ReactDOM.render(
  <App status="Open" />,
  document.getElementById("root")
);
```

Status is a string, so we might be inclined to use the string check:

```
App.propTypes = {
  status: PropTypes.string.isRequired
};
```

That works well, but if other string values besides Open and Closed are passed in, the property will be validated. The type of check we actually want to enforce is an enum check. An enumeration type is a restricted list of options for a particular field or property. We'll adjust the propTypes object like so:

```
App.propTypes = {
  status: PropTypes.oneOf(["Open", "Closed"])
};
```

Now if anything other than the values from the array that's passed to Prop Types.oneOf is supplied, a warning will appear.

For all the options you can configure for PropTypes in your React app, check out the documentation (*https://oreil.ly/pO2Js*).

# Flow

Flow is a typechecking library that's used and maintained by Facebook Open Source. It's a tool that checks for errors via static type annotations. In other words, if you create a variable that's a particular type, Flow will check to be sure that that value used is the correct type.

Let's fire up a Create React App project:

```
npx create-react-app in-the-flow
```

Then we'll add Flow to the project. Create React App doesn't assume you want to use Flow, so it doesn't ship with the library, but it's smooth to incorporate:

```
npm install --save flow-bin
```

Once installed, we'll add an npm script to run Flow when we type `npm run flow`. In *package.json*, just add this to the `scripts` key:

```
{
  "scripts": {
    "start": "react-scripts start",
    "build": "react-scripts build",
    "test": "react-scripts test",
    "eject": "react-scripts eject",
    "flow": "flow"
  }
}
```

Now running the `flow` command will run typechecking on our files. Before we can use it, though, we need to create a *.flowconfig* file. To do so, we run:

```
npm run flow init
```

This creates a skeleton of a configuration file that looks like this:

```
[ignore]

[include]

[libs]

[lints]

[options]

[strict]
```

In most cases, you'll leave this blank to use Flow's defaults. If you want to configure Flow beyond the basics, you can explore more options in the documentation (*https://flow.org/en/docs/config/*).

One of the coolest features of Flow is that you can adopt Flow incrementally. It can feel overwhelming to have to add typechecking to an entire project. With Flow, this isn't a requirement. All you need to do is add the line //@flow to the top of any files you want to typecheck, then Flow will automatically only check those files.

Another option is to add the VSCode extension for Flow to help with code completion and parameter hints. If you have Prettier or a linting tool set up, this will help your editor handle the unexpected syntax of Flow. You can find that in the marketplace (*https://oreil.ly/zdaPv*).

Let's open the *index.js* file and, for the sake of simplicity, keep everything in the same file. Make sure to add //@flow to the top of the file:

```
//@flow

import React from "react";
import ReactDOM from "react-dom";

function App(props) {
  return (
    <div>
      <h1>{props.item}</h1>
    </div>
  );
}

ReactDOM.render(
  <App item="jacket" />,
  document.getElementById("root")
);
```

Now we'll define the types for the properties:

```
type Props = {
  item: string
};

function App(props: Props) {
  //...
}
```

Then run Flow npm run flow. In certain versions of Flow, you may see this warning:

```
Cannot call ReactDOM.render with root bound to container because null [1] is
incompatible with Element [2]
```

This warning exists because if document.getElementById("root") returns null, the app will crash. To safeguard against this (and to clear the error), we can do one of two things. The first approach is to use an if statement to check to see that root is not null:

```
const root = document.getElementById("root");

if (root !== null) {
  ReactDOM.render(<App item="jacket" />, root);
}
```

Another option is to add a typecheck to the root constant using Flow syntax:

```
const root = document.getElementById("root");

ReactDOM.render(<App item="jacket" />, root);
```

In either case, you'll clear the error and see that your code is free of errors!

*No errors!*

We could trust this fully, but trying to break it feels like a good idea. Let's pass a different property type to the app:

```
ReactDOM.render(<App item={3} />, root);
```

Cool, we broke it! Now we get an error that reads:

```
Cannot create App element because number [1] is incompatible with string [2]
in property item.
```

Let's switch it back and add another property for a number. We'll also adjust the component and property definitions:

```
type Props = {
  item: string,
  cost: number
};

function App(props: Props) {
  return (
    <div>
      <h1>{props.item}</h1>
      <p>Cost: {props.cost}</p>
    </div>
  );
}

ReactDOM.render(
  <App item="jacket" cost={249} />,
  root
);
```

Running this works, but what if we removed the cost value?

```
ReactDOM.render(<App item="jacket" />, root);
```

We'll immediately get an error:

```
Cannot create App element because property cost is missing in props [1] but
exists in Props [2].
```

If `cost` is truly not a required value, we can make it optional in the property definitions using the question mark after the property name, `cost?:`

```
type Props = {
  item: string,
  cost?: number
};
```

If we run it again, we don't see the error.

That's the tip of the iceberg with all of the different features that Flow has to offer. To learn more and to stay on top of the changes in the library, head over to the documentation site (*https://flow.org/en/docs/getting-started/*).

## TypeScript

TypeScript is another popular tool for typechecking in React applications. It's an open source superset of JavaScript, which means that it adds additional features to the language. Created at Microsoft, TypeScript is designed to be used for large apps to help developers find bugs and iterate more quickly on projects.

TypeScript has a growing allegiance of supporters, so the tooling in the ecosystem continues to improve. One tool that we're already familiar with is Create React App, which has a TypeScript template we can use. Let's set up some basic typechecking, similar to what we did with PropTypes and Flow, to get a sense of how we can start using it in our own apps.

We'll start by generating yet another Create React App, this time with some different flags:

```
npx create-react-app my-type --template typescript
```

Now let's tour the features of our scaffolded project. Notice in the `src` directory that the file extensions are *.ts* or *.tsx* now. We'll also find a *.tsconfig.json* file, which contains all of our TypeScript settings. More on that in a bit.

Also, if you take a look at the *package.json* file, there are new dependencies listed and installed related to TypeScript, like the library itself and type definitions for Jest, React, ReactDOM, and more. Any dependency that starts with **@types/** describes the type definitions for a library. That means that the functions and methods in the library are typed so that we don't have to describe all of the library's types.

> If your project doesn't include the TypeScript features, you might be using an old version of Create React App. To get rid of this, you can run `npm uninstall -g create-react-app`.

Let's try dropping our component from the Flow lesson into our project. Just add the following to the *index.ts* file:

```
import React from "react";
import ReactDOM from "react-dom";

function App(props) {
  return (
    <div>
      <h1>{props.item}</h1>
    </div>
  );
}

ReactDOM.render(
  <App item="jacket" />,
  document.getElementById("root")
);
```

If we run the project with npm start, we should see our first TypeScript error. This is to be expected at this point:

```
Parameter 'props' implicitly has an 'any' type.
```

This means we need to add type rules for this App component. We'll start by defining types just as we did earlier for the Flow component. The item is a string, so we'll add that to the AppProps type:

```
type AppProps = {
  item: string;
};

ReactDOM.render(
  <App item="jacket" />,
  document.getElementById("root")
);
```

Then we'll reference AppProps in the component:

```
function App(props: AppProps) {
  return (
    <div>
      <h1>{props.item}</h1>
    </div>
  );
}
```

Now the component will render with no TypeScript issues. It's also possible to destructure props if we'd like to:

```
function App({ item }: AppProps) {
  return (
    <div>
```

```
      <h1>{item}</h1>
    </div>
  );
}
```

We can break this by passing a value of a different type as the `item` property:

```
ReactDOM.render(
  <App item={1} />,
  document.getElementById("root")
);
```

This immediately triggers an error:

```
Type 'number' is not assignable to type 'string'.
```

The error also tells us the exact line where there's a problem. This is extremely useful as we're debugging.

TypeScript helps with more than just property validation, though. We can use TypeScript's *type inference* to help us do typechecking on hook values.

Consider a state value for a `fabricColor` with an initial state of `purple`. The component might look like this:

```
type AppProps = {
  item: string;
};

function App({ item }: AppProps) {
  const [fabricColor, setFabricColor] = useState(
    "purple"
  );
  return (
    <div>
      <h1>
        {fabricColor} {item}
      </h1>
      <button
        onClick={() => setFabricColor("blue")}
      >
        Make the Jacket Blue
      </button>
    </div>
  );
}
```

Notice that we haven't added anything to the type definitions object. Instead, TypeScript is inferring that the type for the `fabricColor` should match the type of its initial state. If we try setting the `fabricColor` with a number instead of another string color `blue`, an error will be thrown:

```
<button onClick={() => setFabricColor(3)}>
```

The error looks like this:

```
Argument of type '3' is not assignable to parameter of type string.
```

TypeScript is hooking us up with some pretty low-effort typechecking for this value. Of course, you can customize this further, but this should give you a start toward adding typechecking to your applications.

For more on TypeScript, check out the official docs (*https://oreil.ly/97_Px*) and the amazing React+TypeScript Cheatsheets on GitHub (*https://oreil.ly/vmran*).

# Test-Driven Development

Test-driven development, or TDD, is a practice—not a technology. It does not mean that you simply have tests for your application. Rather, it's the practice of letting the tests drive the development process. In order to practice TDD, you should follow these steps:

*Write the tests first*
> This is the most critical step. You declare what you're building and how it should work first in a test. The steps you'll use to test are red, green, and gold.

*Run the tests and watch them fail (red)*
> Run the tests and watch them fail before you write the code.

*Write the minimal amount of code required to make the tests pass (green)*
> Focus specifically on making each test pass; do not add any functionality beyond the scope of the test.

*Refactor both the code and the tests (gold)*
> Once the tests pass, it's time to take a closer look at your code and your tests. Try to express your code as simply and as beautifully as possible.[2]

TDD gives us an excellent way to approach a React application, particularly when testing Hooks. It's typically easier to think about how a Hook should work before actually writing it. Practicing TDD will allow you to build and certify the entire data structure for a feature or application independent of the UI.

## TDD and Learning

If you're new to TDD, or new to the language you're testing, you may find it challenging to write a test before writing code. This is to be expected, and it's OK to write the code before the test until you get the hang of it. Try to work in small batches: a little

---

2 For more on this development pattern, see Jeff McWherter's and James Bender's "Red, Green, Refactor" (*https://oreil.ly/Hr6Me*).

bit of code, a few tests, and so on. Once you get used to writing tests, it will be easier to write the tests first.

For the remainder of this chapter, we'll be writing tests for code that already exists. Technically, we're not practicing TDD. However, in the next section, we'll pretend that our code does not already exist so we can get a feel for the TDD workflow.

# Incorporating Jest

Before we can get started writing tests, we'll need to select a testing framework. You can write tests for React with any JavaScript testing framework, but the official React docs recommend testing with Jest, a JavaScript test runner that lets you access the DOM via JSDOM. Accessing the DOM is important because you want to be able to check what is rendered with React to ensure your application is working correctly.

## Create React App and Testing

Projects that have been initialized with Create React App already come with the jest package installed. We can create another Create React App project to get started, or use an existing one:

```
npx create-react-app testing
```

Now we can start thinking about testing with a small example. We'll create two new files in the *src* folder: *functions.js* and *functions.test.js*. Remember, Jest is already configured and installed in Create React App, so all you need to do is start writing tests. In *functions.test.js*, we'll stub the tests. In other words, we'll write what we think the function should do.

We want our function to take in a value, multiply it by two, and return it. So we'll model that in the test. The test function is the function that Jest provides to test a single piece of functionality:

*functions.test.js*

```
test("Multiplies by two", () => {
  expect();
});
```

The first argument, Multiplies by two, is the test name. The second argument is the function that contains what should be tested and the third (optional) argument specifies a timeout. The default timeout is five seconds.

The next thing we'll do is stub the function that will multiply numbers by two. This function will be referred to as our *system under test* (*SUT*). In *functions.js*, create the function:

```
export default function timesTwo() {...}
```

We'll export it so that we can use the SUT in the test. In the test file, we want to import the function, and we'll use **expect** to write an assertion. In the assertion, we'll say that if we pass 4 to the **timesTwo** function, we expect that it should return 8:

```
import { timesTwo } from "./functions";

test("Multiplies by two", () => {
  expect(timesTwo(4)).toBe(8);
});
```

Jest "matchers" are returned by the **expect** function and used to verify results. To test the function, we'll use the **.toBe** matcher. This verifies that the resulting object matches the argument sent to **.toBe**.

Let's run the tests and watch them fail using **npm test** or **npm run test**. Jest will provide specific details on each failure, including a stack trace:

```
FAIL  src/functions.test.js
  ✕ Multiplies by two (5ms)

  ● Multiplies by two

    expect(received).toBe(expected) // Object.is equality

    Expected: 8
    Received: undefined

      2 |
      3 | test("Multiplies by two", () => {
    > 4 |   expect(timesTwo(4)).toBe(8);
        |                       ^
      5 | });
      6 |

      at Object.<anonymous> (src/functions.test.js:4:23)

Test Suites: 1 failed, 1 total
Tests:       1 failed, 1 total
Snapshots:   0 total
Time:        1.048s
Ran all test suites related to changed files.
```

Taking the time to write the tests and run them to watch them fail shows us that our tests are working as intended. This failure feedback represents our to-do list. It's our job to write the minimal code required to make our tests pass.

Now if we add the proper functionality to the *functions.js* file, we can make the tests pass:

```
export function timesTwo(a) {
  return a * 2;
}
```

The .toBe matcher has helped us test for equality with a single value. If we want to test an object or array, we could use .toEqual. Let's go through another cycle with our tests. In the test file, we'll test for equality of an array of objects.

We have a list of menu items from the Guy Fieri restaurant in Las Vegas. It's important that we build an object of their ordered items so the customer can get what they want and know what they're supposed to pay. We'll stub the test first:

```
test("Build an order object", () => {
  expect();
});
```

Then we'll stub our function:

```
export function order(items) {
  // ...
}
```

Now we'll use the order function in the test file. We'll also assume that we have a starter list of data for an order that we need to transform:

```
import { timesTwo, order } from "./functions";

const menuItems = [
  {
    id: "1",
    name: "Tatted Up Turkey Burger",
    price: 19.5
  },
  {
    id: "2",
    name: "Lobster Lollipops",
    price: 16.5
  },
  {
    id: "3",
    name: "Motley Que Pulled Pork Sandwich",
    price: 21.5
  },
  {
    id: "4",
    name: "Trash Can Nachos",
    price: 19.5
  }
];

test("Build an order object", () => {
  expect(order(menuItems));
});
```

Remember that we'll use `toEqual` because we're checking the value of an object instead of an array. What do we want the result to equal? Well, we want to create an object that looks like this:

```
const result = {
  orderItems: menuItems,
  total: 77
};
```

So we just add that to the test and use it in the assertion:

```
test("Build an order object", () => {
  const result = {
    orderItems: menuItems,
    total: 77
  };
  expect(order(menuItems)).toEqual(result);
});
```

Now we'll complete the function in the *functions.js* file:

```
export function order(items) {
  const total = items.reduce(
    (price, item) => price + item.price,
    0
  );
  return [
    orderItems: items,
    total
  };
}
```

And when we check out the terminal, we'll find that are tests are now passing! Now this might feel like a trivial example, but if you were fetching data, it's likely that you'd test for shape matches of arrays and objects.

Another commonly used function with Jest is `describe()`. If you've used other testing libraries, you might have seen a similar function before. This function is typically used to wrap several related tests. For example, if we had a few tests for similar functions, we could wrap them in a describe statement:

```
describe("Math functions", () => {
  test("Multiplies by two", () => {
    expect(timesTwo(4)).toBe(8);
  });
  test("Adds two numbers", () => {
    expect(sum(4, 2)).toBe(6);
  });
  test("Subtracts two numbers", () => {
    expect(subtract(4, 2)).toBe(2);
  });
});
```

When you wrap tests in the `describe` statement, the test runner creates a block of tests, which makes the testing output in the terminal look more organized and easier to read:

```
Math functions
    ✓ Multiplies by two
    ✓ Adds two numbers
    ✓ Subtracts two numbers (1ms)
```

As you write more tests, grouping them in `describe` blocks might be a useful enhancement.

This process represents a typical TDD cycle. We wrote the tests first, then wrote code to make the tests pass. Once the tests pass, we can take a closer look at the code to see if there's anything that's worth refactoring for clarity or performance. This approach is very effective when working with JavaScript (or really any other language).

# Testing React Components

Now that we have a basic understanding of the process behind writing tests, we can start to apply these techniques to component testing in React.

React components provide instructions for React to follow when creating and managing updates to the DOM. We can test these components by rendering them and checking the resulting DOM.

We're not running our tests in a browser; we're running them in the terminal with Node.js. Node.js does not have the DOM API that comes standard with each browser. Jest incorporates an npm package called `jsdom` that's used to simulate a browser environment in Node.js, which is essential for testing React components.

For each component test, it's likely that we'll need to render our React component tree to a DOM element. To demonstrate this workflow, let's revisit our `Star` component in *Star.js*:

```
import { FaStar } from "react-icons/fa";

export default function Star({ selected = false }) {
  return (
    <FaStar color={selected ? "red" : "grey"} id="star" />
  );
}
```

Then in *index.js*, we'll import and render the star:

```
import Star from "./Star";

ReactDOM.render(
  <Star />,
  document.getElementById("root")
);
```

Now let's write our test. We already wrote the code for the star, so we won't be partaking in TDD here. If you had to incorporate tests into your existing apps, this is how you'd do it. In a new file called *Star.test.js*, start by importing React, ReactDOM, and the Star:

```
import React from "react";
import ReactDOM from "react-dom";
import Star from "./Star";

test("renders a star", () => {
  const div = document.createElement("div");
  ReactDOM.render(<Star />, div);
});
```

We'll also want to write the tests. Remember, the first argument we supply to test is the name of the test. Then we're going to perform some setup by creating a div that we can render the star to with ReactDOM.render. Once the element is created, we can write the assertion:

```
test("renders a star", () => {
  const div = document.createElement("div");
  ReactDOM.render(<Star />, div);
  expect(div.querySelector("svg")).toBeTruthy();
});
```

We'll expect that if we try to select an svg element inside of the created div, the result will be truthy. When we run the test, we should see that the test passes. Just to verify that we aren't getting a valid assertion when we shouldn't be, we can change the selector to find something fake and watch the test fail:

```
expect(
  div.querySelector("notrealthing")
).toBeTruthy();
```

The documentation (*https://oreil.ly/ah7ZU*) provides more detail about all of the custom matchers that are available so that you can test exactly what you want to test.

When you generated your React project, you may have noticed that a few packages from @testing-library were installed in addition to the basics like React and React-DOM. React Testing Library is a project that was started by Kent C. Dodds as a way to enforce good testing practices and to expand the testing utilities that were part of the React ecosystem. Testing Library is an umbrella over many testing packages for libraries like Vue, Svelte, Reason, Angular, and more—it's not just for React.

One potential reason you might choose React Testing Library is to get better error messages when a test fails. The current error we see when we test the assertion:

```
expect(
  div.querySelector("notrealthing")
).toBeTruthy();
```

is:

```
expect(received).toBeTruthy()

Received: null
```

Let's punch this up by adding React Testing Library. It's already installed in our Create React App project. To begin, we'll import the toHaveAttribute function from @testing-library/jest-dom:

```
import { toHaveAttribute } from "@testing-library/jest-dom";
```

From there, we want to extend the functionality of expect to include this function:

```
expect.extend({ toHaveAttribute });
```

Now instead of using toBeTruthy, which gives us hard-to-read messages, we can use toHaveAttribute:

```
test("renders a star", () => {
  const div = document.createElement("div");
  ReactDOM.render(<Star />, div);
  expect(
    div.querySelector("svg")
  ).toHaveAttribute("id", "hotdog");
});
```

Now when we run the tests, we see an error telling us exactly what's what:

```
expect(element).toHaveAttribute("id", "hotdog")
// element.getAttribute("id") === "hotdog"

Expected the element to have attribute:
  id="hotdog"
Received:
  id="star"
```

It should be pretty straightforward to fix this now:

```
expect(div.querySelector("svg")).toHaveAttribute(
  "id",
  "star"
);
```

Using more than one of the custom matchers just means that you need to import, extend, and use:

```
import {
  toHaveAttribute,
  toHaveClass
} from "@testing-library/jest-dom";

expect.extend({ toHaveAttribute, toHaveClass });

expect(you).toHaveClass("evenALittle");
```

There's an even faster way to do this, though. If you find yourself importing too many of these matchers to list or keep track of, you can import the extend-expect library:

```
import "@testing-library/jest-dom/extend-expect";

// Remove this --> expect.extend({ toHaveAttribute, toHaveClass });
```

The assertions will continue to run as expected (pun intended). Another fun fact about Create React App is that, in a file called *setupTests.js* that ships with CRA, there's a line that has already included the extend-expect helpers. If you look at the *src* folder, you'll see that *setupTests.js* contains:

```
// jest dom adds custom jest matchers for asserting on DOM nodes.
// allows you to do things like:
// expect(element).toHaveTextContent(/react/i)
// learn more: https://github.com/testing-library/jest-dom
import "@testing-library/jest-dom/extend-expect";
```

So if you're using Create React App, you don't even have to include the import in your test files.

## Queries

Queries are another feature of the React Testing Library that allow you to match based on certain criteria. In order to demonstrate using a query, let's adjust the Star component to include a title. This will allow us to write a common style of test—one that matches based on text:

```
export default function Star({ selected = false }) {
  return (
    <>
      <h1>Great Star</h1>
      <FaStar
        id="star"
        color={selected ? "red" : "grey"}
      />
    </>
  );
}
```

Let's pause to think about what we're trying to test. We want the component to render, and now we want to test to see if the h1 contains the correct text. A function that's part of React Testing Library, `render`, will help us do just that. `render` will replace our need to use `ReactDOM.render()`, so the test will look a bit different. Start by importing `render` from React Testing Library:

```
import { render } from "@testing-library/react";
```

`render` will take in one argument: the component or element that we want to render. The function returns an object of queries that can be used to check in with values in that component or element. The query we'll use is `getByText`, which will find the first matching node for a query and throw an error if no elements match. To return a list of all matching nodes, use `getAllBy` to return an array:

```
test("renders an h1", () => {
  const { getByText } = render(<Star />);
  const h1 = getByText(/Great Star/);
  expect(h1).toHaveTextContent("Great Star");
});
```

`getByText` finds the h1 element via the regular expression that's passed to it. Then we use the Jest matcher `toHaveTextContent` to describe what text the h1 should include.

Run the tests, and they'll pass. If we change the text passed to the `toHaveTextContent()` function, the test will fail.

## Testing Events

Another important part of writing tests is testing events that are part of components. Let's use and test the `Checkbox` component we created in Chapter 7:

```
export function Checkbox() {
  const [checked, setChecked] = useReducer(
    checked => !checked,
    false
  );

  return (
    <>
      <label>
        {checked ? "checked" : "not checked"}
        <input
          type="checkbox"
          value={checked}
          onChange={setChecked}
        />
      </label>
    </>
  );
}
```

This component uses `useReducer` to toggle a checkbox. Our aim here is to create an automated test that will click this checkbox and change the value of `checked` from the default `false` to `true`. Writing a test to check the box will also fire `useReducer` and test the hook.

Let's stub the test:

```
import React from "react";

test("Selecting the checkbox should change the value of checked to true", () => {
  // .. write a test
});
```

The first thing we need to do is select the element that we want to fire the event on. In other words, which element do we want to click on with the automated test? We'll use one of Testing Library's queries to find the element we're looking for. Since the input has a label, we can use `getByLabelText()`:

```
import { render } from "@testing-library/react";
import { Checkbox } from "./Checkbox";

test("Selecting the checkbox should change the value of checked to true", () => {
  const { getByLabelText } = render(<Checkbox />);
});
```

When the component first renders, its label text reads not `checked`, so we can search via a regular expression to find a match with the string:

```
test("Selecting the checkbox should change the value of checked to true", () => {
  const { getByLabelText } = render(<Checkbox />);
  const checkbox = getByLabelText(/not checked/);
});
```

Currently, this regex is case sensitive, so if you wanted to search for any case, you could add an `i` to the end of it. Use that technique with caution depending on how permissive you want the query selection to be:

```
const checkbox = getByLabelText(/not checked/i);
```

Now we have our checkbox selected. All we need to do now is fire the event (click the checkbox) and write an assertion to make sure that the `checked` property is set to `true` when the checkbox is clicked:

```
mport { render, fireEvent } from "@testing-library/react"

test("Selecting the checkbox should change the value of checked to true", () => {
  const { getByLabelText } = render(<Checkbox />);
  const checkbox = getByLabelText(/not checked/i);
  fireEvent.click(checkbox);
  expect(checkbox.checked).toEqual(true);
});
```

You also could add the reverse toggle to this checkbox test by firing the event again and checking that the property is set to `false` on toggle. We changed the name of the test to be more accurate:

```
test("Selecting the checkbox should toggle its value", () => {
  const { getByLabelText } = render(<Checkbox />);
  const checkbox = getByLabelText(/not checked/i);
  fireEvent.click(checkbox);
  expect(checkbox.checked).toEqual(true);
  fireEvent.click(checkbox);
  expect(checkbox.checked).toEqual(false);
});
```

In this case, selecting the checkbox is pretty easy. We have a label we can use to find the input we want to check. In the event that you don't have such an easy way to access a DOM element, Testing Library gives you another utility you can use to check in with any DOM element. You'll start by adding an attribute to the element you want to select:

```
<input
  type="checkbox"
  value={checked}
  onChange={setChecked}
  data-testid="checkbox" // Add the data-testid= attribute
/>
```

Then use the query `getByTestId`:

```
test("Selecting the checkbox should change the value of checked to true", () => {
  const { getByTestId } = render(<Checkbox />);
  const checkbox = getByTestId("checkbox");
  fireEvent.click(checkbox);
  expect(checkbox.checked).toEqual(true);
});
```

This will do the same thing but is particularly useful when reaching out to DOM elements that are otherwise difficult to access.

Once this `Checkbox` component is tested, we can confidently incorporate it into the rest of the application and reuse it.

## Using Code Coverage

*Code coverage* is the process of reporting on how many lines of code have actually been tested. It provides a metric that can help you decide when you've written enough tests.

Jest ships with Istanbul, a JavaScript tool used to review your tests and generate a report that describes how many statements, branches, functions, and lines have been covered.

---

To run Jest with code coverage, simply add the coverage flag when you run the jest command:

```
npm test -- --coverage
```

This report tells you how much of your code in each file has been executed during the testing process and reports on all files that have been imported into tests.

Jest also generates a report that you can run in your browser, which provides more details about what code has been covered by tests. After running Jest with coverage reporting, you'll notice that a *coverage* folder has been added to the root. In a web browser, open this file: */coverage/lcov-report/index.html*. It will show you your code coverage in an interactive report.

This report tells you how much of the code has been covered, as well as the individual coverage based on each subfolder. You can drill down into a subfolder to see how well the individual files within have been covered. If you select the *components/ui* folder, you'll see how well your user interface components are covered by testing.

You can see which lines have been covered in an individual file by clicking on the filename.

Code coverage is a great tool to measure the reach of your tests. It's one benchmark to help you understand when you've written enough unit tests for your code. It's not typical to have 100% code coverage in every project. Shooting for anything above 85% is a good target.[3]

Testing can often feel like an extra step, but the tooling around React testing has never been better. Even if you don't test all of your code, starting to think about how to incorporate testing practices can help you save time and money when building production-ready applications.

---

3 See Martin Fowler's article, "Test-Coverage" (*https://oreil.ly/Hbb-D*).

# CHAPTER 11

# React Router

When the web started, most websites consisted of a series of pages that users could navigate through by requesting and opening separate files. The location of the current file or resource was listed in the browser's location bar. The browser's forward and back buttons would work as expected. Bookmarking content deep within a website would allow users to save a reference to a specific file that could be reloaded at the user's request. On a page-based, or server-rendered, website, the browser's navigation and history features simply work as expected.

In a single-page app, all of these features become problematic. Remember, in a single-page app, everything is happening on the same page. JavaScript is loading information and changing the UI. Features like browser history, bookmarks, and forward and back buttons will not work without a routing solution. *Routing* is the process of defining endpoints for your client's requests.[1] These endpoints work in conjunction with the browser's location and history objects. They're used to identify requested content so that JavaScript can load and render the appropriate user interface.

Unlike Angular, Ember, or Backbone, React doesn't come with a standard router. Recognizing the importance of a routing solution, engineers Michael Jackson and Ryan Florence created one named simply React Router. The React Router has been adopted by the community as a popular routing solution for React apps.[2] It's used by companies including Uber, Zendesk, PayPal, and Vimeo.[3]

In this chapter, we'll introduce React Router and leverage its features to handle routing on the client.

---

[1] Express.js documentation, "Basic routing" (*https://oreil.ly/jD1HC*).

[2] The project has been starred over 20,000 times on GitHub (*https://oreil.ly/ThNG9*).

[3] See "Sites Using React Router" (*https://oreil.ly/staEF*).

# Incorporating the Router

To demonstrate the capabilities of the React Router, we'll build a classic starter website complete with About, Events, Products, and Contact Us sections. Although this website will feel as though it has multiple pages, there's only one—it's an SPA, a single-page application (see Figure 11-1).

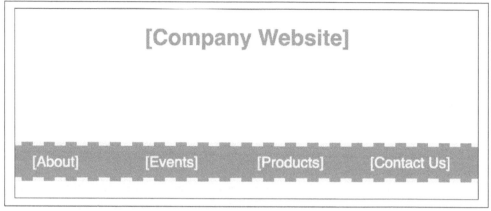

*Figure 11-1. Simple website with link navigation*

The sitemap for this website consists of a home page, a page for each section, and an error page to handle 404 Not Found errors (see Figure 11-2).

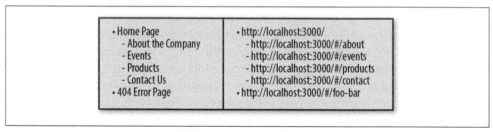

*Figure 11-2. Sitemap with local links*

The router will allow us to set up routes for each section of the website. Each *route* is an endpoint that can be entered into the browser's location bar. When a route is requested, we can render the appropriate content.

To start, let's install React Router and React Router DOM. React Router DOM is used for regular React applications that use the DOM. If you're writing an app for React Native, you'll use `react-router-native`. We're going to install these packages at their experimental versions because React Router 6 is not officially out at the time of this printing. Once released, you can use the packages without that designation.

```
npm install react-router@experimental react-router-dom@experimental
```

We'll also need a few placeholder components for each section or page in the sitemap. We can export these components from a single file called *pages.js*:

```
import React from "react";

export function Home() {
  return (
    <div>
      <h1>[Company Website]</h1>
    </div>
  );
}

export function About() {
  return (
    <div>
      <h1>[About]</h1>
    </div>
  );
}

export function Events() {
  return (
    <div>
      <h1>[Events]</h1>
    </div>
  );
}

export function Products() {
  return (
    <div>
      <h1>[Products]</h1>
    </div>
  );
}

export function Contact() {
  return (
    <div>
      <h1>[Contact]</h1>
    </div>
  );
}
```

With these pages stubbed out, we need to adjust the *index.js* file. Instead of rendering the App component, we'll render the Router component. The Router component passes information about the current location to any children that are nested inside of it. The Router component should be used once and placed near the root of our component tree:

```
import React from "react";
import { render } from "react-dom";
import App from "./App";

import { BrowserRouter as Router } from "react-router-dom";

render(
  <Router>
    <App />
  </Router>,
  document.getElementById("root")
);
```

Notice that we're importing BrowserRouter as Router. The next thing we need to do is set up our route configuration. We're going to place this in the *App.js* file. The wrapper component for any routes we want to render is called Routes. Inside of Routes, we'll use a Route component for each page we want to render. We also want to import all of the pages from the *./pages.js* file:

```
import React from "react";
import { Routes, Route } from "react-router-dom";
import {
  Home,
  About,
  Events,
  Products,
  Contact
} from "./pages";

function App() {
  return (
    <div>
      <Routes>
        <Route path="/" element={<Home />} />
        <Route
          path="/about"
          element={<About />}
        />
        <Route
          path="/events"
          element={<Events />}
        />
        <Route
          path="/products"
          element={<Products />}
        />
        <Route
          path="/contact"
          element={<Contact />}
        />
      </Routes>
    </div>
```

```
  );
}
```

These routes tell the Router which component to render when the window's location changes. Each Route component has path and element properties. When the browser's location matches the path, the element will be displayed. When the location is /, the router will render the Home component. When the location is /products, the router will render the Products component.

At this point, we can run the app and physically type the routes into the browser's location bar to watch the content change. For example, type *http://localhost:3000/about* into the location bar and watch the About component render.

It's probably not realistic to expect our users to navigate the website by typing routes into the location bar. The react-router-dom provides a Link component that we can use to create browser links.

Let's modify the home page to contain a navigation menu with a link for each route:

```
import { Link } from "react-router-dom";

export function Home() {
  return (
    <div>
      <h1>[Company Website]</h1>
      <nav>
        <Link to="about">About</Link>
        <Link to="events">Events</Link>
        <Link to="products">Products</Link>
        <Link to="contact">Contact Us</Link>
      </nav>
    </div>
  );
}
```

Now users can access every internal page from the home page by clicking on a link. The browser's back button will take them back to the home page.

## Router Properties

The React Router passes properties to the components it renders. For instance, we can obtain the current location via a property. Let's use the current location to help us create a 404 Not Found component. First, we'll create the component:

```
export function Whoops404() {
  return (
    <div>
      <h1>Resource not found</h1>
    </div>
```

```
    );
  }
```

Then we'll add this to our route configuration in *App.js*. If we visit a route that doesn't exist, like `highway`, we want to display the `Whoops404` component. We'll use the * as the path value and the component as the element:

```
function App() {
  return (
    <div>
      <Routes>
        <Route path="/" element={<Home />} />
        <Route
          path="/about"
          element={<About />}
        />
        <Route
          path="/events"
          element={<Events />}
        />
        <Route
          path="/products"
          element={<Products />}
        />
        <Route
          path="/contact"
          element={<Contact />}
        />
        <Route path="*" element={<Whoops404 />} />
      </Routes>
    </div>
  );
}
```

Now if we visit *localhost:3000/highway*, we'll see the 404 page component render. We also could display the value of the route that we've visited by using the location value. Since we're living in a world with React Hooks, there's a hook for that. In the `Whoops404` component, create a variable called `location` that returns the value of the current location (i.e., properties about which page you're navigated to). Then use the value of `location.pathname` to display the route that's being visited:

```
export function Whoops404() {
  let location = useLocation();
  console.log(location);
  return (
    <div>
      <h1>
        Resource not found at {location.pathname}
      </h1>
    </div>
  );
}
```

If you log the location, you can explore that object further.

This section introduced the basics of implementing and working with the React Router. Router is used once and wraps all components that will use routing. All Route components need to be wrapped with a Routes component, which selects the component to render based on the window's present location. Link components can be used to facilitate navigation. These basics can get you pretty far, but they just scratch the surface of the router's capabilities.

## Nesting Routes

Route components are used with content that should be displayed only when specific URLs are matched. This feature allows us to organize our web apps into eloquent hierarchies that promote content reuse.

Sometimes, as users navigate our apps, we want some of the UI to stay in place. In the past, solutions such as page templates and master pages have helped web developers reuse UI elements.

Let's consider the simple starter website. We might want to create subpages for the About page that will display additional content. When the user selects the About section, they should be defaulted to the Company page under that section. The outline looks like this:

- Home Page
  - **About the Company**
    - **Company (default)**
    - **History**
    - **Services**
    - **Location**
  - Events
  - Products
  - Contact Us
- 404 Error Page

The new routes that we need to create will reflect this hierarchy:

- *http://localhost:3000/*
  - *http://localhost:3000/about*
    - *http://localhost:3000/about*
    - *http://localhost:3000/about/history*

— *http://localhost:3000/about/services*

— *http://localhost:3000/about/location*

— *http://localhost:3000/events*

— *http://localhost:3000/products*

— *http://localhost:3000/contact*

- *http://localhost:3000/hot-potato*

We also need to remember to stub placeholder components for our new sections: Company, Services, History, and Location. As an example, here's some text for the Services component that you can reuse for the other two:

```
export function Services() {
  <section>
    <h2>Our Services</h2>
    <p>
      Lorem ipsum dolor sit amet, consectetur
      adipiscing elit. Integer nec odio. Praesent
      libero. Sed cursus ante dapibus diam. Sed
      nisi. Nulla quis sem at nibh elementum
      imperdiet. Duis sagittis ipsum. Praesent
      mauris. Fusce nec tellus sed augue semper
      porta. Mauris massa. Vestibulum lacinia arcu
      eget nulla. Class aptent taciti sociosqu ad
      litora torquent per conubia nostra, per
      inceptos himenaeos. Curabitur sodales ligula
      in libero.
    </p>
  </section>;
}
```

With those components created, we can configure the router starting with the *App.js* file. If you want to create a page hierarchy with the routes, all you need to do is nest the Route components inside of each other:

```
import {
  Home,
  About,
  Events,
  Products,
  Contact,
  Whoops404,
  Services,
  History,
  Location
} from "./pages";

function App() {
  return (
    <div>
```

```
          <Routes>
            <Route path="/" element={<Home />} />
            <Route path="about" element={<About />}>
              <Route
                path="services"
                element={<Services />}
              />

              <Route
                path="history"
                element={<History />}
              />
              <Route
                path="location"
                element={<Location />}
              />
            </Route>
            <Route
              path="events"
              element={<Events />}
            />
            <Route
              path="products"
              element={<Products />}
            />
            <Route
              path="contact"
              element={<Contact />}
            />
            <Route path="*" element={<Whoops404 />} />
          </Routes>
        </div>
    );
}
```

Once you've wrapped the nested routes with the About `Route` component, you can visit these pages. If you open *http://localhost:3000/about/history*, you'll just see the content from the `About` page, but the `History` component doesn't display. In order to get that to display, we'll use another feature of React Router DOM: the `Outlet` component. `Outlet` will let us render these nested components. We'll just place it anywhere we want to render child content.

In the `About` component in *pages.js*, we'll add this under the `<h1>`:

```
import {
  Link,
  useLocation,
  Outlet
} from "react-router-dom";

export function About() {
  return (
```

```
      <div>
        <h1>[About]</h1>
        <Outlet />
      </div>
    );
  }
```

Now this `About` component will be reused across the entire section and will display the nested components. The location will tell the app which subsection to render. For example, when the location is *http://localhost:3000/about/history*, the `History` component will be rendered inside of the `About` component.

## Using Redirects

Sometimes you want to redirect users from one route to another. For instance, we can make sure that if users try to access content via *http://localhost:3000/services*, they get redirected to the correct route: *http://localhost:3000/about/services*.

Let's modify our application to include redirects to ensure that our users can access the correct content:

```
import {
  Routes,
  Route,
  Redirect
} from "react-router-dom";

function App() {
  return (
    <div>
      <Routes>
        <Route path="/" element={<Home />} />
        // Other Routes
        <Redirect
          from="services"
          to="about/services"
        />
      </Routes>
    </div>
  );
}
```

The `Redirect` component allows us to redirect the user to a specific route.

When routes are changed in a production application, users will still try to access old content via old routes. This typically happens because of bookmarks. The `Redirect` component provides us with a way to load the appropriate content for users, even if they're accessing our site via an old bookmark.

Throughout this section, we've created a route configuration using the `Route` component. If you love this structure, feel free to ignore this next section, but we wanted to make sure that you knew how to create a route configuration a different way. It's also possible to use the hook `useRoutes` to configure your application's routing.

If we wanted to refactor our application to use `useRoutes`, we'd make the adjustments in the `App` component (or anywhere where the routes are set up). Let's refactor it:

```
import { useRoutes } from "react-router-dom";

function App() {
  let element = useRoutes([
    { path: "/", element: <Home /> },
    {
      path: "about",
      element: <About />,
      children: [
        {
          path: "services",
          element: <Services />
        },
        { path: "history", element: <History /> },
        {
          path: "location",
          element: <Location />
        }
      ]
    },
    { path: "events", element: <Events /> },
    { path: "products", element: <Products /> },
    { path: "contact", element: <Contact /> },
    { path: "*", element: <Whoops404 /> },
    {
      path: "services",
      redirectTo: "about/services"
    }
  ]);
  return element;
}
```

The official docs call the config `element`, but you can choose to call it whatever you like. It's also totally optional to use this syntax. `Route` is a wrapper around `useRoutes`, so you're actually using this either way. Choose whichever syntax and style works best for you!

## Routing Parameters

Another useful feature of the React Router is the ability to set up *routing parameters*. Routing parameters are variables that obtain their values from the URL. They're extremely useful in data-driven web applications for filtering content or managing display preferences.

Let's revisit the color organizer and improve it by adding the ability to select and display one color at a time using React Router. When a user selects a color by clicking on it, the app should render that color and display its `title` and `hex` value.

Using the router, we can obtain the color ID via the URL. For example, this is the URL we'll use to display the color "lawn" because the ID for lawn is being passed within the URL:

```
http://localhost:3000/58d9caee-6ea6-4d7b-9984-65b145031979
```

To start, let's set up the router in the *index.js* file. We'll import the `Router` and wrap the `App` component:

```
import { BrowserRouter as Router } from "react-router-dom";

render(
  <Router>
    <App />
  </Router>,
  document.getElementById("root")
);
```

Wrapping the `App` passes all of the router's properties to the component and any other components nested inside of it. From there, we can set up the route configuration. We'll use the `Routes` and `Route` components instead of `useRoutes`, but remember that this is always an option if you prefer that syntax. Start by importing `Routes` and `Route`:

```
import { Routes, Route } from "react-router-dom";
```

Then add to the `App`. This application will have two routes: the `ColorList` and the `ColorDetails`. We haven't built `ColorDetails` yet, but let's import it:

```
import { ColorDetails } from "./ColorDetails";

export default function App() {
  return (
    <ColorProvider>
      <AddColorForm />
      <Routes>
        <Route
          path="/"
          element={<ColorList />}
        />
        <Route
          path=":id"
          element={<ColorDetails />}
        />
      </Routes>
```

```
      </ColorProvider>
   );
}
```

The `ColorDetails` component will display dynamically based on the `id` of the color. Let's create the `ColorDetails` component in a new file called *ColorDetails.js*. To start, it'll be a placeholder:

```
import React from "react";

export function ColorDetails() {
  return (
    <div>
      <h1>Details</h1>
    </div>
  );
}
```

How do we know if this is working? The easiest way to check is to open the React Developer tools and find the `id` of one of the colors that is being rendered. If you don't have a color yet, then add one and take a look at its `id`. Once you have the `id`, you can append that to the `localhost:3000` URL. For example, `localhost:3000/00fdb4c5-c5bd-4087-a48f-4ff7a9d90af8`.

Now, you should see the `ColorDetails` page appear. Now we know that the router and our routes are working, but we want this to be more dynamic. On the `ColorDetails` page, we want to display the correct color based on the `id` that's found in the URL. To do that, we'll use the `useParams` hook:

```
import { useParams } from "react-router-dom";

export function ColorDetails() {
  let params = useParams();
  console.log(params);
  return (
    <div>
      <h1>Details</h1>
    </div>
  );
}
```

If we log `params`, we'll see that this is an object that contains any parameters that are available on the router. We'll destructure this object to grab the `id`, then we can use that `id` to find the correct color in the `colors` array. Let's use our `useColors` hook to make this happen:

```
import { useColors } from "./";

export function ColorDetails() {
  let { id } = useParams(); // destructure id
```

```
    let { colors } = useColors();

    let foundColor = colors.find(
      color => color.id === id
    );
    console.log(foundColor);

    return (
      <div>
        <h1>Details</h1>
      </div>
    );
  }
```

Logging `foundColor` shows us that we've found the correct color. Now all we need to do is display the data about that color in the component:

```
  export function ColorDetails() {
    let { id } = useParams();
    let { colors } = useColors();

    let foundColor = colors.find(
      color => color.id === id
    );

    return (
      <div>
        <div
          style={{
            backgroundColor: foundColor.color,
            height: 100,
            width: 100
          }}
        ></div>
        <h1>{foundColor.title}</h1>
        <h1>{foundColor.color}</h1>
      </div>
    );
  }
```

Another feature we want to add to the color organizer is the ability to navigate to the `ColorDetails` page by clicking on the color in the list. Let's add this functionality to the `Color` component. We're going to use another router hook called `useNavigate` to open the details page when we click on the component. We'll import it first from `react-router-dom`:

```
  import { useNavigate } from "react-router-dom";
```

Then we'll call `useNavigate`, which will return a function we can use to navigate to another page:

```
  let navigate = useNavigate();
```

Now in the `section`, we'll add an `onClick` handler to navigate to the route based on the color `id`:

```
let navigate = useNavigate();

return (
  <section
    className="color"
    onClick={() => navigate(`/${id}`)}
  >
    // Color component
  </section>
);
```

Now, when we click on the `section`, we'll be routed to the correct page.

Routing parameters are an ideal tool to obtain data that affects the presentation of your user interface. However, they should only be used when you want users to capture these details in a URL. For example, in the case of the color organizer, users can send other users links to specific colors or all the colors sorted by a specific field. Users can also bookmark those links to return specific data.

In this chapter, we reviewed the basic usage of the React Router. In the next chapter, we'll learn how to use routing on the server.

# CHAPTER 12

# React and the Server

So far, we've built small applications with React that run entirely in the browser. They've collected data in the browser and saved the data using browser storage. This makes sense because React is a view layer; it's intended to render UI. However, most applications require at least the existence of some sort of a backend, and we will need to understand how to structure applications with a server in mind.

Even if you have a client application that's relying entirely on cloud services for the backend, you still need to get and send data to these services. There are specific places where these transactions should be made and libraries that can help you deal with the latency associated with HTTP requests.

Additionally, React can be rendered *isomorphically*, which means that it can be in platforms other than the browser. This means we can render our UI on the server before it ever gets to the browser. Taking advantage of server rendering, we can improve the performance, portability, and security of our applications.

We start this chapter with a look at the differences between isomorphism and universalism and how both concepts relate to React. Next, we'll look at how to make an isomorphic application using universal JavaScript. Finally, we'll improve the color organizer by adding a server and rendering the UI on the server first.

## Isomorphic Versus Universal

The terms *isomorphic* and *universal* are often used to describe applications that work on both the client and the server. Although these terms are used interchangeably to describe the same application, there's a subtle difference between them that's worth investigating. *Isomorphic* applications are applications that can be rendered on multiple platforms. *Universal* code means that the exact same code can run in multiple environments.[1]

Node.js will allow us to reuse the same code we've written in the browser in other applications such as servers, CLIs, and even native applications. Let's take a look at some universal JavaScript:

```
const userDetails = response => {
  const login = response.login;
  console.log(login);
};
```

The `printNames` function is universal. The exact same code can be invoked in the browser or on a server. This means that if we constructed a server with Node.js, we could potentially reuse code between the two environments. Universal JavaScript is JavaScript that can run on the server or in the browser without error (see Figure 12-1).

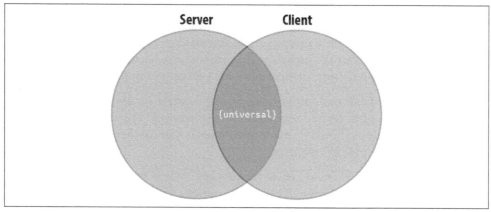

*Figure 12-1. Client and server domains*

## Client and Server Domains

The server and the client are completely different domains, so all of our JavaScript code won't automatically work between them. Let's take a look at creating an AJAX request with the browser:

```
fetch("https://api.github.com/users/moonhighway")
  .then(res => res.json())
  .then(console.log);
```

Here, we're making a fetch request to the GitHub API, converting the response to JSON, then calling a function on the JSON results to parse it.

---

1 Gert Hengeveld, "Isomorphism vs Universal JavaScript" (*https://oreil.ly/i70W2*), Medium.

However, if we try to run the exact same code with Node.js, we get an error:

```
fetch("https://api.github.com/users/moonhighway")
^

ReferenceError: fetch is not defined
at Object.<anonymous> (/Users/eveporcello/Desktop/index.js:7:1)
at Module._compile (internal/modules/cjs/loader.js:1063:30)
at Object.Module._extensions..js (internal/modules/cjs/loader.js:1103:10)
at Module.load (internal/modules/cjs/loader.js:914:32)
at Function.Module._load (internal/modules/cjs/loader.js:822:14)
at Function.Module.runMain (internal/modules/cjs/loader.js:1143:12)
at internal/main/run_main_module.js:16:11
```

This error occurs because Node.js does not have a built-in `fetch` function like the browser does. With Node.js, we can use `isomorphic-fetch` from npm, or use the built-in `https` module. Since we've already used the `fetch` syntax, let's incorporate `isomorphic-fetch`:

```
npm install isomorphic-fetch
```

Then we'll just import `isomorphic-fetch` with no changes to the code:

```
const fetch = require("isomorphic-fetch");

const userDetails = response => {
  const login = response.login;
  console.log(login);
};

fetch("https://api.github.com/users/moonhighway")
  .then(res => res.json())
  .then(userDetails);
```

Loading data from an API with Node.js requires the use of core modules. It requires different code. In these samples, the `userDetails` function is universal, so the same function works in both environments.

This JavaScript file is now isomorphic. It contains universal JavaScript. All of the code is not universal, but the file itself will work in both environments. It can run it with Node.js or include it in a `<script>` tag in the browser.

Let's take a look at the `Star` component. Is this component universal?

```
function Star({
  selected = false,
  onClick = f => f
}) {
  return (
    <div
      className={
        selected ? "star selected" : "star"
      }
```

```
          onClick={onClick}
        ></div>
    );
}
```

Sure it is; remember, the JSX compiles to JavaScript. The Star component is simply a function:

```
function Star({
  selected = false,
  onClick = f => f
}) {
  return React.createElement("div", {
    className: selected
      ? "star selected"
      : "star",
    onClick: onClick
  });
}
```

We can render this component directly in the browser, or render it in a different environment and capture the HTML output as a string. ReactDOM has a renderToString method that we can use to render UI to an HTML string:

```
// Renders html directly in the browser
ReactDOM.render(<Star />);

// Renders html as a string
let html = ReactDOM.renderToString(<Star />);
```

We can build isomorphic applications that render components on different platforms, and we can architect these applications in a way that reuses JavaScript code universally across multiple environments. Additionally, we can build isomorphic applications using other languages such as Go or Python—we're not restricted to Node.js.

## Server Rendering React

Using the ReactDOM.renderToString method allows us to render UI on the server. Servers are powerful; they have access to all kinds of resources that browsers do not. Servers can be secure and access secure data. You can use all of these added benefits to your advantage by rendering initial content on the server.

The app we'll server render is our Recipes app that we built in Chapter 5. You can run Create React App and place this code over the contents of the *index.js* file:

```
import React from "react";
import ReactDOM from "react-dom";
import "./index.css";
import { Menu } from "./Menu";

const data = [
```

```
{
  name: "Baked Salmon",
  ingredients: [
    {
      name: "Salmon",
      amount: 1,
      measurement: "lb"
    },
    {
      name: "Pine Nuts",
      amount: 1,
      measurement: "cup"
    },
    {
      name: "Butter Lettuce",
      amount: 2,
      measurement: "cups"
    },
    {
      name: "Yellow Squash",
      amount: 1,
      measurement: "med"
    },
    {
      name: "Olive Oil",
      amount: 0.5,
      measurement: "cup"
    },
    {
      name: "Garlic",
      amount: 3,
      measurement: "cloves"
    }
  ],
  steps: [
    "Preheat the oven to 350 degrees.",
    "Spread the olive oil around a glass baking dish.",
    "Add the yellow squash and place in the oven for 30 mins.",
    "Add the salmon, garlic, and pine nuts to the dish.",
    "Bake for 15 minutes.",
    "Remove from oven. Add the lettuce and serve."
  ]
},
{
  name: "Fish Tacos",
  ingredients: [
    {
      name: "Whitefish",
      amount: 1,
      measurement: "l lb"
    },
    {
```

```
        name: "Cheese",
        amount: 1,
        measurement: "cup"
      },
      {
        name: "Iceberg Lettuce",
        amount: 2,
        measurement: "cups"
      },
      {
        name: "Tomatoes",
        amount: 2,
        measurement: "large"
      },
      {
        name: "Tortillas",
        amount: 3,
        measurement: "med"
      }
    ],
    steps: [
      "Cook the fish on the grill until hot.",
      "Place the fish on the 3 tortillas.",
      "Top them with lettuce, tomatoes, and cheese."
    ]
  }
];

ReactDOM.render(
  <Menu
    recipes={data}
    title="Delicious Recipes"
  />,
  document.getElementById("root")
);
```

The components will live in a new file called *Menu.js*:

```
function Recipe({ name, ingredients, steps }) {
  return (
    <section
      id={name.toLowerCase().replace(/ /g, "-")}
    >
      <h1>{name}</h1>
      <ul className="ingredients">
        {ingredients.map((ingredient, i) => (
          <li key={i}>{ingredient.name}</li>
        ))}
      </ul>
      <section className="instructions">
        <h2>Cooking Instructions</h2>
        {steps.map((step, i) => (
          <p key={i}>{step}</p>
```

```
      ))}
    </section>
  </section>
);
}

export function Menu({ title, recipes }) {
  return (
    <article>
      <header>
        <h1>{title}</h1>
      </header>
      <div className="recipes">
        {recipes.map((recipe, i) => (
          <Recipe key={i} {...recipe} />
        ))}
      </div>
    </article>
  );
}
```

Throughout the book, we've rendered components on the client. Client-side rendering is typically the first approach we'll use when building an app. We serve up the
Create React App *build* folder, and the browser runs the HTML and makes calls to the
*script.js* file to load any JavaScript.

Doing this can be time consuming. The user might have to wait to see anything load
for a few seconds depending on their network speed. Using Create React App with an
Express server, we can create a hybrid experience of client- and server-side rendering.

We're rendering a Menu component that renders several recipes. The first change we'll
make to this app is to use ReactDOM.hydrate instead of ReactDOM.render.

These two functions are the same except hydrate is used to add content to a container that was rendered by ReactDOMServer. The order of operations will look like
this:

1. Render a static version of the app, allowing users to see that something has happened and the page has "loaded."
2. Make the request for the dynamic JavaScript.
3. Replace the static content with the dynamic content.
4. User clicks on something and it works.

We're rehydrating the app after a server-side render. By rehydrate, we mean statically
loading the content as static HTML and then loading the JavaScript. This allows users
to experience perceived performance. They'll see that something is happening on the
page, and that makes them want to stay on the page.

Next, we need to set up our project's server, and we'll use Express, a lightweight Node server. Install it first:

```
npm install express
```

Then we'll create a server folder called *server* and create an *index.js* file inside of that. This file will build a server that will serve up the *build* folder but also preload some static HTML content:

```
import express from "express";
const app = express();

app.use(express.static("./build"));
```

This imports and statically serves the *build* folder. Next, we want to use `renderTo String` from `ReactDOM` to render the app as a static HTML string:

```
import React from "react";
import ReactDOMServer from "react-dom/server";
import { Menu } from "../src/Menu.js";

const PORT = process.env.PORT || 4000;

app.get("/*", (req, res) => {
  const app = ReactDOMServer.renderToString(
    <Menu />
  );
});

app.listen(PORT, () =>
  console.log(
    `Server is listening on port ${PORT}`
  )
);
```

We'll pass the `Menu` component to this function because that's what we want to render statically. We then want to read the static *index.html* file from the built client app, inject the app's content in the `div`, and send that as the response to the request:

```
app.get("/*", (req, res) => {
  const app = ReactDOMServer.renderToString(
    <Menu />
  );

  const indexFile = path.resolve(
    "./build/index.html"
  );

  fs.readFile(indexFile, "utf8", (err, data) => {
    return res.send(
      data.replace(
        '<div id="root"></div>',
        `<div id="root">${app}</div>`
```

```
      )
    );
  });
});
```

Once we've completed this, we'll need to do some configuration with webpack and Babel. Remember, Create React App can take care of compiling and building out of the box, but we need to set up and enforce different rules with the server project.

Start by installing a few dependencies (OK, a lot of dependencies):

```
npm install @babel/core @babel/preset-env babel-loader nodemon npm-run-all
webpack webpack-cli webpack-node-externals
```

With Babel installed, let's create a `.babelrc` with some presets:

```
{
  "presets": ["@babel/preset-env", "react-app"]
}
```

You'll add `react-app` because the project uses Create React App, and it has already been installed.

Next, add a webpack configuration file for the server called *webpack.server.js*:

```
const path = require("path");
const nodeExternals = require("webpack-node-externals");

module.exports = {
  entry: "./server/index.js",
  target: "node",
  externals: [nodeExternals()],
  output: {
    path: path.resolve("build-server"),
    filename: "index.js"
  },
  module: {
    rules: [
      {
        test: /\.js$/,
        use: "babel-loader"
      }
    ]
  }
};
```

The babel-loader will transform JavaScript files as expected, and `nodeExternals` will scan the *node_modules* folder for all `node_modules` names. Then, it will build an external function that tells webpack not to bundle those modules or any submodules.

Also, you might run into a webpack error due to a version conflict between the version you've installed with Create React App and the version we just installed. To fix the conflict, just add a *.env* file to the root of the project and add:

```
SKIP_PREFLIGHT_CHECK=true
```

Finally, we can add a few extra npm scripts to run our dev commands:

```
{
  "scripts": {
    //...
    "dev:build-server": "NODE_ENV=development webpack --config webpack.server.js
    --mode=development -w",
    "dev:start": "nodemon ./server-build/index.js",
    "dev": "npm-run-all --parallel build dev:*"
  }
}
```

1. `dev:build-server`: Passes `development` as an environment variable and runs `web pack` with the new server config.

2. `dev:start`: Runs the server file with `nodemon`, which will listen for any changes.

3. `dev`: Runs both processes in parallel.

Now when we run `npm run dev`, both of the processes will run. You should be able to see the app running on `localhost:4000`. When the app runs, the content will load in sequence, first as prerendered HTML and then with the JavaScript bundle.

Using a technique like this can mean faster load times and will yield a boost in perceived performance. With users expecting page-load times of two seconds or less, any improved performance can mean the difference between users using your website or bouncing to a competitor.

# Server Rendering with Next.js

Another powerful and widely used tool in the server rendering ecosystem is Next.js. Next is an open source technology that was released by Zeit to help engineers write server-rendered apps more easily. This includes features for intuitive routing, statically optimizing, automatic splitting, and more. In the next section, we'll take a closer look at how to work with Next.js to enable server rendering in our app.

To start, we'll create a whole new project, running the following commands:

```
mkdir project-next
cd project-next
npm init -y
npm install --save react react-dom next
mkdir pages
```

Then we'll create some npm scripts to run common commands more easily:

---

```
{
  //...
  "scripts": {
    "dev": "next",
    "build": "next build",
    "start": "next start"
  }
}
```

In the *pages* folder, we'll create an *index.js* file. We'll write our component, but we won't worry about importing React or ReactDOM. Instead, we'll just write a component:

```
export default function Index() {
  return (
    <div>
      <p>Hello everyone!</p>
    </div>
  );
}
```

Once we've created this, we can run npm run dev to see the page running on local host:3000. It displays the expected component.

You'll also notice there's a small lightning bolt icon in the lower righthand corner of the screen. Hovering over this will display a button that reads Prerendered Page. When you click on it, it will take you to documentation about the Static Optimization Indicator. This means that the page fits the criteria for automatic static optimization, meaning that it can be prerendered. There are no data requirements that block it. If a page is automatically statically optimized (a mouthful, but useful!), the page is faster to load because there's no server-side effort needed. The page can be streamed from a CDN, yielding a super-fast user experience. You don't have to do anything to pick up on this performance enhancement.

What if the page does have data requirements? What if the page cannot be prerendered? To explore this, let's make our app a bit more robust and build toward a component that fetches some remote data from an API. In a new file called *Pets.js*:

```
export default function Pets() {
  return <h1>Pets!</h1>;
}
```

To start, we'll render an h1. Now we can visit localhost:3000/pets to see that our page is now loaded on that route. That's good, but we can improve this by adding links and a layout component that will display the correct content for each page. We'll create a header that can be used on both pages and will display links:

```
import Link from "next/link";

export default function Header() {
  return (
    <div>
      <Link href="/">
        <a>Home</a>
      </Link>
      <Link href="/pets">
        <a>Pets</a>
      </Link>
    </div>
  );
}
```

The Link component is a wrapper around a couple of links. These look similar to the
links we created with React Router. We can also add a style to each of the <a> tags:

```
const linkStyle = {
  marginRight: 15,
  color: "salmon"
};

export default function Header() {
  return (
    <div>
      <Link href="/">
        <a style={linkStyle}>Home</a>
      </Link>
      <Link href="/pets">
        <a style={linkStyle}>Pets</a>
      </Link>
    </div>
  );
}
```

Next, we'll incorporate the Header component into a new file called *Layout.js*. This
will dynamically display the component based on the correct route:

```
import Header from "./Header";

export function Layout(props) {
  return (
    <div>
      <Header />
      {props.children}
    </div>
  );
}
```

The Layout component will take in props and display any additional content in the
component underneath the Header. Then in each page, we can create content blocks

that can be passed to the Layout component when rendered. For example, the *index.js* file would now look like this:

```
import Layout from "./Layout";

export default function Index() {
  return (
    <Layout>
      <div>
        <h1>Hello everyone!</h1>
      </div>
    </Layout>
  );
}
```

We'll do the same in the *Pets.js* file:

```
import Layout from "./Layout";

export default function Pets() {
  return (
    <Layout>
      <div>
        <h1>Hey pets!</h1>
      </div>
    </Layout>
  );
}
```

Now if we visit the homepage, we should see the header, then when we click the Pets link, we should see the Pets page.

When we click on the lightning bolt button in the lower righthand corner, we'll notice that these pages are still being prerendered. This is to be expected as we continue to render static content. Let's use the Pets page to load some data and see how this changes.

To start, we'll install isomorphic-unfetch like we did earlier in the chapter:

```
npm install isomorphic-unfetch
```

We'll use this to make a fetch call to the Pet Library API. Start by importing it in the *Pages.js* file:

```
import fetch from "isomorphic-unfetch";
```

Then we're going to add a function called getInitialProps. This will handle fetching and loading the data:

```
Pets.getInitialProps = async function() {
  const res = await fetch(
    `http://pet-library.moonhighway.com/api/pets`
  );
```

```
    const data = await res.json();
    return {
      pets: data
    };
  };
```

When we return the data as the value for `pets`, we then can map over the data in the component.

Adjust the component to map over the `pets` property:

```
export default function Pets(props) {
  return (
    <Layout>
      <div>
        <h1>Pets!</h1>
        <ul>
          {props.pets.map(pet => (
            <li key={pet.id}>{pet.name}</li>
          ))}
        </ul>
      </div>
    </Layout>
  );
}
```

If `getInitialProps` is present in the component, Next.js will render the page in response to each request. This means that the page will be server-side rendered instead of statically prerendered, so the data from the API will be current on each request.

Once we're satisfied with the state of the application, we can run a build with `npm run build`. Next.js is concerned with performance, so it will give us a full rundown of the number of kilobytes present for each file. This is a quick spot-check for unusually large files.

Next to each file, we'll see an icon for whether a site is server-rendered at runtime ($\lambda$), automatically rendered as HTML ($\bigcirc$), or automatically generated as static HTML + JSON ($\bullet$).

Once you've built the app, you can deploy it. Next.js is an open source product of Zeit, a cloud-hosting provider, so the experience of deploying with Zeit is the most straightforward. However, you can use many different hosting providers to deploy your application.

To recap, there are some important bits of terminology that are important to understand when setting out to build your own apps:

*CSR (client-side rendering)*
Rendering an app in a browser, generally using the DOM. This is what we do with an unmodified Create React App.

*SSR (server-side rendering)*
Rendering a client-side or universal app to HTML on the server.

*Rehydration*
Loading JavaScript views on the client to reuse the server-rendered HTML's DOM tree and data.

*Prerendering*
Running a client-side application at build time and capturing initial state as static HTML.

# Gatsby

Another popular site generator that's based on React is Gatsby. Gatsby is taking over the world as a straightforward way to create a content-driven website. It aims to offer smarter defaults to manage concerns like performance, accessibility, image handling, and more. And if you're reading this book, it's likely that you might work on a Gatsby project at some point!

Gatsby is used for a range of projects, but it's often used to build content-driven websites. In other words, if you have a blog or static content, Gatsby is a great choice, particularly now that you know React. Gatsby can also handle dynamic content like loading data from APIs, integration with frameworks, and more.

In this section, we'll start building a quick Gatsby site to demonstrate how it works. Essentially, we'll build our small Next.js app as a Gatsby app:

```
npm install -g gatsby-cli
gatsby new pets
```

If you have yarn installed globally, the CLI will ask you whether to use yarn or npm. Either is fine. Then you'll change directory into the *pets* folder:

```
cd pets
```

Now you can start the project with `gatsby develop`. When you visit `localhost:8000`, you'll see your Gatsby starter site running. Now you can take a tour of the files.

If you open up the project's *src* folder, you'll see three subfolders: *components*, *images*, and *pages*.

Within the *pages* folder, you'll find a *404.js* error page, an *index.js* page (the page that renders when you visit `localhost:8000`), and a *page-2.js* that renders the content of the second page.

If you visit the *components* folder, this where the magic of Gatsby is located. Remember when we built the `Header` and `Layout` components with Next.js? Both of these components are already created as templates in the *components* folder.

A few particularly interesting things to note:

*layout.js*
> This contains the `Layout` component. It uses the `useStaticQuery` hook to query some data about the site using GraphQL.

*seo.js*
> This component lets us access the page's metadata for search engine optimization purposes.

If you add additional pages to the *pages* folder, this will add additional pages to your site. Let's try it and add a *page-3.js* file to the *pages* folder. Then we'll add the following code to that file to stand up a quick page:

```
import React from "react";
import { Link } from "gatsby";

import Layout from "../components/layout";
import SEO from "../components/seo";

const ThirdPage = () => (
  <Layout>
    <SEO title="Page three" />
    <h1>Hi from the third page</h1>
    <Link to="/">Go back to the homepage</Link>
  </Layout>
);

export default ThirdPage;
```

We'll use the `Layout` component to wrap the content so that it's displayed as `children`. Not only does `Layout` display the dynamic content, but as soon as we create it, the page is autogenerated.

That's the tip of the iceberg with what you can do with Gatsby, but we'll leave you with some information about some of its additional features:

*Static content*
> You can build your site as static files, which can be deployed without a server.

*CDN support*
> It's possible to cache your site on CDNs all over the world to improve performance and availability.

*Responsive and progressive images*
> Gatsby loads images as blurry placeholders, then fades in the full assets. This tactic, popularized by Medium, allows users to see something rendering before the full resource is available.

*Prefetching of linked pages*
> All of the content needed to load the next page will load in the background before you click on the next link.

All of these features and more are used to ensure a seamless user experience. Gatsby has made a lot of decisions for you. That could be good or bad, but these constraints aim to let you focus on your content.

# React in the Future

While Angular, Ember, and Vue continue to have substantial marketshare in the JavaScript ecosystem, it's hard to argue with the fact that React is currently the most widely used and influential library for building JavaScript apps. In addition to the library itself, the wider JavaScript community, as evidenced particularly by Next.js and Gatsby, has embraced React as the tool of choice.

So where do we go from here? We'd encourage you to use these skills to build your own projects. If you're looking to build mobile applications, you can check out React Native. If you're looking to declaratively fetch data, you can check out GraphQL. If you're looking to build content-based websites, dig deeper into Next.js and Gatsby.

There are a number of avenues you can travel down, but these skills you've picked up in React will serve you well as you set out to build your own applications. When you're doing so, we hope that this book will serve as a reference and a foundation. Although React and its related libraries will almost certainly go through changes, these are stable tools that you can feel confident about using right away. Building apps with React and functional, declarative JavaScript is a lot of fun, and we can't wait to see what you'll build.

# Index

## About the Authors

**Alex Banks** and **Eve Porcello** are software engineers, instructors, and cofounders of Moon Highway, a curriculum development company in Northern California. They've created courses for LinkedIn Learning and egghead.io, are frequent conference speakers, and teach workshops to engineers all over the world.

## Colophon

The animal on the cover of *Learning React* is a wild boar and its babies (*Sus scrofa*). The wild boar, also known as wild swine or Eurasian wild pig, is native to Eurasia, North Africa, and the Greater Sunda Islands. Because of human intervention, they are one of the widest-ranging mammals in the world.

Wild boars have short thin legs and bulky bodies with short, massive trunks. Their necks are short and thick, leading to a large head that accounts for up to a third of the body's length. Adult sizes and weights vary depending on environmental factors such as access to food and water. Despite their size, they can run up to 25 miles per hour and jump to a height of 55–59 inches. In the winter, their coat consists of coarse bristles that overlay short brown downy fur. These bristles are longer along the boar's back and shortest around the face and limbs.

Wild boars have a highly developed sense of smell; they have been used for drug detection in Germany. They also have an acute sense of hearing, which contrasts with their weak eyesight and lack of color vision. The boars are unable to recognize a human standing 30 feet away.

Boars are social animals that live in female-dominated groups. Breeding lasts from around November to January. Males go through several bodily changes in preparation of mating, including the development of a subcutaneous armor that helps during confrontations with rivals; they travel long distances, eating very little on the way, to locate a sow. Average litters contain four to six piglets.

Many of the animals on O'Reilly covers are endangered; all of them are important to the world.

The cover illustration is by Karen Montgomery, based on a black-and-white engraving from *Meyers Kleines Lexicon*. The cover fonts are Gilroy Semibold and Guardian Sans. The text font is Adobe Minion Pro; the heading font is Adobe Myriad Condensed; and the code font is Dalton Maag's Ubuntu Mono.

# O'REILLY®

# There's much more
# where this came from.

Experience books, videos, live online
training courses, and more from O'Reilly
and our 200+ partners—all in one place.

Learn more at oreilly.com/online-learning

Milton Keynes UK
Ingram Content Group UK Ltd.
UKHW030907191024
449883UK00004B/8